# كَلِمَاتُ القُرآن

# KALIMATUL-QUR'AN

## A DICTIONARY OF THE QUR'ANIC WORDS

*Compiled by*:

**Ash-Shaikh Hasanin Muhammad Makhluf**

*Translated by*:

**Duraid & Faiz Fatouhi**

KITAB BHAVAN

NEW DELHI-110 002. [INDIA]

Kalimatul Qur'an A Dictionary of The Qur'anic Words

**KITAB BHAVAN**
Publishers, Distributors, Exporters & Importers
1784, Kalan Mahal, Darya Ganj,
New Delhi - 1100 02 (India)

Phone : (91-11) 23277392, 23274686,
: (91-11) 23263383
Mob : +91-9953098606

Website : www.kitabbhavan.net
Email : info@kitabbhavan.net
nasri@vsnl.com



First Published in India : 1999
Reprint : 2022

ISBN - 10 : 81-7151-280-1
ISBN - 13 : 978-81-7151-280-5

Book Code No. : K00074

Batch ID : SPRFNS130722

*Printed & Published in India by :*

Moonis Ali Nasri for Kitab Bhavan
1784, Kalan Mahal, Darya Ganj,
New Delhi - 1100 02 [India]

## CONTENTS

بسمِ اللهِ الرَّحمن الرَّحيم

# INTRODUCTION

Praise be to Allah, the Cherisher and Sustainer of the worlds, and prayer and peace be upon the last Messenger and the best of all of the creation and on his family and companions and their followers to the Day of Judgment.

This is an interpretation for those words of the Qûr'an that require interpretation and explanation. It explains the meanings of those words and helps in understanding the verse in which they occur. The words have been listed according to the order of the verse in the Surahs (Qûr'anic chapters). To the left of each word is the number of the verse to which the word belongs, and to its right is its meaning, in brevity and accuracy, with simplicity and clarity. Therefore, this book is a companion for those who are resident, provision for those who are travelling. It is light to carry, simple to understand, near to grasp. When it is sought for help, it offers its help to those who need it without difficulty or hardship.

I ask the Almighty Allah that He accepts this book as purely done for the sake of His Noble Countenance, that He makes me and those who help in publishing, on account of it, among those who kept the trust and discharged some of the duties toward His Great Book, and that He erases with it the sins and increases the rewards. Allah is Hearer, Responsive, Bountiful.

Hasanin Muhammad Makhluf

بِسْمِ اللهِ الرَّحمن الرَّحيم

# TRANSLATORS' NOTE

Praise be to Allah, the Cherisher and Sustainer of the worlds, Who has said in the Holy Qûr'an :

" We have sent it down as an Arabic Qûr'an in order that you may learn wisdom. " [12:2]

And prayer and peace be upon the seal of the Prophets, Muhammad صلى الله عليه وسلم , who has said :

" The best among you are those who learn the Qûr'an and teach it. " [Al-Bukhari]

In conformity with the sayings of the Almighty Allah and His Messenger صلى الله عليه وسلم, we have the honour to present to the Muslim readers a translation of the famous book " Kalimatul-Qûr'an ". This book was compiled by the famous Egyptian Shaikh, Hasanin Muhammad Makhluf, whose piety and knowledge made this book well-known in the Arabic countries, and that led to its re-printing for many times.

In this translation we have tried to present simple and clear meanings of the words of the original book, following a shortened and accurate method and avoiding any repetition as much as possible. We have also added a transliteration to each word in the book, which shows the right way of pronouncing that word.

Finally, we hope that this humble work may avail the readers and extend their knowledge of the Holy Qûr'an.

Duraid & Faiz Fatouhi

# TRANSLITERATION

The following table shows the system that has been used in transliterating the letters of the Arabic words:

| | | | | | |
|---|---|---|---|---|---|
| أ | ......... | a | ض | ......... | d |
| ب | ......... | b | ط | ......... | t |
| ت | ......... | t | ظ | ......... | z |
| ث | ......... | th | ع | ......... | ‘ |
| ج | ......... | j | غ | ......... | gh |
| ح | ......... | h | ف | ......... | f |
| خ | ......... | kh | ق | ......... | q |
| د | ......... | d | ك | ......... | k |
| ذ | ......... | dh | ل | ......... | l |
| ر | ......... | r | م | ......... | m |
| ز | ......... | z | ن | ......... | n |
| س | ......... | s | هه ه | ......... | h |
| ش | ......... | sh | و | ......... | w |
| ص | ......... | s | ي | ......... | y |

| | | | |
|---|---|---|---|
| **short vowels** | | *fatha* | **a** |
| | | *kasra* | **i** |
| | | *damma* | **u** |
| | ء | *hamza* | **’** |

# LIST OF ABBREVIATIONS

| | | |
|---|---|---|
| *ap.* | : | active participle |
| *dl.* | : | dual |
| *fg.* | : | feminine gender |
| *i.e.,* | : | that is |
| *im.* | : | imperative |
| *lit.* | : | literally |
| *mg.* | : | masculine gender |
| *ni.* | : | negative imperative |
| *pl.* | : | plural |
| *pp.* | : | passive participle |
| *pv.* | : | passive voice |
| *sr.* | : | singular |
| *tr.* | : | transliteration |
| *v;* | : | verse |

## MANNERS OF RECITING THE HOLY QÛR'AN

1. Cleansing the mouth with Miswak (tooth-stick) before reciting the Holy Qûr'an

2. Reciting in a clean, pure place whether in the mosque or any other place.

3. Facing the Qiblah (direction towards the Ka'ba) during recitation.

4. Starting recitation by saying Isti'adhah (seeking Allah's protection from Satan).
The Almighty Allah says," So when you want to recite the Qûr'an, seek refuge with Allah from Satan, the outcast (the cursed one) ".
[16:98]

5. Pronouncing the Basmalah (saying: In the name of Allah, Most Gracious, Most Merciful) at the beginning of each Surah with the exception of Surat At-Tawba.

6. Submitting to Allah and considering the contents of the recited verses of Qûr'an.
The Almighty Allah says," Do they not then earnestly seek to understand the Qûr'an, or are their hearts locked up by them ".
[47:24]
The Almighty Allah also says," (Here is) a Book which We have sent down unto you, full of blessings, that they may meditate on its signs ".
[38:29]

7. Reciting the Qûr'an in slow, measured rhythmic tones.
Chanting and improving the voice in reciting the Holy Qûr'an.
The Almighty Allah says," And recite the Qûr'an in slow, measured rhythmic tones ".
[73:4]

Abu Huraira رضي الله عنه reported that Allah's Messenger صلى الله عليه وسلم said, " He does not belong to us who does not chant the Qûr'an".

[Al-Bukhari]

Abu Huraira رضي الله عنه reported that Allah's Messenger صلى الله عليه وسلم said, " Allah has not listened to anything as He does to a Prophet with a good voice reciting the Qûr'an aloud ".

[Agreed upon]

8. Reciting the Holy Qûr'an slowly and without hastening.

Abu Wa'il reported ," We went to 'Abdullah in the morning and a man said,' Yesterday I recited all the Mufassil Surahs '. On that 'Abdullah said,' That is very quick, and we have the (Prophet's صلى الله عليه وسلم) recitation, and I remember very well the recitation of those Surahs which the Prophet صلى الله عليه وسلم used to recite, and they were eighteen Surahs from the Mufassil starting with (Alif Lam Mim) ' ".

[Al-Bukhari]

9. Reading the Qûr'an with some prolongation

Qatadah رضي الله عنه reported that Anas Ibn Malik was asked,"How was the recitation (of the Qûr'an) of the Prophet صلى الله عليه وسلم?" He replied," It was characterized by the prolongation of certain sound "

[Al-Bukhari]

Um Salamah رضي الله عنها described the recitation of the Prophet صلى الله عليه وسلم as," Recitation in a manner in which it is explained letter by letter ".

[Abu Dawud]

10. Stopping on verses of mercy and verses of punishment for supplication

Hudhaifa رضي الله عنه reported," One night I prayed along with the Prophet صلى الله عليه وسلم. The Prophet صلى الله عليه وسلم started with Al-Baqarah which he recited; then An-Nisa' which he recited; then Al-'Imran which he recited slowly. When he came to a verse speaking of glorification of Allah, he would glorify Him. When he came to a verse speaking of supplication of Allah, he would supplicate Him. When he came to a verse speaking of seeking Allah's protection, he would seek Allah's protection ".

[Agreed upon]

11. Weeping, felling grieve and affection in reciting the Holy Qûr'an.

The Almighty Allah says," And when they listen to the revelation received by the Apostle, you will see their eyes overflowing with tears, for they recognize the truth: they pray,' Our Lord! We believe: writes us down among the witnesses ' "

[5:83]

The Almighty Allah says," Say, ' Whether you believe in it or not, it is true that those who were given knowledge beforehand, when it is recited to them, they fall down on their faces in humble prostration'. And they say, ' Glory to our Lord! Truly has the promise of our Lord been fulfilled! They fall down on their faces in tears, and it increases their (earnest) humility ' "

[17:107-109]

12. Prostrating during recitation

'Umar رضي الله عنه was truly reported that in Friday prayer he recited on the rostrum Surat An-Nahl. When he came to a verse of prostration, he prostrated and so did the people along with him. In the next Friday prayer, he recited the Holy Qûr'an. When he came to a verse of prostration, he said, " O you people! When you come to a verse of prostration, you may prostrate and if you did, you would act properly. And, if you did not you would not encumber a sin. 'Umar did not prostrate "

[Al-Bukhari]

13. Moderation between reciting the Holy Qûr'an loudly and reciting it quietly.

The Almighty Allah says," Neither speak your prayer aloud, nor speak it in a low tone, but seek a middle course between ".

[17:110]

‘Uqbah Ibn Amir رضي الله عنـــه heard the Prophet صلى الله عليه وسلم as saying,“ He who recites the Qûr'an loudly is like him who gives Sadaqa openly, and he who recites the Qûr'an quietly is like him who gives Sadaqa secretly ”.

[Abu Dawud]

14. Avoiding laughter, shout and talk during recitation.
The Almighty Allah says,“ When the Qûr’an is read, listen to it with attention, and hold your peace, that you may receive Mercy ”.

[7:204]

15. When reciting in a particular mode it is one of the manners of recitation to continue reciting in the same mode and in the same company.

16. Reciting and completing the recitation of the Qûr'an several times.
‘Abdullah Ibn ‘Amr رضي الله عنـه reported, “Allah’s Apostle صلى الله عليه وسـلم said to me,‘ Recite the whole Qûr'an in one month time’. I said,‘ But I have power (to do more than that) ’. Then Allah’s Apostle صلـى الله عليـه وسـلم said,‘ Then finish the recitation of the Qûr'an in seven days, and do not finish it in less than this period’”.

[Agreed upon]

## THE VIRTUES OF SPECIAL SURAHS AND VERSES

1. Abu Sa'id Rafi'i Ibn Al-Mu'ala رضي الله عنه said," Allah's Apostle صلى الله عليه وسلم said,' Shall I not teach you the most superior Surah in the Qûr'an before you leave the mosque? ' He took me by the hand. We were about to leave and I said,' O Apostle of Allah! You said you will teach me the most superior Surah in the Qûr'an'. The Prophet صلى الله عليه وسلم said,' (It is) Praise be to Allah, the Lord of the world, (Surat Al-Fatiha) which consists of seven repeatedly recited verses and the Magnificent Qûr'an which was given to me'".

[Al-Bukhari]

2. Ibn 'Abbas رضي الله عنه reported that while Jibril عليه السلام was sitting with the Prophet صلى الله عليه وسلم he heard a creaking sound above him, and after raising his head he said," This is a gate opened in heaven today which has never been open before ". Then when an angel descended through it he said," This is an angel came down to earth, he has never come down before ". He gave a salutation and said," Rejoice in two lights brought to you which have not been brought to any Prophet before you: Fatihat Al-Kitab and the last verses of Surat Al-Baqarah. You will not recite a letter of them without being given the blessing it contains."

[Muslim]

3. Abu Hurairah رضي الله عنه reported that the Prophet صلى الله عليه وسلم said," Do not make your houses graveyards. The devil flies from the house in which Surat Al-Baqarah is recited ".

[Muslim]

4. Ubayy Ibn Ka'b رضي الله عنه reported that Allah's Apostle صلى الله عليه وسلم said," Abal-Mundhir, do you know which verse of Allah's Book that you have is greatest? " I replied," Allah, there is no god but He, the Living, the Eternal ". Thereupon he struck me on the breast and said," My knowledge be pleasant for you, Abal-Mundhir ".

[Muslim]

5. Abu Mas'ud Al-Badri رضي الله عنه reported that the Prophet صلى الله عليه وسلم said," If anyone recites the last two verses of Surat Al-Baqarah at night, that will be sufficient for him ".

[Agreed upon]

6. Abu Umamah Al-Bahili رضي الله عنه reported that he heard Allah's Messenger صلى الله عليه وسلم as saying," Recite the Qûr'an, for on the Day of Resurrection it will come as an intercessor for those who recite it. Recite the two shining ones Al-Baqarah and Surat Al-'Imran, for on the Day of Resurrection they will come as two clouds or two shades, or two flocks or birds in ranks pleading for those who recite them. Recite Surat Al-Baqarah, for reading it produces blessing, and abandoning it produces regret, and the slothful are unable to recite it ".

[Muslim]

7. Abu Darda' رضي الله عنه reported that the Prophet صلى الله عليه وسلم said," If anyone learns by heart ten verses at the beginning of Surat Al-Kahf, he will be protected from the Dajjal ".
In another version: " ...at the end of Surat Al-Kahf ".

[Muslim]

8. Abu Sa'id رضي الله عنه reported that the Prophet صلى الله عليه وسلم said," If anyone recites Surat Al-Kahf on Friday, light will shine brightly for him till the next Friday ".

[Al-Bayhaqi]

9. Ibn Mas'ud رضي الله عنه reported that the Prophet صلى الله عليه وسلم said," Surat Tabarak prevents (whoever reads it) from the punishment of the grave ".

[Al-Hakim]

10. Ibn 'Umar رضي الله عنه reported that the Prophet صلى الله عليه وسلم said," Whoever feels pleased to see the Day of Resurrection as if seeing it with his own eyes, should may recite Surat At-Takwir, Al-Infitar and Al-Inshiqaq ".

[At-Tirmidhi]

11. Abu Sa'id Al-Khudri رضي الله عنه reported that the Prophet صلى الله عليه وسلم said regarding the verse," Say He is Allah, the One and Only " (Surat Al-Ikhlas): " By Him in whose Hand my life is, this Surah is equal to one-third of the Qûr'an ".

In another wording: The Prophet صلى الله عليه وسلم said to his companions," Is it difficult for any of you to recite one-third of the Qûr'an in one night? " The suggestion was difficult for them so the said," Who among us has the power to do so, O Messenger of Allah?" Allah's Apostle صلى الله عليه وسلم replied, " Say: He is Allah, the One and Only Allah, the Eternal, Absolute, (Surat Al-Ikhlas) is equal to one-third of the Qûr'an".

[Al-Bukhari]

12. Mu'ad Ibn Anas رضي الله عنه reported that the Prophet صلى الله عليه وسلم said," If someone recites,' Say: He is Allah, the One' eleven times, Allah will build for him a palace in Paradise ".

[Ahmad]

13. 'Uqbah Ibn Amir رضي الله عنه reported that Allah's Messenger صلى الله عليه وسلم said," What wonderful verses have been sent down tonight! The like of them has never been seen. They are:' Say: I seek refuge in the Lord of the dawn ', and ' Say: I seek refuge in the Lord of men ' ".

[Muslim]

14. 'A'isha رضي الله عنها reported that whenever the Prophet صلى الله عليه وسلم went to bed every night, he used to cup his hands together and blow over them after reciting Surat Al-Ikhlas, Surat Al-Falaq and Surat An-Nas, and then rub his hands over whatever parts of his body he was able to rub, starting with his head, face and front of his body. He صلى الله عليه وسلم used to do that three times.

[Agreed upon]

15. 'A'isha رضي الله عنها reported that whenever Allah's Apostle صلى الله عليه وسلم became sick, he would recite Mu'audhat (Surat Al-Falaq Surat An-Nas) and then blow his breath over his body. But when he became seriously ill I used to recite (these two Surahs) and rub his hands over his body hoping for their blessings.

[Al-Bukhari]

# VIRTUES OF THE HOLY QÛR'AN IN PROPHETIC SAYINGS

1. Abu Ummamah رضي الله عنه reported that Allah's Messenger صلى الله عليه وسلم said," Recite the Qur'an for on the Day of Resurrection it will comes as intercessor for those who recite it ".

[Muslim]

2. Al-Nawwas Ibn Sam'an رضي الله عنه reported that Allah's Messenger صلى الله عليه وسلم said," On the Day of Resurrection, the Qûr'an and those who acted according to it will be brought with Surat Al-Baqarah and Surat Al-'Imran preceding them and pleading for the one who recited them ".

[Muslim]

3. 'Uthman Ibn 'Affan رضي الله عنه reported that Allah's Messenger صلى الله عليه وسلم said," The best among you are those who learn the Qûr'an and teach it (to others) ".

[Al-Bukhari]

4. 'A'isha رضي الله عنها reported that Allah's Messenger صلى الله عليه وسلم said," He who falters when reciting the Qûr'an and finds it difficult for him will have a double reward ".

[Agreed upon]

5. Abu Musa Al-Ash-'ari رضي الله عنه reported that Allah's Messenger صلى الله عليه وسلم said," The example of a believer who recites the Qûr'an and acts on it is like a citron which tastes and smells nice. And the believer who does not recite the Qûr'an is like a date which tastes good but has no smell. And the example of a hypocrite who recites the Qûr'an is like the Raihana (a good smelling plant) which tastes good but smells bitter. And the example of a hypocrite who does not recite the Qûr'an is like the colocynth which tastes bitter and has no smell ".

[Agreed upon]

6. ‘Umar Ibn Al-Khattab رضـي الله عنـه reported that Allah’s Messenger صلى الله عليه وسـلم said,“ By this Book, Allah exalts some people and lowers others ”.

[Agreed upon]

7. Ibn ‘Umar رضي الله عنـه reported that the Prophet صلى الله عليه وسلم said,“ Do not wish to be except like one of two men. A man whom Allah has given the knowledge of the Qûr'an and he recites it during the hours of the night and during the hours of the day, and a man whom Allah has given money and he spends it (in giving charity) during the night and the day ”.

[Agreed upon]

8. Al-Bara’ Ibn ‘Azib رضـي الله عنـه reported: A man was reciting Surat Al-Kahf and his horse was tied with two ropes besides him. A cloud came and spread over that man, and it kept on coming closer to him till his horse started jumping (as if afraid of something). When it was morning, the man came to the Prophet صلى الله عليه وسـلم and told him about that incident. The Prophet صلى الله عليـه وسـلم said,“ That was Al-Sakina (tranquility) which descended because of (the recitation of) the Qûr’an ”.

[Agreed upon]

9. Ibn ‘Abbas رضي الله عنه reported that Allah’s Messenger صلى الله عليه وسـلم said,“ Anyone who has nothing of the Qûr'an within him is like a ruined house ”.

[At-Tirmidhi]

10. ‘Abdullah Ibn ‘Amr رضـي الله عنـه reported that Allah’s Messenger صلى الله عليه وسـلم said,“ The one who was devoted to the Qûr'an will be told (on the Day of Resurrection) to recite carefully as he recited carefully when he was in the world, for he will reach his abode when he comes to the last verse he recites ”.

[An-Nasa’i]

11. ‘Uqbah Ibn ‘Amir رضي الله عنه reported that: When we were in the Suffa, Allah’s Messenger صلى الله عليه وسلم came out and asked, “Which of you would like to go out every morning to Buthan or Al-‘Aqiq and bring two large humped she-camels withsout being guilty of sin or severing ties of relationship? ” We replied, “Messenger of Allah, we would all like that ”. He صلى الله عليه وسلم said,“ Does not one of you go out in the morning to the mosque and teach or recite two verses of Allah’s Book? That is better for him than two she-camels, and three verses are better for him than three she-camels, and four verses are better for him than four she-camels, and so on than their numbers in camels ”.

[Muslim]

12. Ibn Mas‘ud رضي الله عنه reported that Allah’s Messenger صلى الله عليه وسلم said,“ The one of you who is most versed in Allah’s Book should act as Imam for the people ”.

[Muslim]

13. Jabir Ibn ‘Abdullah رضي الله عنه reported that the Prophet صلى الله عليه وسلم put two men killed in Uhud in one grave. He صلى الله عليه وسلم asked who most acted according to the Qûr'an. He who was pointed to was buried first in the grave.

[At-Tirmidhi]

14. ‘Imran Ibn Husain رضي الله عنه reported that when he came upon a reader who was reciting the Qûr'an and then asking for payment, he told that reader that he had heard Allah’s Messenger صلى الله عليه وسلم say,“ When anyone recites the Qûr'an, let him ask reward for it from Allah, for (in the future) there will come a people who will recite the Qûr'an and ask a reward for it from men ”.

[At-Tirmidhi]

15. Ibn Mas‘ud رضي الله عنه reported that Allah’s Messenger صلى الله عليه وسلم said,“ If anyone recites a letter of Allah’s Book, he will be credited with a good deed, and a good deed gets a tenfold reward. I do not say that Alif Lam Mim are one letter, but Alif is a letter, Lam is a letter and Mim is a letter ”.

[At-Tirmidhi]

| V. | WORD | TR. | MEANING |
|---|---|---|---|

## سُورَةُ الفَاتِحَةِ

## [1] SURAT AL-FATIHA
THE OPENING CHAPTER

| | | | |
|---|---|---|---|
| 1 | بِسْمِ اللَّه | *Bismillah* | In the name of Allah |
| 1 | الرَّحْمَانِ | *Ar-Rahman* | The Most Gracious |
| 1 | الرَّحْيِمِ | *Ar-Rahim* | The Most Merciful |
| 2 | الحَمْدُ للَّهِ | *Al-Hamdu lillah* | Praise be to Allah |
| 2 | رَبِّ الْعَالَمِينَ | *Rabbil-'Alamin* | The Cherisher and Sustainer of the worlds |
| 4 | مَالِكِ | *Malik* | Owner, master |
| 4 | يَوْمِ الدِّينِ | *Yawmid-Din* | The Day of Judgment |
| 5 | إِيَّاكَ | *'Iyyaka* | You (Alone) |
| 5 | نَعْبُدُ | *Na'-bud* | We worship |
| 5 | نَسْتَعِينُ | *Nasta-'in* | We ask for help |
| 6 | اهْدِنَا الصِّرَاطَ الْمُسْتَقِيمَ | *Ihdinas-siratal-Mustaqim* | *im.* Show us the straight way |
| 7 | الَّذِينَ | *Al-Ladhina* | Those |
| 7 | أَنْعَمْتَ | *'An-'amta* | You have bestowed Your Grace |
| 7 | عَلَيْهِم | *'Alay-him* | On them |
| 7 | المَغضُوبِ عَلَيهِم | *Al-maghdubi 'alay-him* | Those whose portion is wrath |
| 7 | الضَّالِّينَ | *Ad-dallin* | Those who go astray |

| V. | WORD | TR. | MEANING |
|---|---|---|---|

## سُورَةُ البَقَرةِ

## [2] SURAT AL-BAQARAH

## THE HEIFER

| | | | |
|---|---|---|---|
| 2 | ذَلِكَ الْكِتَابُ | *Dhalikal-Kitab* | This is the Book (the Holy Qur'an) |
| 2 | لَا رَيْبَ فِيهِ | *La rayba fih* | Whereof there is no doubt |
| 2 | هُدًى | *Huda* | Guidance |
| 2 | لِلْمُتَّقِينَ | *Lil-Muttaqin* | To those who fear Allah |
| 5 | عَلَى هُدًى | *'Ala Huda* | On (true) guidance |
| 7 | خَتَمَ اللَّهُ | *Khatamallah* | Allah has set a seal |
| 7 | غِشَاوَةٌ | *Ghishawah* | Veil |
| 9 | يُخَادِعُونَ | *Yukhadi'un* | They deceive |
| 10 | مَرَضًا | *Marada* | Disease |
| 14 | خَلَوْا إِلَى شَيَاطِينِهِمْ | *Khalaw 'ila shayatinihim* | They are alone with their evil ones |
| 15 | يَمُدُّهُمْ | *Yamuddu-hum* | (Allah) Gives them rope |
| 15 | طُغْيَانِهِمْ | *Tughyanihim* | Their trespasses |
| 15 | يَعْمَهُونَ | *Ya'-mahun* | They wander like blind ones (hither and thither) |
| 17 | مَثَلُهُمْ | *Mathaluhum* | Their similitude |
| 17 | اسْتَوْقَدَ نَارًا | *Istawqada nara* | Kindled a fire |
| 18 | بُكْمٌ | *Bukm* | *pl.* Dumb |
| 19 | كَصَيِّبٍ | *Kasayyib* | Like a rain-laden cloud |

| V. | WORD | TR. | MEANING |
|---|---|---|---|
| 20 | يَخْطَفُ | *Yakhtaf* | Snatches away |
| 20 | أَبْصَارَهُمْ | *'Absarahum* | Their sight |
| 20 | قَامُوا | *Qamu* | They stood still |
| 22 | الْأَرْضَ فِرَاشًا | *Al-'arda fira-sha* | (Allah has made) the earth (your) couch |
| 22 | السَّمَاءَ بِنَاءً | *As-sama-'a bina-'a* | (Allah has made) the heaven (your) canopy |
| 22 | أَندَادًا | *Andada* | Rivals |
| 23 | ادْعُوا | *Id-'u* | *Im.pl.* Call |
| 23 | شُهَدَاءَكُمْ | *shuhada-'akum* | Your witnesses |
| 25 | مُتَشَابِهًا | *Mutashabiha* | Mutually resembling one another |
| 29 | اسْتَوَىٰ إِلَى السَّمَاءِ | *Istawa 'ilas-Sama'* | (Allah) turned to the heaven |
| 29 | فَسَوَّاهُنَّ | *Fa-sawwa-hunn* | And (Allah) made them |
| 30 | يَسْفِكُ | *Yasfik* | Sheds |
| 30 | دمَاء | *Dima'* | Blood |
| 30 | نُسَبِّحُ بِحَمْدِكَ | *Nusabbihu bi-Hamdik* | Wc celebrate Your praises |
| 30 | نُقَدِّسُ لَكَ | *Nu-qaddisu lak* | We glorify Your holy (name) |
| 34 | اسْجُدُوا لِآدَمَ | *Isjudu li-Adam* | *im.pl.* Bow down to Adam |
| 35 | رَغَدًا | *Raghada* | With pleasure |
| 36 | فَأَزَلَّهُمَا الشَّيْطَانُ | *Fa-adhalla-humash-shaytann* | Then Satan made them slip |
| 40 | إِسْرَائِيلَ | *Israil* | The agnomen of |

| V. | WORD | TR. | MEANING |
|---|---|---|---|
| | | | Ya'qub عليه السلام |
| 40 | فَارْهَبُونِ | *Farhabun* | *im.pl.* And fear Me |
| 42 | لَا تَلْبِسُوا | *La talbisu* | *ni.pl.* Do not cover |
| 44 | بِرّ | *Birr* | Right conduct |
| 45 | إِنَّهَا لَكَبِيرَةٌ | *Innaha lakabira* | It is indeed hard |
| 45 | خَاشِعِينَ | *Khashi-'in* | *Ap.* Those who are humble |
| 46 | يَظُنُّونَ | *Yazun-nun* | They bear in mind |
| 47 | عَالَمِينَ | *'Alamin* | Mankind and jinns |
| 48 | لَا تَجْزِي نَفْسٌ | *La tajzi nafs* | (When) one soul shall not avail (another) |
| 48 | عَدْلٌ | *'Adl* | Compensation |
| 49 | يَسُومُونَكُمْ | *Yasumuna-kum* | They afflict you |
| 49 | يَسْتَحْيُونَ نِسَاءَكُمْ | *Yas-tahyuna nisa-'akum* | They let your women-folk live |
| 49 | بَلَاءٌ | *Bala'* | Trial |
| 50 | فَرَقْنَا | *Faraqna* | We divided |
| 51 | اتَّخَذْتُمْ الْعِجْلَ | *At-takhadhtu-mul-'ijl* | You took the calf (for worship) |
| 53 | الْفُرْقَانَ | *Al-Furqan* | The criterion (between right and wrong) |
| 54 | بَارِئِكُمْ | *Bari-'ikum* | *pl.* Your Maker |
| 54 | فَاقْتُلُوا أَنفُسَكُمْ | *Faqtulu 'anfusakum* | *im.pl* And slay yourselves(the wrong-doers) |
| 55 | جَهْرَةً | *Jahrata* | Manifestly |
| 55 | صَّاعِقَةُ | *Sa'iqa* | Thunderbolt |

| V. | WORD | TR. | MEANING |
|---|---|---|---|
| 57 | غَمَام | *Ghamam* | Clouds |
| 57 | مَنّ | *Mann* | A kind of sweet gum |
| 57 | سَلْوَى | *Salwa* | Quails |
| 58 | رَغَدًا | *Raghada* | With pleasure |
| 58 | قُولُوا حِطَّةٌ | *Qulu hitta* | *Im.pl* Say : "Forgive us" |
| 59 | رِجْزًا | *Rijza* | Plague |
| 60 | فَانفَجَرَتْ | *Fan-fajarat* | Then gushed forth |
| 60 | مَشْرَبَهُمْ | *Mashrabahum* | Their own place for water |
| 60 | لَا تَعْثَوْا فِي الْأَرْضِ | *La ta'thaw fil-'ard* | *ni.pl* Do not act corruptly on the earth |
| 60 | مُفْسِدِينَ | *Mufsidin* | *ap*. Those who do mischief |
| 61 | فُومِهَا | *Fumiha* | Its (wheat or garlic) |
| 61 | ضُرِبَتْ عَلَيْهِمْ | *Duribat 'alayhim* | They were covered |
| 61 | ذِلَّةُ | *Dhila* | Humiliation |
| 61 | مَسْكَنَةُ | *Mas-kanah* | Misery |
| 61 | بَاءُوا بِغَضَبٍ | *Ba-'u bi-ghadab* | They drew on themselves the wrath (of Allah) |
| 62 | هَادُوا | *Hadu* | They became Jews |
| 62 | صَّابِئِينَ | *Sabi-'in* | Sabians (a past nation used to live in Iraq) |
| 63 | مِيثَاقَكُمْ | *Mithaqakum* | *pl.* Your covenant |
| 65 | خَاسِئِينَ | *Khasi-'in* | Those who are Despised and |

| V. | WORD | TR. | MEANING |
|---|---|---|---|
| | | | rejected |
| 66 | فَجَعَلْنَاهَا نَكَالًا | *Faja-'alnaha nakala* | So We made it an example |
| 67 | هُزُوًا | *Huzuwa* | Laughing-stock |
| 68 | لَا فَارِضٌ وَلَا بِكْرٌ | *La-faridun wa la bikr* | (A heifer) neither too old nor too young |
| 68 | عَوَانٌ بَيْنَ ذَٰلِكَ | *Awanum-bayna dhalik* | Between the two conditions (i.e., middle-aged) |
| 69 | فَاقِعٌ لَوْنُهَا | *Faqi-'ul-lawnuha* | Bright in its (yellow) colour |
| 71 | لَا ذَلُولٌ | *La-dhalul* | Not trained |
| 71 | تُثِيرُ الْأَرْضَ | *Tuthirul-'ard* | Tills the soil |
| 71 | حَرْثَ | *Harth* | Fields |
| 71 | مُسَلَّمَةٌ | *Musallama* | Sound |
| 71 | لَا شِيَةَ فِيهَا | *La-shiyata fiha* | Without blemish |
| 72 | فَادَّارَأْتُمْ فِيهَا | *Faddara'-tum fiha* | And fell into a dispute among yourselves |
| 74 | يَتَفَجَّرُ | *Yatafajjar* | Gushes forth |
| 74 | يَشَّقَّقُ | *Yash-shaqqaq* | Splits asunder |
| 75 | يُحَرِّفُونَهُ | *Yuharri-funah* | They pervert it |
| 76 | خَلَا بَعْضُهُمْ | *Khala ba'-duhum* | They met (each other) in private |
| 76 | فَتَحَ اللَّهُ عَلَيْكُمْ | *Fatahallahu 'alaykum* | Allah has revealed to you |
| 78 | أُمِّيُّونَ | *Ummiyyun* | *pl.* Illiterate |
| 78 | أَمَانِيَّ | *'Amaniyy* | *pl.* Desire |
| 79 | فَوَيْلٌ | *Fa-wayl* | Then woe |

| V. | WORD | TR. | MEANING |
|---|---|---|---|
| 81 | كَسَبَ سَيِّئَةً | *Kasab sayyi'a* | Earned Evil |
| 81 | أَحَاطَتْ بِهِ | *'ahatat bih* | Surrounded him |
| 85 | تَظَاهَرُونَ عَلَيْهِمْ | *Tazaharuna 'alayhim* | *pl.* You assist (their enemies) against them |
| 85 | أُسَارَى | *'Usara* | Captives |
| 85 | تُفَادُوهُمْ | *Tufaduhum* | *pl.* You ransom them |
| 85 | خِزْيٌ | *Khizy* | Disgrace |
| 87 | قَفَّيْنَا مِنْ بَعْدِهِ بِالرُّسُلِ | *Qaffayna mim-ba'-dihi birrusul* | We followed him up with a succession of Messengers |
| 87 | بِرُوحِ الْقُدُسِ | *Bi-ruhil-qudus* | With the holy spirit |
| 88 | قُلُوبُنَا غُلْفٌ | *Qulubuna ghulf* | Our hearts are wrapped (i.e., do not hear or understand Allah's Word) |
| 89 | يَسْتَفْتِحُونَ | *Yastafti-hun* | They pray for victory |
| 90 | اشْتَرَوْا بِهِ أَنفُسَهُمْ | *'Sh-taraw bihi 'anfusahum* | (The price) for which they sold their souls |
| 90 | بَغْيًا | *Baghya* | In insolent envy |
| 90 | فَبَاءُوا بِغَضَبٍ | *Faba-'u bi-ghadab* | They drew on themselves wrath |
| 92 | اتَّخَذْتُمُ الْعِجْلَ | *At-takhadhtumul-'ijl* | *pl.* You worshipped the calf |
| 96 | يُعَمَّرُ | *Yu-'ammar* | Is allowed to live |
| 100 | نَبَذَهُ | *Nabadhah* | Threw it aside |

| V. | WORD | TR. | MEANING |
|---|---|---|---|
| 102 | تَتْلُو الشَّيَاطِينُ | *Tatlush-shayya-tin* | Satans recite over |
| 102 | نَحْنُ فِتْنَةٌ | *Nahnu-fitna* | We are for trial |
| 102 | خَلَاقٍ | *Khalaq* | Share in the happiness (of the Hereafter) |
| 102 | شَرَوْا بِهِ أَنفُسَهُمْ | *Sharaw bihi 'anfusa-hum* | (the price) for which they sold their souls |
| 104 | لَا تَقُولُوا رَاعِنَا | *La taqulu ra'ina* | *ni.pl.* Do not say : "Ra'ina" [in Hebrew it means "an insult"] |
| 104 | قُولُوا انظُرْنَا | *Qulunzurna* | *im.* Say : " 'Unzurna" [which means look upon us] |
| 105 | اللَّهُ ذُو الْفَضْلِ الْعَظِيمِ | *Allahu dhul-Fadlil-'azim* | Allah is the Owner of Great Bounty |
| 106 | مَا نَنسَخْ مِنْ آيَةٍ | *Ma nansakh min 'aya* | None of Our revelations do We abrogate |
| 106 | نُنسِهَا | *Nunsiha* | (None of Our revelations) do We cause to be forgotten |
| 107 | وَلِيٌّ | *Waliyy* | Patron |
| 108 | سَوَاءَ السَّبِيلِ | *Sawa-'assbil* | Even way |
| 111 | أَمَانِيُّهُمْ | *'Amaniyyuhum* | Their (vain) desires |
| 112 | أَسْلَمَ وَجْهَهُ لِلَّهِ | *'Aslam wajhahu lillah* | Submitted his whole self to Allah |
| 114 | خِزْيٌ | *Khizy* | Disgrace |
| 115 | فَثَمَّ وَجْهُ اللَّهِ | *Fa-thamma Waj-* | There is Allah's |

| V. | WORD | TR. | MEANING |
|---|---|---|---|
| | | *hullah* | Face |
| 116 | سُبْحَانَهُ | *Subhanah* | Glory be to Him |
| 116 | لَهُ قَانِتُونَ | *Lahu qanitun* | (All) surrender with obedience (in worship) to Him |
| 117 | بَدِيعُ | *Badi'* | The Originator |
| 117 | قَضَى أَمْرًا | *Qada 'amra* | He decreed a matter |
| 117 | كُنْ فَيَكُونُ | *Kun fayakun* | Be, and it is |
| 122 | عَالَمِينَ | *'Alamin* | Mankind and jinns |
| 123 | لَا تَجْزِي نَفْسٌ | *La-tajzi nafs* | One soul shall not avail (another) |
| 123 | عَدْلٌ | *'Adl* | Compensation |
| 124 | ابْتَلَى | *Ibtala* | Tried |
| 124 | بِكَلِمَاتٍ | *Bi-kalimat* | With certain Commands |
| 124 | فَأَتَمَّهُنَّ | *Fa-'atammahunn* | He (Ibrahim عليه السلام) fulfilled them |
| 125 | مَثَابَةً لِلنَّاسِ | *Mathabatal-linnas* | A place of assembly for men |
| 125 | عَهِدْنَا | *'Ahidna* | We covenanted |
| 125 | بَيْتِي | *Baytiy* | My House (the Ka'ba) |
| 126 | أَضْطَرُّهُ | *'Adtarruhu* | I shall compel him |
| 128 | مُسْلِمَيْنِ لَكَ | *Muslimayni lak* | (Make us)Submissive unto You |
| 128 | أَرِنَا مَنَاسِكَنَا | *'Arina mana sikana* | Show us our places for the celebration of (due) rites |
| 129 | يُزَكِّيهِمْ | *Yuzakkihim* | Purifies them |

| V. | WORD | TR. | MEANING |
|---|---|---|---|
| 130 | يَرْغَبُ عَنْ | *Yarghabu 'an* | Turns away from |
| 130 | سَفِهَ نَفْسَهُ | *Safiha nafsah* | Debased his soul with folly |
| 131 | أَسْلِمْ | *'Aslim* | Submitted (his will to Allah) |
| 132 | دِينَ | *Din* | (True) religion |
| 134 | خَلَتْ | *Khalat* | Passed away |
| 135 | حَنِيفًا | *Hanifa* | The true |
| 136 | الْأَسْبَاط | *Al-'asbat* | The twelve sons of Ya'qub عليه السلام |
| 138 | صِبْغَةَ اللَّهِ | *Sibghatallah* | The religion of Allah (Islam) |
| 142 | سُّفَهَاءُ | *Sufaha'* | Fools (Jews, pagans, and hypocrites) |
| 142 | مَا وَلَّاهُمْ | *Ma wallahum* | What has turned them? |
| 142 | عَنْ قِبْلَتِهِمْ | *'An-qiblati-him* | From their Qibla [prayer direction (towards Jerusalem)] |
| 143 | أُمَّةً وَسَطًا | *'Ummatanw-wasata* | A nation justly balanced |
| 143 | يَنقَلِبُ عَلَى عَقِبَيْهِ | *Many-yanqalibu 'ala 'aqibayh* | Turns on his (two) heels |
| 143 | لَكَبِيرَةً | *Lakabira* | Indeed it is great (heavy) |
| 143 | لِيُضِيعَ إِيمَانَكُمْ | *Liyudi-'a 'imanakum* | (Allah would never) make your faith (prayers) to be lost |
| 144 | شَطْرَ الْمَسْجِدِ الْحَرَامِ | *Shatral-masjidil-Haram* | Towards the Sacred Mosque |

| V. | WORD | TR. | MEANING |
|---|---|---|---|
| 147 | مُمْتَرِينَ | *Mumtarin* | Doubters |
| 151 | يُزَكِّيكُمْ | *Yuzakkikum* | Purifies you |
| 151 | الْكِتَابَ وَالْحِكْمَةَ | *Al-Kitaba wal-Hikma* | The Book (i.e.,the Holy Qur'an) and the Hikma (i.e, Sunna and jurisprudence) |
| 155 | لَنَبْلُوَنَّكُمْ | *Lanablu-wannakum* | We shall test you |
| 157 | صَلَوَاتٌ مِنْ رَبِّهِمْ | *Salawatum-mir-Rabbihim* | Blessings from their Lord |
| 158 | شَعَائِرِ اللَّهِ | *Sha-'a-'irillah* | The Symbols of Allah |
| 158 | اعْتَمَرَ | *I'-tamar* | Visited the House(in a period other than that of Hajj) |
| 158 | فَلَا جُنَاحَ عَلَيْهِ | *Fala junaha 'alayh* | It is not a sin on him |
| 158 | يَطَّوَّفَ بِهِمَا | *Yat-tawwafa bihima* | Compasses them round (As-Saffa and Al-Marwa) |
| 159 | يَلْعَنُهُمُ اللَّهُ | *Yal-'anu-humullah* | Allah curses them |
| 162 | يُنظَرُونَ | *Yunzarun* | They will be reprieved |
| 164 | بَثَّ فِيهَا | *Baththa fiha* | He scattered therein |
| 164 | تَصْرِيفِ الرِّيَاحِ | *Tas-rifir-riyah* | Veering of winds |
| 165 | أَندَادًا | *'Andad* | Rivals |
| 166 | تَقَطَّعَتْ بِهِمُ الْأَسْبَابُ | *Taqatta-'at bihimul-'asbab* | All the relation between them was cut off |

| V. | WORD | TR. | MEANING |
|---|---|---|---|
| 167 | كَرَّةً | *Karra* | One more chance |
| 167 | حَسَرَاتٍ | *Hasarat* | Regrets |
| 168 | خُطُوَاتِ الشَّيْطَانِ | *Khutuwatish-shay-tan* | The footsteps of Satan |
| 169 | يَأْمُرُكُمْ بِالسُّوءِ | *Ya'-murukum-bis-su'* | He (Satan) commands you what is evil |
| 169 | فَحْشَاءِ | *Fah-sha'* | Shameful |
| 170 | أَلْفَيْنَا | *'Al-fayna* | We found |
| 171 | يَنْعِقُ | *Yan-'iq* | Shouts |
| 171 | بُكْمٌ | *Bukm* | *pl.* Dumb |
| 173 | دَمَ | *Dam* | Blood |
| 173 | لَحْمَ الْخِنزِيرِ | *Lahmal-khin-zir* | The flesh of swine |
| 173 | مَا أُهِلَّ بِهِ لِغَيْرِ اللَّهِ | *Ma 'u-hilla bihi li-ghayrillah* | That which is slaughtered as a scrifice for others than Allah |
| 173 | اضْطُرَّ | *'Idturr* | *pv.* Is forced by necessity |
| 173 | غَيْرَ بَاغٍ | *Ghayra bagh* | Without wilful disobedience |
| 173 | وَلَا عَادٍ | *Wa la 'ad* | Nor transgressing due limits |
| 174 | ثَمَنًا قَلِيلًا | *Thamanan-qalila* | Miserable profit |
| 174 | لَا يُزَكِّيهِمْ | *La yuzakkihim* | (Allah) does not purify them |
| 176 | شِقَاقٍ | *Shiqaq* | Schism |
| 176 | بَعِيدٍ | *Ba'id* | Far |
| 177 | ابْنَ السَّبِيلِ | *'Ibnas-sabil* | Wayfarer |

| V. | WORD | TR. | MEANING |
|---|---|---|---|
| 177 | فِي الرِّقَابِ | *Fir-riqab* | For the ransom of slaves |
| 177 | صَابِرِينَ | *Sabirin* | Those who are patient |
| 177 | بَأْسَاء | *Ba'-sa'* | Pain (or suffering) |
| 177 | ضَرَّاء | *Darra'* | Adversity |
| 177 | حِينَ الْبَأْسِ | *Hinal-ba's* | At the time of fighting (during the battles) |
| 178 | كُتِبَ عَلَيْكُمْ | *Kutiba 'alaykum* | It is prescribed for you |
| 178 | عُفِيَ لَهُ مِنْ أَخِيهِ | *'Ufiya lahu min 'akhih* | If any remission is made by the relative of the slain |
| 180 | تَرَكَ خَيْرًا | *Taraka khay-ra* | Left wealth |
| 180 | وَصِيَّةً | *Wasiyya* | Will |
| 182 | جَنَفًا | *Janafa* | Unjust |
| 182 | إِثْمًا | *'Ithma* | Wrong-doing |
| 184 | يُطِيقُونَهُ | *Yuti-qunah* | Those who can do it |
| 184 | تَطَوَّعَ خَيْرًا | *Tatawwa-'a khay-ra* | (He) gave more (ransom) of his own free will |
| 185 | لِتُكَبِّرُوا اللَّهَ | *Litukabbirullah* | To glorify Allah |
| 187 | رَفَثُ | *Rafath* | To approach one's wife |
| 187 | هُنَّ لِبَاسٌ لَكُمْ | *Hunna libasul-lakum* | They are your garments |
| 187 | حُدُودُ اللَّهِ | *Hududullah* | Limits set by Allah |
| 188 | تُدْلُوا بِهَا | *Tadlu biha* | Use it (your property) as a bait |

| V. | WORD | TR. | MEANING |
|---|---|---|---|
| 191 | ثَقِفْتُمُوهُمْ | *Thaqif-tumuhum* | *pl.* You found them |
| 191 | فِتْنَةُ | *Fitna* | Polytheism |
| 191 | عِنْدَ الْمَسْجِدِ الْحَرَامِ | *'Indal-Masjidil-Haram* | At the Sacred Mosque |
| 194 | حُرُمَاتُ | *Hurumat* | Prohibited things |
| 195 | تَهْلُكَةِ | *Tahluka* | Destruction |
| 196 | أُحْصِرْتُمْ | *'Uh-sirtum* | *pl.* You are prevented |
| 196 | فَمَا اسْتَيْسَرَ | *Famas-taysar* | *pl.* You may find |
| 196 | مِنَ الْهَدْيِ | *Minal-hady* | Anything that can be offered as a scrifice |
| 196 | لَا تَحْلِقُوا رُءُوسَكُمْ | *La tah-liqu ru-'usakum* | *ni.pl.* Do not shave your heads |
| 196 | يَبْلُغَ الْهَدْيُ مَحِلَّهُ | *Yablughal-hadyu mahillah* | The offering reachs the place of scrifice |
| 196 | فِدْيَةٌ | *Fidya* | Compensation |
| 196 | نُسُكٍ | *Nusuk* | Scrifice |
| 197 | فَرَضَ | *Farad* | Duty |
| 197 | فَلَا رَفَثَ | *Fala rafth* | Let there be no obscenity |
| 197 | لَا جِدَالَ فِي الْحَجِّ | *La jidala fil-Hajj* | Let there be no wrangling in the Hajj |
| 198 | جُنَاحٌ | *Junah* | Crime |
| 198 | فَضْلًا | *Fadla* | Bounty |
| 198 | أَفَضْتُمْ | *'Afadtum* | *pl.* You pour down |
| 198 | الْمَشْعَرِ الْحَرَامِ | *Al-Mash-'aril-Haram* | The Sacred Monument (i.e., Muzdalifa a well |

| V. | WORD | TR. | MEANING |
|---|---|---|---|
| | | | known place near Makka) |
| 200 | مَنَاسِكَكُمْ | *Manasika-kum* | *pl.* Your rites |
| 200 | خَلَاقٍ | *Khalaq* | Portion |
| 201 | فِي الدُّنْيَا حَسَنَةً | *Fid-dunya hasanata* | Good in this world |
| 201 | فِي الْآخِرَةِ حَسَنَةً | *Fil-'akhirati hasanata* | Good in the Hereafter |
| 204 | أَلَدُّ الْخِصَامِ | *'Aladdul-khisam* | The most contentious of enemies |
| 205 | حَرْثَ | *Harth* | Crops |
| 206 | أَخَذَتْهُ الْعِزَّةُ بِالْإِثْمِ | *'Akhadhat-hul-'izzatu bil-'ithm* | He is led by arrogance to (more) crime |
| 206 | فَحَسْبُهُ جَهَنَّمُ | *Fahasbuhu Jahannam* | Enough for him is Hell |
| 206 | لَبِئْسَ الْمِهَادُ | *La-bi'-sal-mihad* | An evil bed indeed (to lie on) |
| 207 | يَشْرِي نَفْسَهُ | *Yashri naf-sah* | Sells himself |
| 208 | فِي السِّلْمِ | *Fis-silm* | Into Islam |
| 208 | خُطُوَاتِ الشَّيْطَانِ | *Khutuwatish-Shay-tan* | The footsteps of Satan |
| 209 | زَلَلْتُمْ | *Zalaltum* | *pl.* You backslide |
| 210 | ظُلَلٍ مِنَ الْغَمَامِ | *Zulalim-minal-ghamam* | Canopies of clouds |
| 212 | بِغَيْرِ حِسَابٍ | *Bi-ghayri hisab* | Without measure |
| 213 | بَغْيًا | *Baghya* | Selfish contumacy |
| 214 | مَثَلُ الَّذِينَ خَلَوْا | *Matha-lulladhina khalawa* | Like those who passed away |
| 214 | زُلْزِلُوا | *Zul-zilu* | They were shaken |

| V. | WORD | TR. | MEANING |
|---|---|---|---|
| 216 | كُرْهٌ لَكُمْ | *Kurhul-lakum* | *pl.* You dislike it |
| 217 | كَبِيرٌ | *Kabir* | Grave (offence) |
| 217 | فِتْنَةُ | *Fitna* | Polytheism |
| 217 | حَبِطَتْ | *Habitat* | Came to nothing |
| 219 | مَيْسِرِ | *Maysir* | Gambling |
| 219 | عَفْوَ | *'Afw* | Superfluous |
| 220 | لَأَعْنَتَكُمْ | *La-'a'-natakum* | He could have put you into difficulties |
| 222 | أَذًى | *'Adha* | Hurt and pollution |
| 223 | حَرْثٌ | *Harth* | Tilth |
| 223 | أَنَّى شِئْتُمْ | *'An-na shi'-tum* | When or how you will |
| 224 | عُرْضَةً لِأَيْمَانِكُمْ | *'Urdatal-li-'ay-manikum* | Excuse in your oaths |
| 225 | بِاللَّغْوِ فِي أَيْمَانِكُمْ | *Bil-laghwi fi 'ay-manikum* | Thoughtlessness in your oaths |
| 226 | يُؤْلُونَ مِنْ نِسَائِهِمْ | *Yu'-luna minnisa-'ihim* | They take an oath for abstention from their wives |
| 226 | تَرَبُّصُ | *Tarabbus* | To wait |
| 226 | فَاءُوا | *Fa-'u* | They return |
| 228 | ثَلَاثَةَ قُرُوءٍ | *Thalathata quru'* | Three menstrual periods |
| 228 | بُعُولَتُهُنَّ | *Bu-'ulatuhunn* | Their husbands |
| 228 | دَرَجَةٌ | *Daraja* | Degree |
| 229 | الطَّلَاقُ مَرَّتَانِ | *'At-talaqu marratan* | A divorce is only permissible twice |
| 229 | تَسْرِيحٌ بِإِحْسَانٍ | *Tasrihum-bi-'ihsan* | Separate with kindness |

| V. | WORD | TR. | MEANING |
|---|---|---|---|
| 229 | تِلْكَ حُدُودُ اللّٰهِ | *Tilka hududullah* | These are the limits ordained by Allah |
| 231 | فَبَلَغْنَ أَجَلَهُنَّ | *Fabalaghna 'ajalahunn* | They fulfilled the term of their 'Iddat (i.e., prescribed period) |
| 231 | لَا تُمْسِكُوهُنَّ ضِرَارًا | *La tumsikuhunna dirara* | *ni.pi.* Do not take them back to injure them |
| 231 | آيَاتِ اللّٰهِ | *'Ayatillah* | The Verses (Laws) of Allah |
| 231 | هُزُوًا | *Huzuwa* | Jest |
| 232 | فَلَا تَعْضُلُوهُنَّ | *Fala ta'-duluhunn* | *ni.pl.* Do not prevent them |
| 232 | أَزْكَى لَكُمْ | *'Azka lakum* | More virtuous and purer for you |
| 233 | وُسْعَهَا | *Wus-'aha* | Its ability |
| 233 | وَعَلَى الْوَارِثِ | *Wa 'alal-warith* | And on the (father's) heir |
| 233 | أَرَادَا فِصَالًا | *'Arada fisala* | They both decided on weaning |
| 235 | عَرَّضْتُمْ بِهِ | *'Arradtum-bih* | *pl.* You made an indirect offer |
| 235 | أَكْنَنْتُمْ | *'Aknantum* | *pl.* You kept secret |
| 235 | لَا تُوَاعِدُوهُنَّ سِرًّا | *La tuwa-'iduhunna sirra* | *ni.pl.* Do not make a secret contract with them |
| 235 | حَتَّى يَبْلُغَ الْكِتَابُ أَجَلَهُ | *Hatta yablughal-kitabu 'ajalah* | Till the term prescribed is fulfilled |
| 236 | فَرِيضَةً | *Farida* | Dower |
| 236 | مَتِّعُوهُنَّ | *Matti-'uhunn* | Bestow on them (a suitable gift) |

| V. | WORD | TR. | MEANING |
|---|---|---|---|
| 236 | مُوسِعِ | *Musi‘* | Wealthy |
| 236 | قَدَرُهُ | *Qadaruh* | According to his means |
| 236 | مُقْتِرِ | *Muqtir* | Poor |
| 238 | الصَّلَاةِ الْوُسْطَى | *As-salatil-wusta* | The ‘Asr prayer |
| 238 | قَانِتِينَ | *Qanitin* | *ap.* Those who are obedient to Allah |
| 239 | فَرِجَالًا | *Fa-rijala* | *im.pl.* (Pray) on foot |
| 241 | لِلْمُطَلَّقَاتِ مَتَاعٌ | *Lil-mutallaqati mata‘* | For divorced women is a suitable gift |
| 245 | قَرْضًا حَسَنًا | *Qardan hasana* | Beautiful loan |
| 245 | يَقْبِضُ وَيَبْسُطُ | *Yaqbidu wa yab-sut* | (Allah) decreases or increases (your provisions) |
| 246 | مَلَإِ | *Mala'* | Cheifs |
| 246 | هَلْ عَسَيْتُمْ | *Hal ‘asaytum* | Is it not possible that you? |
| 247 | أَنَّى يَكُونُ | *'Ana yakun* | How can he be? |
| 247 | زَادَهُ بَسْطَةً فِي الْعِلْمِ | *Zadahu basta-tan-fil-‘ilm* | (Allah) increased him abundantly in knowledge |
| 248 | التَّابُوتُ | *At-ta-but* | The Ark of the Covenant |
| 248 | فِيهِ سَكِينَةٌ | *Fihi sakina* | Wherein is peace and reassurance |
| 249 | فَصَلَ طَالُوتُ | *Fasala Talut* | Talut set forth |
| 249 | مُبْتَلِيكُم | *Mubtalikum* | (Allah) will test you |
| 249 | اغْتَرَفَ | *Ightaraf* | He took in the hollow (of his |

| V. | WORD | TR. | MEANING |
|---|---|---|---|
| | | | hand) |
| 249 | لَا طَاقَةَ لَنَا | *La taqata lana* | We have no power |
| 249 | فِئَةٍ | *Fi-'a* | Group |
| 250 | بَرَزُوا | *Barazu* | They advanced |
| 251 | حِكْمَةَ | *Hikma* | Wisdom |
| 253 | بِرُوحِ الْقُدُسِ | *Bi-ruhil-qudus* | With the Holy Spirit |
| 254 | لَا خُلَّةٌ | *La khulla* | No friendship |
| 255 | الْحَيُّ | *Al-hayy* | The Ever Living |
| 255 | الْقَيُّومُ | *Al-qayyum* | The One Who sustains and protects all that exists |
| 255 | سِنَةٌ | *Sina* | Slumber |
| 255 | لَا يَئُودُهُ | *La ya-'uduh* | He feels no fatigue |
| 256 | تَبَيَّنَ الرُّشْدُ | *Ta-bayyanar-rushd* | The Right Path became distinct |
| 256 | غَيِّ | *Ghayy* | Wrong path |
| 256 | طَاغُوتِ | *Taghut* | Anything worshipped beside Allah |
| 256 | الْعُرْوَةِ الْوُثْقَى | *Al-'urwatil-wuthqa* | The most trustworthy hand-hold |
| 256 | لَاانفِصَامَ لَهَا | *Lan-fisama laha* | That never breaks |
| 258 | الَّذِي حَاجَّ إِبْرَاهِيمَ | *Al-lathi hajja 'Ibra-him* | One who disputed with Ibrahim عليه السلام |
| 258 | بُهِتَ | *Buhit* | He (the disbeliever) was utterly |

| V. | WORD | TR. | MEANING |
|---|---|---|---|
| | | | defeated |
| 259 | خَاوِيَةٌ عَلَى عُرُوشِهَا | *Khawi-yatun 'ala uru-shiha* | All in ruins |
| 259 | أَنَّى يُحْيِي | *'Anna yuhyi* | How shall He bring it to life |
| 259 | لَمْ يَتَسَنَّهْ | *Lam yata-sannah* | They show no signs of change |
| 259 | نُنشِزُهَا | *Nun-shizuha* | We bring them together |
| 260 | فَصُرْهُنَّ إِلَيْكَ | *Fasur-hunna 'ilayk* | *im.* Cause them to incline towards you (then cut them into pieces) |
| 262 | مَنًّا | *Man-na* | Reminding (others)of (one's) generosity |
| 262 | أَذًى | *'Adha* | Injury |
| 264 | رِئَاءَ النَّاسِ | *Ri-'a-'annas* | To be seen of men |
| 264 | صَفْوَانٍ | *Saf-wan* | Smooth rock |
| 264 | وَابِلٌ | *Wabil* | Heavy rain |
| 264 | صَلْدًا | *Salda* | Bare |
| 265 | تَثْبِيتًا | *Tathbita* | Certainty |
| 265 | جَنَّةٍ بِرَبْوَةٍ | *Jannatim-bi-rabwa* | Garden on a height |
| 265 | أُكُلَهَا | *'Ukulaha* | Its yields |
| 265 | طَلٌّ | *Tall* | Light rain |
| 266 | إِعْصَارٌ | *'I'-sar* | Whirlwind |
| 266 | فِيهِ نَارٌ | *Fihi narr* | In it fire |
| 267 | لَا تَيَمَّمُوا الْخَبِيثَ | *La ta-yamma-mul-khabith* | *ni.pl.* Do not aim at anything which is bad |

| V. | WORD | TR. | MEANING |
|---|---|---|---|
| 267 | تُغْمِضُوا فِيهِ | *Tugh-midu fih* | *pl.* You close eyes in it |
| 273 | أُحْصِرُوا | *'Uh-siru* | They were restricted from travel |
| 273 | ضَرْبًا | *Darba* | To move about |
| 273 | تَعَفُّفِ | *Ta-'affuf* | Modesty |
| 273 | بِسِيمَاهُمْ | *Bi-sima-hum* | By their (unfailing) mark |
| 273 | إِلْحَافًا | *'Il-hafa* | Importunately |
| 275 | يَتَخَبَّطُهُ الشَّيْطَانُ | *Yata-khab-batuhush-shay-tan* | Satan beats him (and leads him to insanity) |
| 275 | مَسِّ | *Mass* | Madness |
| 276 | يَمْحَقُ اللَّهُ الرِّبَا | *Yamha-qulla-hur-riba* | Allah will deprive usury of all blessing |
| 276 | يُرْبِي الصَّدَقَاتِ | *Yur-bis-sadaqat* | (Allah) will give increase for deeds of charity |
| 279 | فَأْذَنُوا بِحَرْبٍ | *Fa'dhanu bi-harb* | Then take notice of war |
| 280 | عُسْرَةٍ | *'Us-ra* | Difficulty |
| 280 | نَظِرَةٌ | *Nazi-ra* | To grant time |
| 282 | يُمْلِلْ | *Umlil* | Dictates |
| 282 | يَبْخَسْ | *Yabkhas* | Diminishes |
| 282 | شَيْئًا | *Shay-'a* | Anything |
| 282 | أَنْ يُمِلَّ هُوَ | *'Any-yumilla huwa* | To dictate by himself |
| 282 | لَا يَأْبَ | *La ya'-b* | Should not refuse |

| V. | WORD | TR. | MEANING |
|---|---|---|---|
| 282 | لَا تَسْأَمُوا | *La tas-'amu* | *ni.pl.* You should not become weary |
| 282 | أَقْسَطُ | *'Aqsat* | Juster |
| 282 | أَقْوَمُ لِلشَّهَادَةِ | *'Aqwamu lish-shahada* | More suitable as evidence |
| 282 | أَدْنَى | *'Adna* | More convenient |
| 282 | فُسُوقٌ | *Fusuq* | Wickedness |
| 285 | غُفْرَانَكَ | *Ghufranak* | Your forgiveness |
| 286 | وُسْعَهَا | *Wus-'aha* | Its ability |
| 286 | إِصْرًا | *'Is-ra* | Burden |

| V. | WORD | TR. | MEANING |
|---|---|---|---|

## سُورَةُ آلَ عِمران

## [3] SURAT AL-'IMRAN

## THE FAMILY OF 'IMRAN

| | | | |
|---|---|---|---|
| 3 | أَنْزَلَ الْفُرْقَانَ | *'Anzalal-Furqan* | (Allah) sent down the Cirterion (of Judgment between right and wrong) |
| 4 | اللَّهُ عَزِيزٌ | *Allahu 'Aziz* | Allah is Exalted in Might |
| 7 | آيَاتٌ مُحْكَمَاتٌ | *'Ayatum-muhkamat* | Clear Verses |
| 7 | أُمُّ الْكِتَابِ | *'Ummul-Kitab* | The foundation (or fundamental part) of the Book |
| 7 | مُتَشَابِهَاتٌ | *Mutasha-bihat* | Not entirely clear |
| 7 | زَيْغٌ | *Zay-gh* | Deviation |
| 7 | تَأْوِيلِهِ | *Ta'-wilah* | Its interpretation |
| 8 | لَا تُزِغْ قُلُوبَنَا | *La tuzigh qulu-bana* | *Ni.* Let not our hearts deviate (from the truth) |
| 11 | كَدَأْبِ | *Kada'-b* | Like the behaviour (of the people of Pharaoh) |
| 12 | بِئْسَ الْمِهَادُ | *Bi'-sal-mihad* | An evil bed indeed to lie on (i.e., Hell) |
| 13 | عِبْرَةً | *'Ibra* | Lesson |
| 14 | حُبُّ الشَّهَوَاتِ | *Hubbush-shahawat* | The love of worldly desires |
| 14 | مُقَنْطَرَةِ | *Muqan-tara* | Heaped-up |
| 14 | مُسَوَّمَةِ | *Musawwama* | Branded |
| 14 | أَنْعَامِ | *'An-'am* | Cattle |

| V. | WORD | TR. | MEANING |
|---|---|---|---|
| 14 | حَرْث | *Harth* | Well-tilled land |
| 14 | حُسْنُ الْمَآب | *Husunul-ma-'ab* | The best of the goals (to return to) |
| 17 | قَانِتِينَ | *Qanitin* | *Ap.* Those who worship (Allah) devoutly |
| 17 | بِالْأَسْحَارِ | *Bil-'as-har* | In the early hours of the morning |
| 18 | قَائِمًا بِالْقِسْطِ | *Qa-'imam-bil-qist* | He is standing firm on justice |
| 19 | دِينَ | *Din* | Religion |
| 19 | الْإِسْلَامُ | *Al-'islam* | Submission to the Will of Allah |
| 19 | بَغياً | *Baghya* | Envy |
| 20 | أَسْلَمْتُ وَجْهِي لِلَّهِ | *'As-lamtu wajhia lillah* | I have submitted my whole self to Allah |
| 20 | أُمِّيِّينَ | *'Ummiy-yin* | Unlettered people (the Pagan Arabs) |
| 24 | غَرَّهُمْ | *Gharrahum* | Deceived them |
| 24 | مَّاكَانُوا يَفْتَرُونَ | *Ma ka-nu yaftarun* | What they used to froge |
| 27 | تُولِجُ | *Tulij* | You make (the night) enter into (the day) |
| 27 | بِغَيْرِ حِسَاب | *Bi-ghayri hisab* | Without measure |
| 28 | أَوْلِيَاءَ | *'Awliya'* | Supporters,helpers |
| 28 | تَتَّقُوا مِنْهُمْ | *Tattaqu minhum* | *Pl.* You may guard yourselves from them |
|  | تُقَاةً | *Tuqat* | By way of precaution |

| V. | WORD | TR. | MEANING |
|---|---|---|---|
| 28 | يُحَذِّرُكُمُ اللَّهُ نَفْسَهُ | *Yuhadhdhiru-kumullah Nafsah* | Allah cautions you (to fear) Himself |
| 30 | مُحْضَرًا | *Muh-dara* | Confronted |
| 33 | آلَ عِمْرَانَ | *Al-'Imran* | 'Isa عليه السلام and his mother , Maryam the daughter of 'Imran |
| 35 | مُحَرَّرًا | *Muharrara* | Dedicated ( for Allah's service) |
| 36 | أُعِيذُهَا بِكَ | *'U-'idhuha bik* | I commend her to Your protection |
| 37 | كَفَّلَهَا زَكَرِيَّا | *Kaffalaha Zakariyya* | (Allah) put her under the care of Zakariya عليه السلام |
| 37 | مِحْرَابَ | *Mihrab* | Chamber |
| 37 | أَنَّى لَكِ هَذَا | *'Ana laki hadha* | From where have you got this? |
| 37 | حِسَابٍ | *Hisab* | Measure |
| 39 | بِكَلِمَةٍ مِّنَ اللَّهِ | *Bi-Kalimatin mminallah* | A worrd from Allah (i.e., the creation of 'Isa عليه السلام) |
| 39 | حَصُورًا | *Hasura* | Chaste |
| 41 | آيَةً | *'Ayah* | Sign |
| 41 | أَلَّا تُكَلِّمَ النَّاسَ | *'Alla tukalli-man-nas* | You shall not speak to mankind |
| 41 | إِلَّا رَمْزًا | *'Illa ramza* | Except with signals |
| 41 | سَبِّحْ | *Sabbih* | *Im*. Glorify (Allah) |
| 41 | عَشِيِّ | *'Ashiyy* | Evening |
| 41 | إِبْكَارِ | *'Ibkar* | Morning |

| V. | WORD | TR. | MEANING |
|---|---|---|---|
| 43 | اقْنُتِي | *'Iqnuti* | *Im.* Worship devoutly |
| 44 | يُلْقُونَ أَقْلَامَهُمْ | *Yulquna 'aqlamahum* | They cast lots with their pens |
| 45 | وَجِيهًا | *Wajiha* | Honourable |
| 46 | فِي الْمَهْدِ | *Fil-mahd* | In the cradle |
| 46 | كَهْلًا | *Kahla* | Maturity |
| 47 | قَضَى أَمْرًا | *Qada 'amra* | Decreed a matter |
| 48 | كِتَابَ | *Kitab* | Book |
| 48 | حِكْمَةَ | *Hikma* | Wisdom |
| 49 | أَخْلُقُ لَكُمْ | *'Akhluqu lakum* | I make for you |
| 49 | أُبْرِئُ الْأَكْمَهَ | *'Ubri-'ul-'akmah* | I heal those born blind |
| 49 | مَا تَدَّخِرُونَ | *Ma tadda-khi-run* | What you store |
| 52 | أَحَسَّ | *'Ahass* | Came to know |
| 52 | الْحَوَارِيُّونَ | *Al-Huwa-riyyun* | Disciples (i.e., the Companions of 'Isa عليه السلام) |
| 54 | مَكَرُوا | *Makaru* | They plotted and planned |
| 54 | مَكَرَ اللَّهُ | *Makaral-lah* | Allah planned |
| 55 | مُتَوَفِّيكَ | *Muta-waffik* | I (Allah) will take you |
| 59 | مَثَلَ عِيسَى | *Mathala 'Iisa* | The similitude of 'Isa عليه السلام |
| 60 | مُمْتَرِينَ | *Mumtarin* | Those who doubt |
| 61 | تَعَالَوْا | *Ta-'alaw* | *Im.pl.* Come |
| 61 | نَبْتَهِلْ | *Nabta-hil* | We invoke the curse (of Allah) |

| V. | WORD | TR. | MEANING |
|---|---|---|---|
| 64 | كَلِمَةٍ سَوَاءٍ | *Kalimatin sawa'* | Commons terms |
| 67 | كَانَ حَنِيفًا مُسْلِمًا | *Kana Hanifa Muslima* | He was upright, and bowed his will to Allah (which is Islam) |
| 68 | وَلِيُّ الْمُؤْمِنِينَ | *Waliyyul-mu'-mìnin* | The Protecter and Helper of the believers |
| 71 | تَلْبِسُونَ | *Tal-bisun* | *Pl.* You mix |
| 75 | عَلَيْهِ قَائِمًا | *'Alayhi qa-'ima* | You constantly stand demanding (of him) |
| 75 | سَبِيلٌ | *Sabil* | Blame |
| 77 | لَا خَلَاقَ لَهُمْ | *La khalaqa lahum* | They shall have no portion |
| 77 | لَا يَنْظُرُ إِلَيْهِمْ | *La yanzuru 'layhim* | He will not look at them |
| 77 | لَا يُزَكِّيهِمْ | *La yuzakki-him* | He will not purify them |
| 78 | يَلْوُونَ | *Yal-wun* | They distort |
| 78 | أَلْسِنَتَهُمْ | *Alsi-natahum* | Their tongues |
| 79 | حُكْمَ | *Hukm* | Knowledge and understanding |
| 79 | كُونُوا رَبَّانِيِّينَ | *Kunu Rab-ba-niyyin* | *Im.pl.* Be you worshippers of Allah |
| 79 | تَدْرُسُونَ | *Tadrusun* | *Pl.* You study |
| 81 | إِصْرِي | *'Isri* | My covenant |
| 83 | لَهُ أَسْلَمَ | *Lahu 'aslam* | ( All creatures ) submitted to Him |
| 84 | الْأَسْبَاطَ | *Al-'Asbat* | The sons of Ya'qub عليه السلام |

| V. | WORD | TR. | MEANING |
|---|---|---|---|
| 88 | وَلَاهُم يُنْظَرُون | *Wa la hum yunzarun* | There will be no respite for them |
| 95 | حَنِيفًا | *Hanifa* | Sane in faith |
| 96 | بَكَّة | *Bak-ka* | Makka |
| 99 | تَبْغُونَهَا عِوَجًا | *Tab-ghuna-ha 'iwaja* | *Pl.* You are seeking to make it crooked |
| 101 | مَنْ يَعْتَصِمْ بِاللّه | *Many-ya'-tasim-billah* | Whoever holds firmly to Allah |
| 102 | حَقَّ تُقَاتِه | *Haqqa tuqa-tih* | As He (Allah) should be feared |
| 103 | اعْتَصِمُوا بِحَبْلِ اللّهِ | *I'tasimu bi-hablil-lah* | *Im.pl.* Hold fast to the Rope of Allah |
| 103 | شَفَا | *Shafa* | Brink |
| 103 | حُفْرَة | *Hufra* | Pit |
| 111 | أَذَى | *'Adha* | Harm |
| 111 | يُوَلُّوكُمْ الْأَدْبَارَ | *Yu-wallukumul-'adbar* | They show you their backs (i.e., they run away) |
| 112 | ضُرِبَتْ عَلَيْهِمِ الذِّلَّةُ | *Duribat 'alayhimudh-dhilla* | Shame was pitched over them |
| 112 | ثُقِفُوا | *Thuqifu* | They were found |
| 112 | حَبْلٍ مِنْ اللّهِ | *Hablim-minallah* | A covenant (of protection) from Allah |
| 112 | حَبْلٍ مِنْ النَّاسِ | *Hablim-minannas* | A covenant (of protection) from men |
| 112 | بَاءُوا بِغَضَبٍ | *Ba-'u bi-ghadab* | They drew on themselves wrath |
| 112 | مَسْكَنَةُ | *Maskanah* | Destitution |
| 113 | لَيْسُوا سَوَاءً | *Laysu sawa'* | They are not alike |

| V. | WORD | TR. | MEANING |
|---|---|---|---|
| 113 | أُمَّةٌ قَائِمَةٌ | *'Ummatun-qa-'ima* | A portion (of people) that stands for the right |
| 116 | لَنْ تُغْنِيَ عَنْهُمْ | *Lan-tughniya 'anhum* | Will not avail them |
| 117 | صِرٌّ | *Sirr* | Extremely cold |
| 117 | حَرْثَ قَوْمٍ | *Hartha qaw-min* | The harvest of men |
| 118 | بِطَانَةً | *Bitana* | Intimate friends |
| 118 | لَا يَأْلُونَكُمْ خَبَالًا | *La ya'-lunakum kha-bala* | They will not fail to corrupt you |
| 118 | وَدُّوا مَا عَنِتُّمْ | *Waddu ma 'anittum* | They (only) desired for you to suffer |
| 119 | خَلَوْا | *Khalaw* | They are alone |
| 119 | غَيْظِ | *Ghayz* | Rage |
| 121 | غَدَوْتَ | *Ghadawt* | You left early in the morning |
| 121 | تُبَوِّئُ | *Tubawwi'* | You assign (positions) |
| 121 | مَقَاعِدَ لِلْقِتَالِ | *Maqa-'ida lil-qital* | Positions for battle |
| 122 | تَفْشَلَا | *Tafshala* | *Dl.* They lose heart |
| 123 | أَذِلَّةٌ | *'Adhillah* | Helpless, weak |
| 124 | يُمِدَّكُمْ | *Yumiddakum* | Helps you |
| 125 | يَأْتُوكُمْ | *Ya'-tukum* | They come to you |
| 125 | مِنْ فَوْرِهِمْ هَذَا | *Min-fawrihim hadha* | Immediately on their arrival |
| 125 | مُسَوِّمِينَ | *Musaw-wimin* | Clearly marked |
| 127 | لِيَقْطَعَ طَرَفًا | *li-yaqta-'a tara-fa* | He might cut off a fringe |
| 127 | يَكْبِتَهُمْ | *Yakbitahum* | He exposes them to infamy |

| V. | WORD | TR. | MEANING |
|---|---|---|---|
| 130 | مُضَاعَفَةً | *Muda-'afah* | Multiplied |
| 134 | سَرَّاءِ | *Sarra'* | Prosperity |
| 134 | ضَرَّاءِ | *Darra'* | Adversity |
| 134 | الْكَاظِمِينَ الْغَيْظَ | *Al-kaziminal-ghayz* | Those who restrain anger |
| 135 | فَعَلُوا | *Fa-'alu* | They committed |
| 135 | فَاحِشَةً | *Fahisha* | Indecency |
| 137 | خَلَتْ | *Khalat* | Passed away |
| 137 | سُنَنٌ | *Sunan* | Examples |
| 139 | لَا تَهِنُوا | *La tahinu* | *Ni.pl.* Lose not heart |
| 140 | قَرْحٌ | *Qarh* | Wound |
| 140 | قَرْحٌ مِثْلُهُ | *Qarhum-mithluh* | Similar wound |
| 140 | نُدَاوِلُهَا | *Nudawiluha* | We give them by turns |
| 141 | يُمَحِّصَ | *Yumahhis* | Purges |
| 141 | يَمْحَقَ | *Yamhaq* | Destroys |
| 145 | كِتَابًا مُؤَجَّلًا | *Kitabam-mu-'ajjala* | Appointed term |
| 146 | كَأَيِّنْ مِنْ نَبِيٍّ | *Ka-'ayyim-min-nabiyy* | How many of the Prophets |
| 146 | رِبِّيُّونَ | *Rib-biyyun* | Godly men |
| 146 | فَمَا وَهَنُوا | *Fama wahanu* | But they never lost heart |
| 146 | مَا اسْتَكَانُوا | *Mastakanu* | They did not give in |
| 150 | اللَّهُ مَوْلَاكُمْ | *Allah maw-lakum* | Allah is your Protector |
| 151 | رُعْبَ | *Ru'b* | Terror |

| V. | WORD | TR. | MEANING |
|---|---|---|---|
| 151 | سُلْطَانًا | *Sultana* | Authority |
| 151 | مَثْوَى الظَّالِمِينَ | *Mathwaz-zalimin* | The home of the wrong-doers |
| 152 | تَحُسُّونَهُمْ | *Tahussu-nahum* | *Pl.* You annihilated them |
| 152 | فَشِلْتُمْ | *Fashiltum* | *Pl.* You lost your courage |
| 152 | لِيَبْتَلِيَكُمْ | *li-yabtali-yakum* | In order to test you |
| 153 | تُصْعِدُونَ | *Tus-'idun* | *Pl.* You ran away |
| 153 | لَا تَلْوُونَ | *La talwun* | *Pl.* You did not cast a side galance |
| 153 | فَأَثَابَكُمْ | *Fa-'athabakum* | He gave you |
| 153 | غَمًّا بِغَمٍّ | *Gham-mam-bi-ghamm* | One distress after another |
| 154 | أَمَنَةً | *'Amanat* | Security |
| 154 | نُعَاسًا | *Nu-'asa* | Slumber |
| 154 | يَغْشَى | *Yaghsha* | Overcomes |
| 154 | بَرَزَ | *Baraz* | Went forth |
| 154 | مَضَاجِعِهِمْ | *Madaji-'ihim* | The place of their death |
| 154 | يُمَحِّصَ | *Yumahhis* | Purges |
| 155 | اسْتَزَلَّهُمُ الشَّيْطَانُ | *Is-tazallahumush-shaytan* | Satan caused them to fail |
| 156 | ضَرَبُوا | *Darabu* | They travelled |
| 156 | غُزًّى | *Ghuzza* | Fighters |
| 159 | فَبِمَا رَحْمَةٍ مِّنَ اللَّهِ | *Fa-bima rahmatim-mi-nallah* | It is part of the Mercy of Allah |
| 159 | لِنْتَ لَهُمْ | *Linta lahum* | You dealt with them gently |

| V. | WORD | TR. | MEANING |
|---|---|---|---|
| 159 | فَظًّا | *Fazza* | Severe and harsh-hearted |
| 159 | لَانْفَضُّوا | *Lan-faddu* | They would have broken away |
| 160 | فَلَا غَالِبَ لَكُمْ | *Fala ghaliba lakum* | None can overcome you |
| 161 | يَغُلَّ | *Yaghull* | Acts dishonestly |
| 168 | فَادْرَءُوا | *Fadra-'u* | *Im.pl.* Then avert |
| 172 | أَصَابَهُمُ الْقَرْحُ | *'Asaba-humul-qarh* | They were wounded (in the battle of Uhud) |
| 178 | نُمْلِي لَهُمْ | *Numli lahum* | We grant them respite |
| 179 | يَجْتَبِي | *Yajtabi* | Chooses |
| 180 | سَيُطَوَّقُونَ مَا بَخِلُوا بِهِ | *Sayu-taw-waquna ma bakhilu bih* | The things which they covetously withhold shall be tied to their necks |
| 183 | عَهِدَ إِلَيْنَا | *'Ahida 'ilayna* | (Allah) took our promise |
| 183 | قُرْبَان | *Qurban* | Sacrifice |
| 184 | الزُّبُر | *Az-Zubur* | Scriptures |
| 185 | زُحْزِحَ عَنِ النَّارِ | *Zuhziha 'aninnar* | *Pv.* is saved far from the Fire |
| 185 | غُرُور | *Ghurur* | Deception |
| 186 | لَتُبْلَوُنَّ | *La-tubla-wunn* | *Pl.* You shall certainly be tried and tested |
| 187 | نَبَذُوهُ | *Na-badhuh* | They threw it away |
| 188 | مَفَازَة | *Mafaza* | Escape, place of refuge |
| 191 | بَاطِلًا | *Batila* | Naught, without |

| V. | WORD | TR. | MEANING |
|---|---|---|---|
| | | | purpose |
| 191 | قِنَا عَذَابَ النَّارِ | *Qina 'adhaban-nar* | *Im.* Give us salvation from the Chastisement of the Fire |
| 192 | أَخْزَيْتَهُ | *'Akh-zaytah* | You disgraced him, You covered him with shame |
| 193 | مُنَادِيًا | *Muna-diya* | A caller ( the Prophet صلى الله عليه وسلم or the Holy Qûr'an) |
| 193 | ذُنُوبَنَا | *Dhunu-bana* | Our sins |
| 193 | كَفِّرْ عَنَّا سَيِّئَاتِنَا | *Kaffir 'anna sayyi-'atina* | *Im.* Blot out from us our iniquities |
| 196 | لَا يَغُرَّنَّكَ | *La yaghurrannak* | *Ni.* Let it not deceive you |
| 196 | تَقَلُّبُ | *Taqal-lub* | (The act of) turning about |
| 197 | مَتَاعٌ قَلِيلٌ | *Mata-'un-qalil* | Brief enjoyment |
| 198 | نُزُلًا | *Nuzula* | Entertainment |
| 200 | صَابِرُوا | *Sabiru* | *Im.pl.* Out do others in patience |
| 200 | رَابِطُوا | *Rabitu* | *Im.pl.* Guard your territory |

| V. | WORD | TR. | MEANING |
|---|---|---|---|

# سُورَةُ النِّسَاءِ

## [4] SURAT AN-NISA'

## THE WOMEN

| | | | |
|---|---|---|---|
| 1 | بَثَّ | *Bathth* | Scattered |
| 1 | أَرْحَام | *'Arham* | Wombs, ties of kinship |
| 1 | رَقِيبًا | *Raqiba* | Watcher |
| 2 | حُوبًا كَبِيرًا | *Huban-kabira* | Great sin |
| 3 | أَلَّا تُقْسِطُوا | *'Alla tuq-situ* | *pl.* You shall not be able to deal justly |
| 3 | طَابَ | *Tab* | Seemed good |
| 3 | رُبَاعَ | *Ruba'* | By fours |
| 3 | أَلَّا تَعْدِلُوا | *'Alla ta'-dilu* | *pl.* You shall not be able to deal justly |
| 3 | ذَلِكَ أَدْنَى أَلَّا تَعُولُوا | *Dhalika 'adna 'alla ta-'ulu* | That will be more suitable, to prevent you from doing injustice |
| 4 | صَدُقَاتِهِنَّ | *Sadu-qa-tihinn* | Their dower |
| 4 | نِحْلَةً | *Nihlah* | Willingly |
| 4 | هَنِيئًا مَرِيئًا | *Hani-'am-mari-'a* | With pleasure and good cheer |
| 5 | قِيَامًا | *Qiyama* | Means of support |
| 6 | ابْتَلُوا الْيَتَامَى | *Ab-talul-yatama* | *im.pl.* Make trial of orphans |
| 6 | آنَسْتُمْ | *Anastum* | *pl.* You found |
| 6 | رُشْدًا | *Rushda* | Sound judgement |

| V. | WORD | TR. | MEANING |
|---|---|---|---|
| 6 | بِدَارًا | *Bidara* | In haste |
| 6 | فَلْيَسْتَعْفِفْ | *Fal-yasta-'fif* | (Let him) claim no remuneration |
| 6 | حَسِيبًا | *Hasiba* | One Who takes an account (i.e., Allah) |
| 7 | مَفْرُوضًا | *Mafruda* | *pp.* Determinate |
| 9 | قَوْلًا سَدِيدًا | *Qawlan-sadida* | Appropriate words |
| 10 | سَيَصْلَوْنَ سَعِيرًا | *Sa-yas-lawna sa-'ira* | They will be burnt in the blazing Fire |
| 11 | يُوصِيكُمُ اللَّهُ | *Yusi-kumullah* | Allah directs you |
| 11 | فَرِيضَةً | *Fari-da* | Ordinance (of Allah) |
| 12 | كَلَالَةً | *Kalala* | Deceased person having left neither parent nor children |
| 17 | بِجَهَالَةٍ | *Bi-jahala* | In ignorance |
| 19 | كَرْهًا | *Karha* | Forcibly, against (one's) will |
| 19 | لَا تَعْضُلُوهُنَّ | *La ta'-duluhunn* | *ni.pl.* Do not treat them with harshness |
| 19 | فَاحِشَةٍ مُبَيِّنَةٍ | *Fa-hishatim-mubayyinah* | Open lewdness |
| 20 | بُهْتَانًا | *Buhtanan* | Wrongfully |
| 21 | أَفْضَى بَعْضُكُمْ إِلَى بَعْضٍ | *'Afda b'a-dukum 'ila ba'dh* | Went in unto each other |
| 21 | مِيثَاقًا غَلِيظًا | *Mithaqan ghaliza* | Solemn covenant |
| 22 | مَقْتًا | *Maqta* | Abomination |

| V. | WORD | TR. | MEANING |
|---|---|---|---|
| 23 | رَبَائِبُكُمْ | *Raba-'ibukum* | *pl.* Your step-daughters |
| 23 | فَلَا جُنَاحَ عَلَيْكُمْ | *Fala junaha 'alay-kum* | Then there is no sin on you |
| 23 | حَلَائِلُ أَبْنَائِكُمْ | *Hala-'ilu 'abna-ikum* | The wives of your sons |
| 24 | مُحْصَنَاتُ | *Muhsanat* | Married women , those who have husbands |
| 24 | مُحْصِنِينَ | *Muhsi-nin* | Those who seek honest wedlock (desiring chastity) |
| 24 | غَيْرَ مُسَافِحِينَ | *Ghayra musa-fihin* | *mg*. Not fornicators |
| 25 | طَوْلًا | *Taw-la* | Sufficiency of means |
| 25 | مُحْصَنَاتُ | *Muhsanat* | Believing free women |
| 25 | فَتَيَاتِكُمْ | *Fataya-tikum* | *pl*. Your slave girls |
| 25 | مُحْصَنَاتٍ | *Muhsanat* | Chaste women |
| 25 | غَيْرَ مُسَافِحَاتٍ | *Ghayra musa-fihat* | *fg*. Not fornicators |
| 25 | مُتَّخِذَاتِ أَخْدَانٍ | *Muttakhi-dhati 'akh-da* | Those (women) who take adulterous (as boy-friends) |
| 25 | خَشِيَ الْعَنَتَ | *Khashiyal-'anat* | Feared sin |
| 26 | سُنَنَ | *Sunan* | Ways |
| 29 | بِالْبَاطِلِ | *Bil-batil* | Unjustly |
| 30 | نُصْلِيهِ نَارًا | *Nuslihi nara* | We shall cast him into the fire |

| V. | WORD | TR. | MEANING |
|---|---|---|---|
| 31 | سَيِّئَاتِكُمْ | *Sayyi-'atikum* | *pl.* Your evil deeds |
| 31 | نُدْخِلْكُمْ | *Nud-khilkum* | We shall admit you |
| 31 | مُدْخَلًا كَرِيمًا | *Mud-khalan-karima* | Noble Entrance (i.e., Paradise) |
| 33 | جَعَلْنَا مَوَالِيَ | *Ja-'alna ma-wa-liy* | We appointed heirs |
| 33 | الَّذِينَ عَقَدَتْ أَيْمَانُكُمْ | *Al-ladhina 'aqadat 'ayamanukum* | Those with whom you made a pledge |
| 34 | الرجال قَوَّامُونَ عَلَى النِّسَاءِ | *Ar-rijalu qawwamuna 'alan-nisa'* | Men are the protectors and maintainers of women |
| 34 | قَانِتَاتٌ | *Qanitat* | Those (women) who are obedient to Allah |
| 34 | حَافِظَاتٌ لِلْغَيْبِ | *Hafi-zatul-lil-ghayb* | Those (women) who guard (their chastity and their husband's property) in (their husband's) absence |
| 34 | مَا حَفِظَ اللَّهُ | *Ma hafi-zallah* | What Allah orders them to guard |
| 34 | نُشُوزَهُنَّ | *Nushu-zahunn* | *fg.* Their disloyalty and ill-conduct |
| 36 | الْجَارِ الْجُنُبِ | *Al-jaril-junub* | Neighbours who are strangers |
| 36 | الصَّاحِبِ بِالْجَنْبِ | *As-sahibi bil-jamb* | Familiar friend, companion |
| 36 | ابْنِ السَّبِيلِ | *Ibnis-sabil* | Way farer |
| 36 | مُخْتَالًا | *Mukh-tala* | Proud, arrogant |

| V. | WORD | TR. | MEANING |
|---|---|---|---|
| 36 | فَخُوراً | *Fakhura* | Vainglorious, boastful |
| 38 | رِئَاءَ النَّاسِ | *Ri-'a-'annas* | To be seen of men |
| 40 | مِثْقَالَ ذَرَّةٍ | *Mithqala dharra* | The weight of an atom (or a small ant) |
| 42 | لَوْ تُسَوَّى بِهِمُ الْأَرْضُ | *Law tu-sawwa bihi-mul-'ard* | (They will wish that) the earth were made one with them |
| 43 | عَابِرِي سَبِيلٍ | *'Abiri sabil* | Passers by |
| 43 | غَائِطِ | *Gha-'it* | Privy |
| 43 | لَامَسْتُمُ النِّسَاءَ | *Lamas-tumun-nisa-'a* | *pl.* You touched women (i.e., by sexual relation) |
| 43 | صَعِيدًا طَيِّبًا | *Sa-'idan tayyiba* | Clean sand |
| 46 | يُحَرِّفُونَ الْكَلِمَ | *Yu-harrifunal-kalim* | They displace words |
| 46 | اسْمَعْ غَيْرَ مُسْمَعٍ | *Isma' ghayra musma'* | *im*. Hear, may you not hear |
| 46 | لَيًّا بِأَلْسِنَتِهِمْ | *Lay-yam-bi-'al-sinatihim* | Twisting their tongues |
| 46 | أَقْوَمَ | *'Aq-wam* | More proper, better |
| 47 | نَطْمِسَ وُجُوهًا | *Nat-misa wujuha* | We efface faces |
| 49 | يُزَكُّونَ أَنفُسَهُمْ | *Yuzakkuna 'anfusahum* | They claim purity for themselves |
| 51 | بِالْجِبْتِ وَالطَّاغُوتِ | *Bil-jibti wat-taghut* | In sorcery and anything worshipped other than Allah |

| V. | WORD | TR. | MEANING |
|---|---|---|---|
| 53 | نَقِيرًا | *Naqira* | Groove in a date-stone, farthing |
| 56 | نَضِجَتْ جُلُودُهُمْ | *Nadijat juluduhum* | Their skins roasted |
| 57 | ظليلا | *Zalila* | Cool and ever deepening |
| 58 | تُؤَدُّوا الْأَمَانَاتِ | *Tu-'addul-'amanat* | *pl.* You render back your trusts |
| 58 | نِعِمَّا يَعِظُكُمْ بِهِ | *Ni-'imma ya-'izukum-bih* | Excellent is the teaching that He gives you |
| 59 | أَحْسَنُ تَأْوِيلًا | *'Ahsanu ta'-wila* | Most suitable for final determination |
| 61 | يَصُدُّونَ عَنْكَ | *Yasudduna 'ank* | They avert their faces from you |
| 65 | شَجَرَ | *Shajar* | Disputed |
| 65 | حَرَجًا | *Haraja* | Resistance |
| 66 | تَثْبِيتًا | *Tathbita* | Strongly |
| 71 | خُذُوا حِذْرَكُمْ | *Khudhu hidhrakum* | *im. pl.* Take your precautions |
| 71 | فَانفِرُوا ثُبَاتٍ | *Fan-firu thubat* | *im. pl.* Go forth in parties |
| 72 | يُبَطِّئَنَّ | *Yubatti-'ann* | Tarries behind |
| 74 | يَشْرُونَ | *Yash-run* | They sell |
| 76 | طَاغُوتِ | *Taghut* | Satan |
| 77 | فَتِيلًا | *Fatila* | Small skin in the cleft of a date-stone (i.e., very least) |
| 78 | بُرُوجٍ | *Buruj* | Towers |

| V. | WORD | TR. | MEANING |
|---|---|---|---|
| 78 | مشيدة | *Mushayyadah* | Built up strong and high |
| 80 | حَفِيظًا | *Hafiza* | Watcher |
| 81 | بَرَزُوا | *Barazu* | They left |
| 81 | بَيَّتَ طَائِفَةٌ | *Bayyata ta-'ifa* | A section spent all night in planning |
| 83 | أَذَاعُوا بِهِ | *'Adha-'u bih* | They divulged it |
| 83 | يَسْتَنْبِطُونَهُ | *Yastam-bitunah* | They investigated it |
| 84 | بَأْسَ | *Ba'-s* | Fury |
| 84 | أَشَدُّ بَأْسًا | *'Ashaddu ba'-sa* | Stronger in might |
| 84 | أَشَدُّ تَنكِيلًا | *'Ashaddu tankila* | Stronger in punishing |
| 85 | كِفْلٌ مِنْهَا | *Kiflum-minha* | Share in its burden |
| 85 | مُقِيتًا | *Muqita* | Able to do everything |
| 86 | حَسِيبًا | *Hasiba* | Careful Account Taker |
| 88 | أَرْكَسَهُمْ | *'Ar-kasahum* | Turned them back |
| 90 | حَصِرَتْ صُدُورُهُمْ | *Hasirat suduruhum* | Their hearts restraining |
| 90 | سَلَمَ | *Salam* | Peace |
| 91 | أُرْكِسُوا | *'Urkisu* | They succumbed |
| 94 | ضَرَبْتُمْ | *Darab-tum* | *pl.* You went out (to fight) |
| 94 | سَلَامَ | *Salaam* | Salutation |
| 94 | عَرَضَ الْحَيَاةِ الدُّنْيَا | *'Aradal-haya-tiddunya* | The perishable goods of the |

| V. | WORD | TR. | MEANING |
|---|---|---|---|
| | | | worldly life |
| 95 | أُولِي الضَّرَرِ | *'Ulid-darar* | Those who are disabled |
| 100 | مُرَاغَمًا | *Mu-raghama* | Dwelling places |
| 101 | يَفْتِنَكُمْ | *Yaftina-kum* | Puts you in distress |
| 102 | تَغْفُلُونَ | *Tagh-fulun* | *pl.* You neglect |
| 103 | كِتَابًا مَوْقُوتًا | *Kitabam-mawquta* | Stated times |
| 104 | لَا تَهِنُوا | *La tahinu* | *ni. pl.* Do not be weak |
| 105 | خَصِيمًا | *Khasima* | Advocate |
| 107 | يَخْتَانُونَ أَنفُسَهُمْ | *Yakh-tanuna 'anfusa-hum* | They deceive themselves |
| 108 | يُبَيِّتُونَ | *Yubayyi-tun* | They plot by night |
| 109 | وَكِيلًا | *Wakila* | Defender |
| 112 | بُهْتَانًا | *Buh-tana* | False charge |
| 114 | نَجْوَاهُمْ | *Naj-wahum* | Their secret talks |
| 115 | يُشَاقِقْ الرَّسُولَ | *Yushaqi-qir-Rasul* | Contends with the Messenger (of Allah) صلى الله عليه وسلم |
| 115 | نُوَلِّهِ مَا تَوَلَّى | *Nu-wallihi ma ta-walla* | We shall leave him in the path he has chosen |
| 117 | إِنَاثًا | *'Inatha* | Female deities |

| V. | WORD | TR. | MEANING |
|---|---|---|---|
| 117 | مَرِيدًا | *Marida* | Persistent rebel |
| 118 | مَفْرُوضًا | *Maf-ruda* | Appointed |
| 119 | يُبَتِّكُنَّ | *Yubatti-kunn* | They will slit |
| 120 | غُرُورًا | *Ghurura* | Deception |
| 121 | مَحِيصًا | *Mahisa* | Escape |
| 122 | قِيلًا | *Qila* | Words |
| 125 | أَسْلَمَ وَجْهَهُ لِلَّهِ | *'Aslama waj-hahu lillah* | He submitted his whole self to Allah |
| 127 | قِسْطِ | *Qist* | Justice |
| 128 | بَعْلِهَا | *Ba'-liha* | Her husband |
| 128 | نُشُوزًا | *Nushuza* | Cruelty or desertion |
| 128 | شُحَّ | *Shuhh* | Greed |
| 129 | أَنْ تَعْدِلُوا | *'An-ta'-dilu* | *pl.* To do justice |
| 130 | سَعَتِهِ | *Sa-'atih* | His (Allah's) Bounty |
| 135 | تَلْوُوا | *Tal-wu* | *pl.* You distort |
| 135 | تُعْرِضُوا | *Tu'-ridu* | *pl.* You refuse |
| 139 | عِزَّةَ | *'Izza* | Honour |
| 141 | يَتَرَبَّصُونَ بِكُمْ | *Yatarab-basu-na bikum* | They wait and watch |
| 141 | فَتْحٌ | *Fat-hu* | Victory |

| V. | WORD | TR. | MEANING |
|---|---|---|---|
| 141 | أَلَمْ نَسْتَحْوِذْ عَلَيْكُمْ | *'alam nastah-widh 'alaykum* | Did we not gain an advantage over you? |
| 143 | مُذَبْذَبِينَ بَيْنَ ذَلِكَ | *Mudhab-dhabina bayna dhalik* | (They are) Wavering between this and that (i.e., wavering between belief and disbelief) |
| 144 | سُلْطَانًا مُبِينًا | *Sul-tanam-mubina* | Open proof |
| 145 | الدَّرْكِ الْأَسْفَلِ | *Fid-darkil-'asfal* | The lowest depth (of the Fire) |
| 153 | جَهْرَةً | *Jah-ra* | Openly, in public |
| 153 | صَّاعِقَةُ | *Sa-'iqa* | Thunder – clap and lightning |
| 154 | لَا تَعْدُوا فِي السَّبْتِ | *La ta'-du fis-Sabt* | *ni. pl.* Do not transgress in the matter of the Sabbath (Saturday) |
| 154 | مِيثَاقًا غَلِيظًا | *Mithaqan ghaliza* | Solemn Covenant |
| 155 | قُلُوبُنَا غُلْفٌ | *Qulubuna ghulf* | Our heart are wrapped (with coverings, i.e., we do not understand) |
| 155 | طَبَعَ اللَّهُ عَلَيْهَا | *Taba-'allah 'alayha* | Allah has set a seal upon (their hearts) |
| 156 | بُهْتَانًا عَظِيمًا | *Buh-ta-nan 'azima* | Grave false charge |
| 157 | شُبِّهَ لَهُمْ | *Shubbiha lahum* | The resemblance (of 'Isa عليه السلام) was put over another man |

| V. | WORD | TR. | MEANING |
|---|---|---|---|
| 162 | الْمُقِيمِينَ الصَّلَاةَ | *Al- muqiminas-Salat* | Those who establish regular prayer |
| 163 | الْأَسْبَاطِ | *Al-'asbat* | The twelve sons of Ya'qub عليه السلام |
| 163 | زَبُورًا | *Zabura* | The Psalms |
| 171 | لَا تَغْلُوا | *La taghlu* | *ni. pl.* Do not exceed the limits |
| 171 | كَلِمَتُهُ | *Kalimatuh* | His Word ("Be!"- and he was) |
| 171 | رُوحٌ مِنْهُ | *Ruhum-minh* | A Spirit proceeding from Him |
| 172 | لَنْ يَسْتَنْكِفَ | *Lany-yas-tankif* | He ('Isa عليه السلام) will never be proud |
| 174 | بُرْهَانٌ | *Bur-han* | (Convincing) proof (i.e., the Prophet Muhammad صلى الله عليه وسلم) |
| 174 | نُورًا مُبِينًا | *Nuram-mubina* | Manifest light (i.e., the Holy Qûr'an) |

| V. | WORD | TR. | MEANING |
|---|---|---|---|

## سُورَةُ المَائِدَةِ

## [5] SURAT AL-MA'IDAH
## THE TABLE SPREAD

| | | | |
|---|---|---|---|
| 1 | عُقُودِ | *'Uqud* | Obligations |
| 1 | غَيْرَ مُحِلِّي | *Ghayra mu-hilli* | Forbidden |
| 1 | صَّيْدِ | *Sayd* | Hunting |
| 1 | وَأَنْتُمْ حُرُمٌ | *Wa 'antum hurum* | While you are in the Sacred Precincts or in the state of pilgrimage |
| 2 | لَا تُحِلُّوا | *La tuhillu* | *ni. pl.* Do not violate |
| 2 | شَعَائِرَ اللَّهِ | *Sha-'a-I'-rallah* | The rites of Allah |
| 2 | الشَّهْرَ الْحَرَامَ | *Ash-Shahral-Ha-ram* | The Sacred Month |
| 2 | الْهَدْيَ | *Al-hady* | Offerings, animals brought for sacrifice |
| 2 | قَلَائِدَ | *Qala-'id* | Garlands (that mark out those animals meant for sacrifice) |
| 2 | آمِّينَ الْبَيْتَ | *'Ammi-nal-Bayt* | Those (people who are) resorting to the Sacred House |
| 2 | لَا يَجْرِمَنَّكُمْ | *La yajri-mannakum* | Let (it) not lead you ( |
| 2 | شَنَآنُ قَوْمٍ | *Shana-'anu qaw-min* | *pl.* (your) Hatred of some people |
| 3 | دَّمُ | *Dam* | Blood |
| 3 | لَحْمُ الْخِنزِيرِ | *Lah-mul-khin-zir* | The flesh of swine |

| V. | WORD | TR. | MEANING |
|---|---|---|---|
| 3 | مَا أُهِلَّ لِغَيْرِ اللَّهِ | *Ma 'uhiilla li-ghayrillah* | The meat on which has been invoked the name of other than Allah |
| 3 | مُنْخَنِقَةُ | *Mun-kha-niqa* | *pp.* Dead by strangling |
| 3 | مَوْقُوذَةُ | *Maw-qudha* | *pp.* Dead by a violent blow |
| 3 | مُتَرَدِّيَةُ | *Muta-raddi-ya* | *pp.* Dead by a headlong fall |
| 3 | نَطِيحَةُ | *Nati-ha* | Killed by goring of horns |
| 3 | مَا أَكَلَ السَّبُعُ | *Ma 'akalas-sabu-'u* | That which has been (partly) eaten by a wild animal |
| 3 | مَا ذَكَّيْتُمْ | *Ma dhakkaytum* | That (animal) which you are able to slaughter (before its death) |
| 3 | النُّصُبِ | *An-nusub* | A stone used by the pagan Arabs on which they made sacrifices |
| 3 | تَسْتَقْسِمُوا | *Tastaq-simu* | *pl.* You draw lots or divine |
| 3 | بِالْأَزْلَامِ | *Bil-'azlam* | By means of arrows |
| 3 | ذَٰلِكُمْ فِسْقٌ | *Dha-likum fisq* | That is impiety |
| 3 | اضْطُرَّ | *Id-turr* | Is driven forcibly |
| 3 | مَخْمَصَةٍ | *Makh-masa* | Severe hunger |
| 3 | مُتَجَانِفٍ لِإِثْمٍ | *Mutaja-nifil-li-'ithm* | One who has an inclination to sin |
| 4 | طَيِّبَاتُ | *Tayyi-bat* | All kinds of lawful |

| V. | WORD | TR. | MEANING |
|---|---|---|---|
| | | | foods |
| 4 | جَوَارِح | *Jawarih* | Beasts and birds of prey |
| 4 | مُكَلِّبِينَ | *Mukalli-bin* | Animals trained for hunting |
| 5 | طَعَامُ | *Ta-'am* | Food |
| 5 | مُتَّخِذِي أَخْدَانٍ | *Mutta-khi-dhi 'akh-dan* | Those (men) who take women as girl-friends |
| 5 | يَكْفُرْ بِالْإِيمَانِ | *Yakfur bil-'iman* | Rejects faith |
| 5 | حَبِطَ عَمَلُهُ | *Habita 'amaluh* | Fruitless is his work |
| 6 | لَامَسْتُمُ النِّسَاءَ | *Lamas-tumun-nisa'* | *pl.* You touched women (did intercourse with them) |
| 6 | صَعِيدًا طَيِّبًا | *Sa-'idan-tayyi-ban* | Clean sand of earth |
| 6 | حَرَجٍ | *Haraj* | Difficulty |
| 7 | مِيثَاقَهُ | *Mithaqah* | His (Allah's) Covenant |
| 8 | شُهَدَاءَ بِالْقِسْطِ | *Shuhada-'a bil-qist* | Just witnesses |
| 11 | يَبْسُطُوا إِلَيْكُمْ أَيْدِيَهُمْ | *Yabsutu 'ilay-kum 'ay-diyahum* | They stretch out their hands against you |
| 12 | نَقِيبًا | *Naqiba* | Chieftains |
| 12 | عَزَّرْتُمُوهُمْ | *'Azzar-tumuhum* | *pl.* You honour and asist them |
| 12 | قَرْضًا حَسَنًا | *Qar-dan Hasana* | Beautiful loan |
| 13 | يُحَرِّفُونَ الْكَلِمَ | *Yuharri-funnal-kalim* | They change the words |
| 13 | نَسُوا حَظًّا | *Nasu haz-za* | They abandoned a |

| V. | WORD | TR. | MEANING |
|---|---|---|---|
| | | | good part |
| 13 | خَائِنَةٍ | *Kha-'ina* | Deceit |
| 14 | فَأَغْرَيْنَا | *Fa-'aghrayna* | So We stirred up |
| 15 | نُورٌ | *Nuur* | Light (i.e., the Prophet Muhammad صلى الله عليه وسلم) |
| 19 | فَتْرَةٍ | *Fatra* | An interval (of time between two messengers) |
| 25 | فَافْرُقْ | *Fafruq* | *im.* So separate |
| 26 | يَتِيهُونَ فِي الْأَرْضِ | *Yatihuna fil-'ard* | In distraction they will wander through the land |
| 26 | لَا تَأْسَ | *La ta'-s* | *ni.* Sorrow not |
| 27 | قُرْبَانًا | *Qurbana* | Sacrifice |
| 29 | تَبُوءَ بِإِثْمِي | *Tabu-'a bi-'ithmi* | You draw on yourself my sin |
| 30 | فَطَوَّعَتْ لَهُ نَفْسُهُ | *Fatawwa-'at lahu nafsuh* | So his soul encouraged him and made fair-seeming to him |
| 31 | يَبْحَثُ فِي الْأَرْضِ | *Yab-hathu fil-'ard* | Scratches the ground |
| 31 | سَوْأَةَ أَخِيهِ | *Saw-'ata 'akhih* | The naked body of his brother |
| 31 | يَاوَيْلَتَا | *Ya-way-lata* | Woe unto me |
| 33 | يُنفَوْا مِنَ الْأَرْضِ | *Yun-faw minal-'ard* | *pv.* Are exiled from the land |
| 35 | وَسِيلَةَ | *Wasila* | Means of approach |
| 38 | نَكَالًا | *Na-kala* | Retribution |

| V. | WORD | TR. | MEANING |
|---|---|---|---|
| 41 | سَمَّاعُونَ لِلْكَذِبِ | *Samma-'una lil-kadhib* | Those who listen much and eagerly to lies |
| 41 | سَمَّاعُونَ لِقَوْمٍ آخَرِينَ | *Samma-'una li-qawmin 'a-kharin* | Those who listen to others |
| 42 | أَكَّالُونَ لِلسُّحْتِ | *'Akka-luna lis-suht* | Those who are fond of devouring anything forbidden |
| 42 | بِالْقِسْطِ | *Bil-qist* | In equity |
| 42 | مُقْسِطِينَ | *Muqsitin* | Those who judge in equity |
| 43 | يَتَوَلَّوْنَ | *Ya-tawal-lawn* | They turn away |
| 44 | أَسْلَمُوا | *'Aslamu* | They submitted themselves to Allah's Will |
| 44 | رَبَّانِيُّونَ | *Rabba-niyyun* | Jewish learned men, rabbies |
| 44 | أَحْبَارُ | *'Ahbar* | Jewish Doctors of Law |
| 46 | قَفَّيْنَا | *Qaf-fayna* | We sent (after) |
| 46 | آثَارِهِمْ | *'A-tha-rihim* | Their footsteps |
| 48 | مُهَيْمِنًا عَلَيْهِ | *Muhay-minan 'alayh* | Trustworthy in highness and a witness over it (old Scriptures) |
| 48 | شِرْعَةً | *Shir-'ata* | Law |
| 48 | مِنْهَاجًا | *Minha-ja* | Open way |
| 48 | لِيَبْلُوكُمْ | *Liyab-luwa-kum* | To test you |
| 49 | أَنْ يَفْتِنُوكَ | *'Any-yafti-nuk* | Lest they beguile you |
| 52 | تُصِيبَنَا دَائِرَةٌ | *Tusi-bana da-'irah* | A change of fortune brings us |

| V. | WORD | TR. | MEANING |
|---|---|---|---|
| | | | disaster |
| 52 | فَتْح | *Fat-h* | Victory |
| 53 | جَهْدَ أَيْمَانِهِمْ | *Jahda 'ayma-nihim* | Their strongest oaths |
| 54 | أَذِلَّةٍ عَلَى الْمُؤْمِنِينَ | *'Adhil-latin 'alal-mu'-minin* | Lowly with the believers |
| 54 | أَعِزَّةٍ عَلَى الْكَافِرِينَ | *'A'-izza-tin 'alal-kafirin* | Mighty against the disbelievers |
| 54 | لَوْمَةَ | *Law-mat* | Blame, reproach |
| 54 | لَائِمٍ | *La-'im* | Blamer |
| 54 | اللَّهُ وَاسِعٌ | *Allahu Wasi'* | Allah is All-Sufficient |
| 57 | هُزُوًا | *Huzuwa* | Mockery |
| 57 | لَعِبًا | *la-'iba* | Fun |
| 59 | تَنقِمُونَ | *Tanqi-mun* | *pl.* You Disapprove |
| 60 | مَثُوبَةً | *Mathu-ba* | Recompense |
| 60 | عَبَدَ الطَّاغُوتَ | *'Abadat-taghut* | Worshipped Evil |
| 60 | سَوَاءِ السَّبِيلِ | *Sa-wa-'is-sabil* | The Right Path (i.e., Islam) |
| 64 | مَغْلُولَةٌ | *Maghlula* | *pp.* Tied up |
| 66 | أُمَّةٌ مُقْتَصِدَةٌ | *'Ummatum-muq-tasi-dah* | Party of the right course |
| 69 | صَابِئُونَ | *Sabi'un* | Sabians |
| 71 | فِتْنَةٌ | *Fitna* | Trial |
| 75 | خَلَتْ | *Khalat* | Passed away |
| 75 | أُمُّهُ صِدِّيقَةٌ | *'Um-muhu siddi-qa* | His mother (Maryam عليها السلام) was a women of truth |

| V. | WORD | TR. | MEANING |
|---|---|---|---|
| 75 | كَانَا يَأْكُلَانِ الطَّعَامَ | *Ka-na ya'-kulanit-ta-'am* | *dl.* They used to eat food |
| 75 | أَنَّى يُؤْفَكُونَ | *'Anna yu'-fakun* | How they are deluded away from the truth |
| 77 | لَا تَغْلُوا | *La taghlu* | *ni. pl.* Do not Exceed the limits |
| 77 | غَيْرَ الْحَقِّ | *Ghay-ral-haqq* | Other than the truth |
| 80 | سَخِطَ اللَّهُ عَلَيْهِمْ | *Sakhi-tallahu 'alayhim* | Allah's Wrath fell upon them |
| 83 | تَفِيضُ مِنَ الدَّمْعِ | *Tafidu mi-naddam'* | Overflows with tears |
| 89 | اللَّغْوِ فِي أَيْمَانِكُمْ | *Bil-laghwi fi 'ay-mani-kum* | (What is) void in your oaths |
| 89 | عَقَّدْتُمُ الْأَيْمَانَ | *'Aqqattu-mul-'ay-man* | *pl.* You took deliberate oaths |
| 90 | رِجْسٌ | *Rijs* | Abomination |
| 93 | جُنَاحٌ | *Ju-nah* | Sin |
| 93 | طَعِمُوا | *Ta-'imu* | They ate |
| 95 | نَعَمِ | *Na-'am* | Eatable animals (sheep, goats, cows, etc.) |
| 95 | بَالِغَ الْكَعْبَةِ | *Balighal-ka'-ba* | To be brought to the Ka'ba |
| 95 | عَدْلُ | *'Adl* | Equivalent |
| 95 | وَبَالَ أَمْرِهِ | *Wabala 'amrih* | The penalty of his deed |
| 96 | سَيَّارَةَ | *Say-yarah* | Travelers |
| 97 | الْبَيْتَ الْحَرَامَ | *Al-baytal-haram* | The Sacred House |
| 97 | قِيَامًا لِلنَّاسِ | *Qi-ya-mal-linnas* | A means of support for men |
| 97 | الشَّهْرَ الْحَرَامَ | *Ash-shahral-* | The Sacred Months |

| V. | WORD | TR. | MEANING |
|---|---|---|---|
| | | *haram* | (i.e., Rajab, Dhul-qa'dah, Dhul-hijjah and Muharram) |
| 103 | بَحِيرَةٍ | *Bahi-ra* | Slit-ear she-camel set free in honour of some idols |
| 103 | سَائِبَةٍ | *Sa-'iba* | She-camel let loose for free pasture for the pagans' idols |
| 103 | وَصِيلَةٍ | *Wasila* | She-camel set free for idols because it has given birth to a she-camel in its first delivery and then again gives birth to a she-camel at its second delivery |
| 103 | حَامٍ | *Ham* | Stallion camel freed from work |
| 104 | حَسْبُنَا | *Has-buna* | Enough for us |
| 105 | امنوا عَلَيْكُمْ أنفسكُمْ | *'A-manu 'alay-kum 'anfusakum* | *im.pl.* Guard your own souls |
| 106 | ضَرَبْتُمْ فِي الْأَرْضِ | *Darabtum fil-'ard* | *pl.* You travel through the earth |
| 106 | لَا نَشْتَرِي بِهِ ثَمَنًا | *La nash-tari bihi thamana* | We wish not for any worldly gain in this |
| 107 | أَحَقُّ | *'Ahaqq* | Truer |
| 108 | وَجْهِهَا | *Waj-hi-ha* | Its true nature |
| 110 | بِرُوحِ الْقُدُسِ | *Bi-ruhil-qudus* | With the Holy Spirit (i.e., Jibril عليه السلام) |

| V. | WORD | TR. | MEANING |
|---|---|---|---|
| 110 | مَهْدِ | *Mahd* | Cradle |
| 110 | كَهْلًا | *Kahla* | Maturity |
| 110 | تَخْلُقُ | *Takh-luq* | You make |
| 110 | أَكْمَهَ | *'Akma* | Those born blind |
| 111 | الْحَوَارِيِّينَ | *Al-hawa-riy-yin* | The disciples (of 'Isa عليه السلام) |
| 112 | مَائِدَةً | *Ma-'ida* | Table spread with food |
| 114 | عِيدًا | *'Iida* | Solemn festival |
| 116 | سُبْحَانَكَ | *Sub-hanak* | Glory to You |
| 117 | تَوَفَّيْتَنِي | *Ta-waffay-tani* | You took me up |

| V. | WORD | TR. | MEANING |
|---|---|---|---|

# سُورَةُ الأَنْعَام

## [6] SURAT AL-AN'AM
## THE CATTLE

| V. | WORD | TR. | MEANING |
|---|---|---|---|
| 1 | بِرَبِّهِمْ يَعْدِلُونَ | *Bi-rabbihim ya'-di-lun* | They hold (others) as equal with their Lord |
| 2 | قَضَى أَجَلًا | *Qada 'ajala* | (Allah) decreed a stated term |
| 2 | أَجَلٌ مُسَمًّى عِنْدَهُ | *'Ajalum-musam-man 'indah* | There is with Him (another) determined term |
| 2 | تَمْتَرُونَ | *Tamtarun* | *pl.* You doubt |
| 3 | وَهُوَ اللَّهُ | *Wa huwal-lah* | And He is Allah (Who should be worship Alone) |
| 5 | أَنْبَاءُ | *'Amba'* | News |
| 6 | قَرْنٍ | *Qarn* | Generation |
| 6 | مَكَّنَّا | *Makkanna* | We had established |
| 6 | مِدْرَارًا | *Mid-rara* | Abundant rain |
| 7 | كِتَابًا فِي قِرْطَاسٍ | *Kitaban-fi qir-tas* | A Message written on parchment |
| 8 | لَا يُنظَرُونَ | *La yun-zarun* | No respite would be granted to them |
| 9 | لَلَبَسْنَا عَلَيْهِمْ مَا يَلْبِسُونَ | *La-labasna 'alay-him-ma yal-bisun* | We would have certainly caused them confusion in a matter which they have already covered with confusion |
| 10 | حَاقَ | *Haq* | Hemmed in |

| V. | WORD | TR. | MEANING |
|---|---|---|---|
| 12 | كَتَبَ | *Katab* | Prescribed |
| 12 | خَسِرُوا أَنفُسَهُمْ | *Khasi-ru 'anfusahum* | They destroyed themselves |
| 13 | سَكَنَ | *Sakan* | Dwelt |
| 14 | فَاطِرِ | *Fatir* | Maker |
| 14 | هُوَ يُطْعِمُ | *Huwa yut-'im* | He (Allah) Who feeds |
| 19 | مَنْ بَلَغَ | *Mam-balagh* | Whom it (i.e., the Holy Qur'an) reaches |
| 23 | فِتْنَتُهُمْ | *Fitnatu-hum* | Their excuse |
| 24 | ضَلَّ عَنْهُمْ | *Zalla 'an-hum* | Disappeared from them |
| 24 | مَا كَانُوا يَفْتَرُونَ | *Ma kanu yaftarun* | (The lie) which they invented |
| 25 | أَسَاطِيرُ الْأَوَّلِينَ | *'Asa-tirul-'awwa-lin* | Tales of the ancients |
| 26 | يَنْأَوْنَ | *Yan-'awn* | They keep away (themselves) |
| 27 | وُقِفُوا عَلَى النَّارِ | *Wuqifu 'alan-nar* | *pv.* They are made to stand by the Fire |
| 30 | وُقِفُوا عَلَى رَبِّهِمْ | *Wuqifu 'ala rabbihim* | *pv.* They are made to stand before their Lord |
| 31 | بَغْتَةً | *Baghta* | Suddenly |
| 31 | فَرَّطْنَا | *Farratna* | We neglected |
| 31 | أَوْزَارَهُمْ | *'Aw-zara-hum* | Their burdens |
| 34 | كَلِمَاتِ اللَّهِ | *Kalima-tillah* | The Words of Allah |
| 35 | كَبُرَ عَلَيْكَ | *Kabura 'alayk* | Hard on you |
| 35 | نَفَقًا فِي الْأَرْضِ | *Nafaqan-fil-'ard* | Tunnel in the ground |

| V. | WORD | TR. | MEANING |
|---|---|---|---|
| 38 | أُمَمٌ أَمْثَالُكُمْ | *'Umamun 'amthalukum* | Communities like you |
| 39 | فِي الظُّلُمَاتِ | *Fiz-zulumat* | In darkness |
| 40 | أَرَأَيْتَكُمْ | *'Ara-'aytakum* | *im.pl.* Tell me |
| 42 | لَعَلَّهُمْ يَتَضَرَّعُونَ | *La-'allahum ya-tadarra-'un* | They might call (Allah) in humility |
| 43 | جَاءَهُمْ بَأْسُنَا | *Ja-'ahum-ba'-suna* | Our Torment reached them |
| 44 | كُلِّ شَيْءٍ | *Kulli shay'* | All (good) things |
| 44 | أَخَذْنَاهُمْ | *'Akhadh-nahum* | We took them to punishment |
| 44 | هم مُبْلِسُونَ | *Hum-mublisun* | Those who are plunged in despair |
| 45 | دَابِرُ | *Dabir* | Roots, remnants |
| 46 | نُصَرِّفُ الْآيَاتِ | *Nusarriful-'ayat* | We explain the Signs by various (symbols) |
| 46 | هُمْ يَصْدِفُونَ | *Hum yas-difun* | They turn aside |
| 50 | خَزَائِنُ اللَّهِ | *Khaza-'inul-lah* | the Treasures of Allah |
| 52 | غَدَاة | *Gha-dat* | Morning |
| 52 | عَشِيِّ | *'A-shiyy* | Evening |
| 53 | فَتَنَّا | *Fatanna* | We tested |
| 54 | بِجَهَالَةٍ | *Bi-jaha-la* | In ignorance |
| 57 | يَقُصُّ الْحَقَّ | *Yaqussul-haqq* | (Allah) declares the Truth |
| 57 | خَيْرُ الْفَاصِلِينَ | *Khayrul-fasilin* | (Allah is) the best of judges |
| 59 | كِتَابٍ مُبِين | *Kitabim-mubin* | Clear record |
| 60 | جَرَحْتُمْ | *Jarahtum* | *pl.* You gained |

| V. | WORD | TR. | MEANING |
|---|---|---|---|
| 61 | لَا يُفَرِّطُونَ | *La yu-farri-tun* | They do not neglect |
| 63 | تَضَرُّعًا | *Tadarru-'a* | In humility |
| 63 | خُفْيَةً | *Khuf-yah* | Secretly |
| 65 | يَلْبِسَكُمْ | *Yal-bisa-kum* | He covers you (*pl*) with confusion |
| 65 | شِيَعًا | *Shiya-'a* | Sect, party |
| 65 | بَأْسَ بَعْضٍ | *Ba'-sa ba'-d* | Violence of one another |
| 68 | يَخُوضُونَ | *Yakhu-dun* | They engage in (vain) discourse |
| 70 | غَرَّتْهُمْ | *Gharrat-hum* | It deceived them |
| 70 | أَنْ تُبْسَلَ نَفْسٌ | *'An-tubsala nafs* | Lets a soul be given up to destruction |
| 70 | تَعْدِلْ كُلَّ عَدْلٍ | *Ta'-dil kulla 'adl* | Offers every ransom |
| 70 | أُبْسِلُوا | *'Ubsilu* | They are given up to destruction |
| 70 | حَمِيمٍ | *Hamim* | Boiling water |
| 71 | اسْتَهْوَتْهُ الشَّيَاطِينُ | *'Is-tah-wat-hush-shayatin* | Satans have made him go astray |
| 71 | أُمِرْنَا لِنُسْلِمَ | *'Umirna linus-lim* | We have been directed to submit ourselves |
| 73 | صُورِ | *Sur* | Trumpet (of the Day of Resurrection) |
| 74 | آزَرَ | *'Azar* | The name of the father of Ibrahim عليه السلام |
| 75 | مَلَكُوتَ | *Malakut* | Kingdom |

| V. | WORD | TR. | MEANING |
|---|---|---|---|
| 76 | جَنَّ عَلَيْهِ اللَّيْلُ | *Janna 'alayhil-layl* | The night covered him over with darkness |
| 76 | أَفَلَ | *'Afal* | Set |
| 77 | بَازِغًا | *Bazi-gha* | Rising in splendour |
| 79 | فَطَرَ السَّمَاوَاتِ | *Fataras-samawat* | He created the heavens |
| 80 | حَاجَّهُ قَوْمُهُ | *Haj-jahu qawmuh* | His people disputed with him |
| 81 | سُلْطَانًا | *Sultana* | Warrant |
| 82 | لَمْ يَلْبِسُوا | *Lam yal-bisu* | They did not mix |
| 82 | بِظُلْمٍ | *Bi-zulm* | With wrong |
| 87 | اجْتَبَيْنَاهُمْ | *Ijta-baynahum* | We chose them |
| 88 | لَحَبِطَ | *Lahabit* | Would be vain |
| 89 | حُكْمَ | *Hukm* | Judgement |
| 90 | اقْتَدِهْ | *Aqtadih* | *im.* Follow |
| 91 | مَا قَدَرُوا اللَّهَ | *Ma qadarul-lah* | They did not estimate Allah |
| 91 | قَرَاطِيسَ | *Qara-tis* | Papers |
| 91 | قُلِ اللَّهُ | *Qulil-lah* | Say: "Allah (sent the Torah down)" |
| 91 | خَوْضِهِمْ | *Khaw-dihim* | Their vain discussions |
| 92 | مُبَارَكٌ | *Muba-rak* | Blessed |
| 92 | أُمَّ الْقُرَى | *'Ummal-qura* | The Mother of Cities (i.e., Makka) |
| 92 | مَنْ حَوْلَهَا | *Man haw-laha* | All those around it |
| 93 | غَمَرَاتِ الْمَوْتِ | *Ghamaratil-mawt* | The agonies of death |

| V. | WORD | TR. | MEANING |
|---|---|---|---|
| 93 | أَخْرِجُوا أَنفُسَكُمْ | *'Akh-riju 'anfu-sakum* | *im.pl.* Yield up your souls |
| 93 | عَذَابَ الْهُونِ | *'Adhabal-hun* | The chastisement of disgrace |
| 94 | خَوَّلْنَاكُم | *Khaw-walanakum* | We bestowed on you |
| 94 | تَقَطَّعَ بَيْنَكُمْ | *Ta-qatta-'a bay-nakum* | All relations between you have been cut off |
| 95 | فَالِقُ الْحَبِّ | *Fali-qul-habb* | The One . Who splits and sprout the seed-grain (i.e., Allah) |
| 96 | فَالِقُ الْإِصْبَاحِ | *Faliqul-'isbah* | The One Who cleaves the day-break (from the dark) (i.e., Allah) |
| 96 | الشَّمْسَ وَالْقَمَرَ حُسْبَانًا | *Ash-shamsa wal-qamara husbana* | The sun and the moon for reckoning |
| 98 | مُسْتَقَرٌّ | *Musta-qarr* | Abode |
| 98 | مُسْتَوْدَعٌ | *Mus-taw-da'* | Repository |
| 99 | خَضِرًا | *Khadira* | Green (crops) |
| 99 | حَبًّا مُتَرَاكِبًا | *Hab-bam-mutarakiba* | Close-compounded grain |
| 99 | طَلْعِهَا | *Tal-'iha* | Its sheaths (or spathes) |
| 99 | قِنْوَانٌ | *Qin-wan* | Clusters |
| 99 | دَانِيَةٌ | *Daniya* | *fg.ap.* That which is near at hand or low |
| 99 | يَنْعِهِ | *Yan-'ih* | Its ripeness |
| 100 | خَرَقُوا لَهُ | *Kharaqu lah* | They falsely attributed to Him |
| 101 | بَدِيعُ | *Badi-'* | Originator |

| V. | WORD | TR. | MEANING |
|---|---|---|---|
| 103 | لَا تُدْرِكُهُ الْأَبْصَارُ | *La tudri-kuhul-'absar* | No vision can grasp Him |
| 104 | بَصَائِرُ | *Basa-'ir* | Proofs |
| 105 | دَرَسْتَ | *Darast* | You have studied |
| 108 | عَدْوًا | *'Adwa* | Out of spite |
| 110 | نَذَرُهُمْ | *Nadharuhum* | We (shall) leave them |
| 110 | طُغْيَانِهِمْ | *Tugh-ya-nihim* | Their trespasses |
| 110 | يَعْمَهُونَ | *Ya'-mahun* | They wander blindly |
| 111 | حَشَرْنَا | *Hashar-na* | We gathered |
| 111 | قُبُلًا | *Qubula* | Before |
| 112 | زُخْرُفَ الْقَوْلِ | *Zukh-rufal-qawl* | Flowery discourses |
| 112 | غُرُورًا | *Ghurura* | Deception |
| 113 | تَصْغَى | *Tasgha* | Incline |
| 113 | يَقْتَرِفُوا | *Yaqtarifu* | They earn |
| 114 | مُمْتَرِينَ | *Mumtarin* | Those who doubt |
| 115 | كَلِمَةُ رَبِّكَ | *Kalimatu-rabbik* | The Word of your Lord (i.e., the Holy Qûr'an) |
| 115 | صِدْقًا وَعَدْلًا | *Sidqanw-wa 'adla* | In truth and in justice |
| 116 | يَخْرُصُونَ | *Yakh-rusun* | They tell lies |
| 120 | ذَرُوا | *Dharu* | *im. pl.* Leave |
| 121 | إِنَّهُ لَفِسْقٌ | *'Innahu-la-fisq* | It is impiety |
| 124 | صَغَارٌ | *Saghar* | Humiliation |
| 125 | يَصَّعَّدُ فِي السَّمَاءِ | *Yassa'-'adu fis-sama'* | Climbs up to the skies |

| V. | WORD | TR. | MEANING |
|---|---|---|---|
| 128 | اسْتَكْثَرْتُمْ مِنَ الْإِنسِ | *Is-takthartum-minal-'ins* | Many did you mislead of men |
| 128 | النَّارُ مَثْوَاكُمْ | *An-naru math-wakum* | The Fire be your dwelling-place |
| 130 | غَرَّتْهُمُ الْحَيَاةُ | *Gharrat-humul-ha-yat* | The life (of this world) deceived them |
| 135 | مَكَانَتِكُمْ | *Maka-natikum* | Whatever you can |
| 136 | ذَرَأَ | *Dhara-'a* | Created |
| 137 | قَتْلَ أَوْلَادِهِمْ | *Qatla 'aw-ladihim* | The Slaughter of their children |
| 137 | لِيُرْدُوهُمْ | *Li-yurduhum* | In order to lead them to their own destruction |
| 137 | لِيَلْبِسُوا عَلَيْهِمْ دِينَهُمْ | *Li-yalbisu 'alay-him dinahum* | In order to cause confusion in their religion |
| 137 | يَفْتَرُونَ | *Yaf-tarun* | They fabricate |
| 138 | حِجْرٌ | *Hijr* | Forbidden |
| 138 | حُرِّمَتْ ظُهُورُهَا | *Hurri-mat zuhuruha* | (Cattle which are) forbidden to be used for burden or any other work |
| 139 | وَصْفَهُمْ | *Was-fahum* | Their (false) attribution |
| 141 | مَعْرُوشَاتٍ | *Ma'-ru-shat* | *pp.* Trellised |
| 141 | غَيْرَ مَعْرُوشَاتٍ | *Ghayra ma'-ru-shat* | *pp.* Un-trellised |
| 141 | مُخْتَلِفًا أُكُلُهُ | *Mukh-talifan 'ukuluh* | Different shape and taste |
| 142 | حَمُولَةً | *Hamu-la* | For burden |
| 142 | فَرْشًا | *Farsha* | For meat |

| V. | WORD | TR. | MEANING |
|---|---|---|---|
| 144 | وَصَّاكُمُ اللّٰهُ بِهٰذا | *Wassa-kumul-lahu bi-hadha* | Allah ordered you such a thing |
| 145 | طَاعِمٍ | *Ta 'imin* | One who eats |
| 145 | اضْطُرَّ | *Id-turra* | *pv.* Forced by necessity |
| 145 | غَيْرَ بَاغٍ وَلَا عَادٍ | *Ghayra bagh wa la 'ad* | Without wilful disobedience nor transgressing due limits |
| 146 | ذِي ظُفُرٍ | *Dhi-zufur* | (Animals) with undivided hoof |
| 146 | شُحُومَ | *Shuhum* | *pl.* Fat |
| 146 | حَوَايَا | *Hawa-ya* | Entrails |
| 146 | مَا اخْتَلَطَ بِعَظْمٍ | *Makh-talata bi-'azm* | What is mixed up with a bone |
| 147 | لَا يُرَدُّ بَأْسُهُ | *La yuraddu ba'-suh* | Never will His Wrath be turned back |
| 149 | الْحُجَّةُ الْبَالِغَةُ | *Al-huj-jatul-ba-lighah* | Perfect proof and argument |
| 150 | هَلُمَّ شُهَدَاءَكُمُ | *Halumma shuhada-'akum* | *im. pl.* Bring forward your witnesses |
| 150 | بِرَبِّهِمْ يَعْدِلُونَ | *Bi-rabbihim ya'-dilun* | They hold others equal (in worship) with their Lord |
| 151 | أَتْلُ | *'Atlu* | I (will) rehearse |
| 151 | إِمْلَاقٍ | *'Imlaq* | Poverty |
| 151 | فَوَاحِشَ | *Fa-wahish* | Indecent deeds |
| 152 | يَبْلُغَ أَشُدَّهُ | *Yab-lugha 'a-shud-dah* | Attains the age of full strength |
| 153 | صِرَاطِي مُسْتَقِيمًا | *Sirati musta-qima* | My Straight Path |

| V. | WORD | TR. | MEANING |
|---|---|---|---|
| 157 | صَدَفَ | *Sadaf* | Turned away |
| 158 | يَأْتِيَ رَبُّكَ | *Ya'-tiya rabbuk* | Your Lord comes |
| 159 | كَانُوا | *Kanu* | They were |
| 159 | شِيَعًا | *Shiya-'a* | Sects |
| 161 | دِينًا قِيَمًا | *Dinan-qiyama* | Right religion |
| 162 | نُسُكِي | *Nu-suki* | My service of sacrifice |
| 165 | خَلَائِفَ الْأَرْضِ | *Khala-'ifal-'ard* | Inheritors of the earth |

| V. | WORD | TR. | MEANING |
|---|---|---|---|

## سُورَةُ الأَعْرَافِ

## [7[ SURAT AL-'ARAF

## THE HEIGHTS

| V. | WORD | TR. | MEANING |
|---|---|---|---|
| 2 | حَرَجٌ | *Hara-j* | Narrowness |
| 4 | كَمْ مِنْ قَرْيَةٍ | *Kam-min-qarya* | How many towns |
| 4 | بَأْسُنَا | *Ba'-suna* | Our punishment |
| 4 | بَيَاتًا | *Ba-yata* | At night |
| 4 | قَائِلُونَ | *Qa-'ilun* | Those who sleep at mid-day |
| 5 | دَعْوَاهُمْ | *Da'-wahum* | Their cry |
| 7 | غَآئِبِينَ | *Gha-'ibin* | *ap.pl.* Absent |
| 8 | ثَقُلَتْ | *Thaqulat* | *fg.* Became heavy |
| 8 | مَوَازِينُ | *Mawa-zin* | Scales |
| 9 | خَفَّتْ | *Khaffat* | *fg.* Became light |
| 10 | مَكَّنَّاكُمْ | *Makkannakum* | We placed you with authority |
| 10 | مَعَايِشَ | *Ma-'a-yish* | Means for the fulfillment of (one's) life |
| 11 | سَاجِدِينَ | *Sajidin* | *ap.* Those who bow down |
| 12 | مَا مَنَعَكَ | *Ma mana-'ak* | What prevented you |
| 13 | صَاغِرِينَ | *Saghirin* | Those humiliated and disgraced |
| 14 | أَنظِرْنِي | *'Anzirni* | *im.* Give me respite |
| 15 | مُنظَرِينَ | *Mun-zarin* | *pp.* Those allowed respite, respited |
| 16 | أَغْوَيْتَ | *'Aghwayt* | You sent astray |

| V. | WORD | TR. | MEANING |
|---|---|---|---|
| 16 | لَأَقْعُدَنَّ لَهُمْ | *La-'aq-'udanna lahum* | I will lie in wait for them |
| 18 | مَذْءُومًا | *Madh-'uma* | *pp.* Despised |
| 18 | مَدْحُورًا | *Mad-hura* | *pp.* Expelled |
| 20 | فَوَسْوَسَ لَهُمَا | *Fa-was-wasa lahuma* | Then he (Satan) whispered suggestions to them both |
| 20 | مَا وُورِيَ عَنْهُمَا | *Ma wu-riya 'an-huma* | That which was hidden from them both |
| 20 | سَوْآتِهِمَا | *Saw-'atihima* | *dl.* Their private parts |
| 21 | قَاسَمَهُمَا | *Qasama-huma* | He swore to them both |
| 22 | فَدَلَّاهُمَا بِغُرُورٍ | *Fadalla-huma bi-ghurur* | So he misled them (*dl.*) with deception |
| 22 | طَفِقَا يَخْصِفَانِ | *Tafiqa yakh-sifan* | *dl.* They began to stick together |
| 26 | أَنزَلْنَا عَلَيْكُمْ | *'Anzal-na 'alay-kum* | We bestowed upon you |
| 26 | يُوَارِي سَوْآتِكُمْ | *Yu-wari saw-'ati-kum* | Covers your private parts |
| 26 | رِيشًا | *Risha* | Adornment |
| 26 | لِبَاسُ التَّقْوَى | *Libasut-taqwa* | Raiment of righteousness |
| 27 | لَا يَفْتِنَنَّكُمْ | *La yafti-nanna-kum* | Let him not seduce you |
| 27 | يَنزِعُ | *Yan-zi-'* | Strips off |
| 29 | أَقِيمُوا | *'Aqimu* | *im. pl.* Set up |
| 29 | عِندَ كُلِّ مَسْجِدٍ | *'Inda kulli mas-jid* | At every time and place of prayer |
| 31 | خُذُوا زِينَتَكُمْ | *Khu-dhu* | *im. pl.* Wear your |

| V. | WORD | TR. | MEANING |
|---|---|---|---|
| | | *zinatakum* | beautiful apparel |
| 33 | بَغْيٍ | *Baghy* | Oppression |
| 37 | أَيْنَ مَا كُنتُمْ تدعون | *'Ayna ma kuntum tad-'un* | Where are the things that you used to invoke |
| 38 | ادَّارَكُوا | *Adda-raku* | They followed each other |
| 38 | عَذَابًا ضِعْفًا | *'Adhaban-di'fa* | Double punishment |
| 40 | جَمَلُ | *Jamal* | Camel |
| 40 | سَمِّ الْخِيَاطِ | *Sammil-khi-yat* | Eye of a needle |
| 41 | مِهَادٌ | *Mihad* | Couch |
| 41 | غَوَاشٍ | *Gha-wash* | Coverings |
| 43 | غِلٍّ | *Ghill* | Rancour |
| 44 | أَذَّنَ | *'Adhdhan* | Proclaimed |
| 44 | مُؤَذِّنٌ | *Mu-'adhdhin* | Crier |
| 45 | يَبْغُونَهَا عِوَجًا | *Yabghunaha 'i-waja* | They desire to make it crooked |
| 46 | حِجَابٌ | *Hijab* | Veil |
| 46 | أَعْرَافِ | *'A'raf* | Heights (elevated places which divide Paradise from Hell) |
| 46 | بِسِيمَاهُمْ | *Bi-si-mahum* | By their marks |
| 50 | أَفِيضُوا عَلَيْنَا | *'Afidu 'alay-na* | *im. pl.* Pour down to us |
| 51 | غَرَّتْهُمُ الْحَيَاةُ الدُّنْيَا | *Gharrat-humul-hayatud-dun-ya* | They were deceived by the life of the world |
| 51 | نَنسَاهُمْ | *Nansa-hum* | We (shall) forget them |
| 51 | وَمَا كَانُوا | *Wa ma kanu* | And as they were |

| V. | WORD | TR. | MEANING |
|---|---|---|---|
| 54 | اسْتَوَى عَلَى الْعَرْشِ | *Is-tawa 'alal- 'arsh* | He settled Himself on the Throne |
| 54 | يُغْشِي اللَّيْلَ النَّهَار | *Yugh-shil-lay-lan-nahar* | He covers the night with the day |
| 54 | يَطْلُبُ | *Yat-lub* | Seeks |
| 54 | حَثِيثًا | *Hathitha* | Rapidly |
| 54 | لَهُ الْخَلْقُ | *La-hul-khalq* | His is the creation |
| 54 | أَمْرُ | *'Amr* | Command |
| 54 | تَبَارَكَ اللَّهُ | *Taba-rakallah* | Blessed be Allah |
| 55 | ادْعُوا رَبَّكُمْ | *'Ud-'u rabba-kum* | *im. pl.* Call on your Lord |
| 56 | رَحْمَةَ اللَّهِ | *Rah-matallah* | The Mercy of Allah |
| 57 | بُشْرًا | *Bushra* | Heralds of glad tidings |
| 57 | أَقَلَّتْ سَحَابًا | *'Aqallat sahaba* | They carried clouds |
| 57 | ثِقَالًا | *Thiqala* | Heavy |
| 57 | بَلَدٍ مَيِّتٍ | *Baladim-mayyit* | Dead land |
| 58 | نَكِدًا | *Nakida* | Scanty |
| 60 | مَلَأُ | *Mala'* | Leaders |
| 62 | أَنصَحُ لَكُمْ | *'Ansahu lakum* | I give you sincere advice |
| 64 | قَوْمًا عَمِينَ | *Qawman 'amin* | Blind people |
| 66 | سَفَاهَةً | *Safaha* | Folly |
| 69 | بَسْطَةً | *Basta* | Increase of stature |
| 69 | آلَاءَ | *'Ala-'* | Benefits, graces |
| 72 | قَطَعْنَا | *Qata'-na* | We cut off |
| 72 | دَابِرَ | *Dabir* | Root |

| V. | WORD | TR. | MEANING |
|---|---|---|---|
| 73 | نَاقَةُ | *Naqa* | She-camel |
| 74 | بَوَّأَكُمْ | *Bawwa-'akum* | He gave you habitations |
| 74 | لَا تَعْثَوْا | *La ta'-thaw* | *ni. pl.* Do not make mischief |
| 77 | عَتَوْا | *'Ataw* | They insolently defied |
| 78 | رَجْفَةُ | *Rajfa* | Earthquake |
| 78 | جَاثِمِينَ | *Jathi-min* | *ap. pl.* Prostrated |
| 82 | يَتَطَهَّرُونَ | *Ya-tatah-harun* | They seek to keep clean and pure |
| 83 | غَابِرِينَ | *Ghabirin* | Those who remained behind (in the torment) |
| 85 | لَا تَبْخَسُوا | *La tab-khasu* | *ni. pl.* Do not withhold |
| 89 | رَبَّنَا افْتَحْ | *Rabbanaf-tah* | *im.* Our Lord! Decide |
| 92 | لَمْ يَغْنَوْا فِيهَا | *Lam yaghnaw fiha* | They had never dwelt there (in their homes) |
| 93 | آسَى | *'Asa* | I lament |
| 94 | بَأْسَاءِ | *Ba'-sa'* | Suffering |
| 94 | ضَرَّاءِ | *Ad-dar-ra'* | Adversity |
| 94 | يَضَّرَّعُونَ | *Yaddarra-'un* | They call in humility |
| 95 | عَفَوا | *'Afaw* | They grew and multiplied |
| 97 | بَأْسُنَا | *Ba'-sunna* | Our Punishment |
| 99 | مَكْرَ اللَّهِ | *Makral-lah* | The Plan of Allah |
| 100 | أَنْ لَوْ نَشَاءُ أَصَبْنَاهُمْ | *'Al-law na-sha-'u 'asab-nahum* | If We so willed, We could punish |

| V. | WORD | TR. | MEANING |
|---|---|---|---|
| | | | them |
| 103 | ظَلَمُوا بِهَا | *zalamu biha* | They wrongfully rejected them |
| 105 | حَقِيقٌ | *Haqiqun* | Proper |
| 108 | نَزَعَ يَدَهُ | *Naza-'a yadah* | He drew out his hand |
| 108 | بَيْضَاءُ | *Bay-da-'* | White |
| 111 | أَرْجِهِ | *'Arjih* | *im.* Put him off (for a time) |
| 111 | حَاشِرِينَ | *Ha-shirin* | *ap.* Those men who collect |
| 116 | سَحَرُوا أَعْيُنَ النَّاسِ | *Saharu 'a'-yunan-nas* | They bewitched the eyes of the people |
| 116 | اسْتَرْهَبُوهُمْ | *Astar-habuhum* | They struck terror into them |
| 117 | تَلْقَفُ | *Talqaf* | Swallows up |
| 117 | يَأْفِكُونَ | *Ya'-fikun* | They fake |
| 118 | فَوَقَعَ الْحَقُّ | *Fa-waqa-'al-haqq* | Thus truth was confirmed |
| 126 | تَنقِمُ مِنَّا | *Tanqimu min-na* | You take vengeance on us |
| 126 | أَفْرِغْ عَلَيْنَا | *'Af-righ 'alay-na* | *im.* Pour out on us |
| 127 | نَسْتَحْيِي | *Nastah-yi* | We will save alive |
| 127 | نِسَاءَهُمْ | *Nisa-'ahum* | Their women |
| 130 | بِالسِّنِينَ | *Bissi-nin* | With years (of drought) |
| 131 | يَطَّيَّرُوا | *Yat-tayyaru* | They ascribe (things) to evil omens |
| 131 | طَائِرُهُمْ عِنْدَ اللَّهِ | *Ta-'iruhum 'indal-lah* | Their evil omens are with Allah (i.e., their punishment in |

| V. | WORD | TR. | MEANING |
|---|---|---|---|
| | | | the Hereafter) |
| 133 | طُوفَان | *Tufan* | Flood, wholesale death |
| 133 | قُمَّل | *Qummal* | Lice |
| 134 | رِجْز | *Rijz* | Plague |
| 135 | يَنكُثُون | *Yan-kuthun* | They break their word |
| 137 | دَمَّرْنَا | *Dammarna* | We destroyed completely |
| 137 | يَعْرِشُون | *Ya'-rishun* | They erect |
| 139 | مُتَبَّرٌ | *Mu-tab-bar* | *pp.* Destroyed, broken up |
| 140 | أَبْغِيكُمْ | *'Ab-ghikum* | I seek for you |
| 141 | يَسُومُونَكُمْ | *Yasumu-nakum* | They afflict you |
| 141 | بَلَاءٌ | *Bala-'* | Momentous trial |
| 143 | تَجَلَّى رَبُّهُ لِلْجَبَلِ | *Tajalla Rabbuhu lil-Jabal* | His Lord manifested Himself To the Mount |
| 143 | دَكًّا | *Dakkan* | Dust |
| 143 | صَعِقًا | *Sa-'iqa* | Unconscious |
| 143 | سُبْحَانَكَ | *Sub-hanak* | Glory be to You |
| 145 | أَلْوَاحِ | *'Alwah* | Tablets |
| 146 | سَبِيلَ الرُّشْدِ | *Sabilar-rushd* | The way of right conduct |
| 146 | سَبِيلَ الغَيِّ | *Sabilal-ghayy* | The way of error |
| 148 | عِجْلًا | *'Ijlan* | Calf |
| 148 | جَسَدًا | *Jasada* | Body |
| 148 | خُوَارٌ | *Khu-war* | Lowing sound |

| V. | WORD | TR. | MEANING |
|---|---|---|---|
| 148 | اتَّخَذُوهُ | *'Itta-khadhuh* | They took it for worship |
| 149 | سُقِطَ فِي أَيْدِيهِمْ | *Suqita fi 'ay-dihim* | They grievously repented |
| 150 | أَسِفًا | *'Asifan* | Grieved |
| 150 | لَا تُشْمِتْ | *La tushmit* | *ni.* Do not make (them) rejoice over (me) |
| 154 | سَكَتَ | *Sakata* | Appeased |
| 155 | أَخَذَتْهُمُ الرَّجْفَةُ | *'Akha-that-humur-rajfa* | They were seized with violent quaking |
| 155 | فِتْنَتُكَ | *Fitna-tuk* | Your trial |
| 156 | هُدْنَا إِلَيْكَ | *Hud-na 'ilayk* | We have turned unto you |
| 157 | إِصْرَهُمْ | *Israhum* | Their heavy burdens |
| 157 | أَغْلَال | *'Aghlal* | Yokes |
| 157 | عَزَّرُوهُ | *'Azza-ruh* | They honoured him |
| 160 | قَطَّعْنَاهُمْ | *Qatta'-nahum* | We divided them |
| 160 | أَسْبَاطًا | *'Asbatan* | Tribes |
| 160 | انْبَجَسَتْ | *Ambaja-sat* | Gushed forth |
| 160 | مَشْرَبَهُمْ | *Mash-rabahum* | Their own place for water |
| 160 | غَمَام | *Ghamam* | Clouds |
| 160 | مَنّ | *Manna* | Manna |
| 160 | سَلْوَى | *Salwa* | Quails |
| 161 | قُولُوا حِطَّةٌ | *Qulu Hittatun* | *im. pl.* Say: "(O Allah) forgive our sins" |

| V. | WORD | TR. | MEANING |
|---|---|---|---|
| 163 | حَاضِرَةَ الْبَحْرِ | *Hadi-ratal-bahr* | Close by the sea |
| 163 | يَعْدُونَ فِي السَّبْتِ | *Ya'-duna fis-Sabt* | They transgress in the matter of the Sabbath (i.e., Saturday) |
| 163 | شُرَّعًا | *Shurra-'an* | Openly |
| 163 | لَا يَسْبِتُونَ | *La yas-bitun* | They have no Sabbath |
| 164 | مَعْذِرَةً إِلَى رَبِّكُمْ | *Ma'-dhiratan 'ila Rabbikum* | In order to be free from guilt before your Lord (Allah) |
| 165 | عَذَابٍ بَئِيسٍ | *'Adhabin-ba-'isin* | Grievous punishment |
| 166 | عَتَوْا | *'Atawa* | They exceeded the limits |
| 166 | قِرَدَةً | *Qiradatan* | Apes |
| 166 | خَاسِئِينَ | *Khasi-'in* | Despised and rejected |
| 167 | يَسُومُهُمْ | *Yasu-muhum* | Afflicts them |
| 169 | عَرَضَ هَذَا الْأَدْنَى | *'Arada hadhal-'adna* | The goods of this low life |
| 169 | دَرَسُوا مَا فِيهِ | *Darasu ma fih* | They studied what is in it |
| 171 | نَتَقْنَا الْجَبَلَ | *Nataqnal-Jabal* | We raised the mount |
| 171 | ظُلَّةٌ | *Zul-latun* | Canopy |
| 175 | انسَلَخَ | *An-salakh* | Passed by |
| 175 | غَاوِينَ | *Ghawin* | Those who go astray |
| 176 | أَخْلَدَ إِلَى الْأَرْضِ | *'Akhlada 'ilal-'ard* | Inclined to the earth |
| 176 | تَحْمِلْ عَلَيْهِ | *Tahmil 'alayh* | You attack him |

| V. | WORD | TR. | MEANING |
|---|---|---|---|
| 176 | يَلْهَثْ | *Yalhath* | He lolls out his tongue |
| 179 | ذَرَأْنَا | *Dhara-'na* | We made |
| 180 | يُلْحِدُونَ | *Yul-hidun* | They deviate from that which is lawful and right |
| 182 | سَنَسْتَدْرِجُهُمْ | *Sanas-tadriju-hum* | We will lead them step by step |
| 183 | أُمْلِي | *'Umli* | I grant respite |
| 183 | كَيْدِي مَتِينٌ | *Kaydi matin* | My scheme is strong |
| 184 | جِنَّةٍ | *Jin-nah* | Madness |
| 187 | أَيَّانَ | *'Ayyan* | When |
| 187 | مُرْسَاهَا | *Mur-saha* | Its appointed time |
| 187 | لَا يُجَلِّي | *La yu-jalli* | Will not reveal |
| 187 | ثَقُلَتْ | *Thaqulat* | Became heavy |
| 187 | حَفِيٌّ | *Ha-fiyyun* | Eager in search |
| 189 | تَغَشَّاهَا | *Taghsh-shahha* | He had sexual relation with her |
| 189 | مَرَّتْ بِهِ | *Marrat bih* | She carried it about |
| 189 | صَالِحًا | *Salihan* | Goodly |
| 190 | جَعَلَا لَهُ شُرَكَاءَ | *Ja-'ala lahu shuraka* | They ascribed partners to Him (Allah) |
| 198 | لَا يُبْصِرُونَ | *La yubsirun* | They see not |
| 199 | خُذْ الْعَفْوَ | *Khudhil-'afw* | *im.* Hold to forgiveness |
| 199 | أْمُرْ بِالْعُرْفِ | *A'-mur bil-'urf* | *im.* Command what is right |
| 200 | نَزْغٌ | *Nazghun* | Suggestion |

| V. | WORD | TR. | MEANING |
|---|---|---|---|
| 201 | مَسَّهُمْ طَائِفٌ | *Massahum ta-'if* | An evil thought assaulted them |
| 201 | تَذَكَّرُوا | *Tadhakkaru* | They remembered |
| 202 | يَمُدُّونَهُمْ فِي الغَيِّ | *Ya-muddu-nahum fil-ghayy* | They plunge them deeper into error |
| 202 | لَا يُقْصِرُونَ | *La yuq-sirun* | They never stop |
| 203 | اجْتَبَيْتَهَا | *Ijtabay-taha* | You have brought it |
| 203 | بَصَائِرُ | *Basa-'ir* | Evidences |
| 206 | لَهُ يَسْجُدُونَ | *Lahu yas-judun* | They prostrate before Him |

| V. | WORD | TR. | MEANING |
|---|---|---|---|

## سُورَةُ الأَنفَال

## [8] SURAT AL-ANFAL
## THE SPOILS OF WAR

| V. | WORD | TR. | MEANING |
|---|---|---|---|
| 1 | أَنْفَال | *Anfal* | Spoils of war |
| 1 | ذَاتَ بَيْنِكُمْ | *Dhata-bay-nikum* | Relations between yourselves |
| 2 | وَجِلَتْ | *Waji-lat* | Filled with fear |
| 2 | يَتَوَكَّلُونَ | *Yata-wakka-lun* | They put their trust |
| 7 | طَائِفَتَيْنِ | *Ta-'ifatayn* | Two parties |
| 7 | ذَاتِ الشَّوْكَةِ | *Dhatish-shawka* | Armed one |
| 9 | مُرْدِفِينَ | *Murdifin* | Ranks on ranks |
| 11 | يُغَشِّيكُمُ النُّعَاسَ | *Yughashshi-kumunnu-'as* | He covers you with drowsiness |
| 11 | أَمَنَةً مِنْهُ | *'Amanatam-minh* | Security from Him |
| 11 | رِجْزَ الشَّيْطَانِ | *Rijzash-Shaytan* | The stain of Satan |
| 11 | يَرْبِطَ | *Yarbit* | Strengthens |
| 12 | أَنِّي مَعَكُمْ | *'Anni ma-'akum* | I am with you |
| 12 | رُعْبَ | *Ru'b* | Terror |
| 12 | كُلَّ بَنَانٍ | *Kulla banan* | All finger-tips |
| 13 | شَاقُّوا | *Shaq-qu* | They contended against |
| 15 | زَحْفًا | *Zahfa* | In hostile array |
| 16 | مُتَحَرِّفًا | *Muta-harrifa* | Stratagem |
| 16 | مُتَحَيِّزًا إِلَى فِئَةٍ | *Muta-hay-yizan 'ila fi-'a* | To retreat to (his own) troop |
| 18 | مُوهِنُ | *Muhin* | *ap.* One who makes (others) weak |

| V. | WORD | TR. | MEANING |
|---|---|---|---|
| 19 | تَسْتَفْتِحُوا | *Tastaf-tihu* | You pray for victory |
| 24 | يُحْيِيكُمْ | *Yuh-yikum* | Gives you life |
| 26 | يَتَخَطَّفَكُمُ النَّاسُ | *Yatakhatta-fakumun-nas* | Men despoil and kidnap you |
| 30 | يُثْبِتُوكَ | *Yuthbituk* | They keep you in bonds |
| 31 | أَسَاطِيرُ الْأَوَّلِينَ | *'Asa-tirul-'awwalin* | Tales of the ancients |
| 35 | مُكَاءً وَتَصْدِيَةً | *Muka-'anw-wa tas-diyah* | Whistling and clapping |
| 36 | حَسْرَةً | *Hasra* | Regret and sigh |
| 37 | يَرْكُمَهُ جَمِيعًا | *Yar-kumahu jami-'a* | Heaps them together |
| 41 | خُمُسَهُ | *Khu-musah* | One-fifth (1/5th) |
| 41 | يَوْمَ الْفُرْقَانِ | *Yawmal-Furqan* | The Day of the Criterion (between right and wrong) [i.e., The battle of Badar] |
| 42 | الْعُدْوَةِ الدُّنْيَا | *Al-'udwatid-dunya* | The near side of the valley |
| 42 | الْعُدْوَةِ الْقُصْوَى | *Al-'udwatil-quswa* | The farther side of the valley |
| 42 | رَكْبُ | *Rakb* | Caravan |
| 43 | لَفَشِلْتُمْ | *La-fashil-tum* | *pl.* You would have discouraged |
| 46 | تَذْهَبَ رِيحُكُمْ | *Tadhhaba rihu-kum* | *pl.* Your power departs |
| 47 | بَطَرًا | *Batara* | Insolently |
| 48 | إِنِّي جَارٌ لَكُمْ | *'Inni jarul-lakum* | I am near to you (for each and every help) |

| V. | WORD | TR. | MEANING |
|---|---|---|---|
| 48 | نَكَصَ عَلَى عَقِبَيْهِ | *Nakasa 'ala 'aqi-bayh* | He turned on his heels |
| 52 | دَأْب | *Da'-b* | Manner |
| 57 | تَثْقَفَنَّهُمْ | *Tathqa-fannahum* | You gain the mastery over them |
| 57 | شَرِّدْ | *Sharrid* | *im.* Disperse |
| 58 | انبِذْ إِلَيْهِمْ | *Ambidh 'ilay-him* | *im.* Throw back to them |
| 58 | عَلَى سَوَاءٍ | *'Ala sawa'* | On equal (terms) |
| 59 | سَبَقُوا | *Sabaqu* | They escaped |
| 60 | قُوَّة | *Quwwa* | Strength |
| 60 | رِبَاطِ الْخَيْلِ | *Ribatil-Khayl* | Steeds of war |
| 61 | جَنَحُوا لِلسَّلْمِ | *Janahu lis-salm* | They inclined towards peace |
| 62 | حَسْبَكَ اللَّهُ | *Hasba-kullah* | Allah suffices you |
| 65 | حَرِّضِ الْمُؤْمِنِينَ | *Harridil-Mu'-minin* | *im.* Rouse the believers |
| 67 | يُثْخِنَ | *Yuth-khin* | Thoroughly subdues |
| 67 | عَرَضَ الدُّنْيَا | *'Aradad-dunya* | Temporal goods of this world |
| 71 | أَمْكَنَ مِنْهُمْ | *'Amkana min-hum* | Gave (you) power over them |
| 75 | أُولُوا الْأَرْحَامِ | *'Ulul-'arham* | Those kindred by blood |
| 75 | أَوْلَى | *'Awla* | Nearer |

# سُورَةُ التَّوبَة

## [9] SURAT AT-TAUBA
## REPENTANCE

| V. | WORD | TR. | MEANING |
|---|---|---|---|
| 1 | بَرَاءةٌ | *Bara-'a* | Immunity, freedom from obligations |
| 1 | عَاهَدتُّمْ | *'A-had-ttum* | *pl.* You contracted |
| 2 | أَرْبَعَةَ أَشْهُرٍ | *'Arba-'ata 'ash-hurin* | Four months |
| 2 | غَيْرُ مُعْجِزِي اللَّهِ | *Ghayru mu'-jizi-lah* | (Those who) cannot frustrate Allah, (those who) cannot escape (from the Punishment of) Allah |
| 3 | أَذَانٌ | *'Adhan* | Announcement |
| 3 | يَوْمَ الْحَجِّ الْأَكْبَرِ | *Yawmal-Hajjil-'Akbar* | The day of the Great Pilgrimage (i.e., the Day of Sacrifice) |
| 4 | لَمْ يَنقُصُوكُمْ | *Lam yanqu-sukum* | They have not (subsequently) failed you in aught |
| 4 | لَمْ يُظَاهِرُوا | *Lam yuza-hiru* | They have not aided |
| 5 | انسَلَخَ | *An-salakh* | Passed |
| 5 | احْصُرُوهُمْ | *Ah-suru-hum* | *im. pl.* Beleaguer them |
| 5 | كُلَّ مَرْصَدٍ | *Kulla marsad* | Every ambush |
| 6 | اسْتَجَارَكَ | *Is-tajarak* | Sought your protection |
| 7 | اسْتَقَامُوا لَكُمْ | *Is-taqamu lakum* | They stood true to |

| V. | WORD | TR. | MEANING |
|---|---|---|---|
| | | | you |
| 8 | يَظْهَرُوا عَلَيْكُمْ | *Yaz-haru 'alay-kum* | They overcome you |
| 8 | لَا يَرْقُبُوا | *La yar-qubu* | They do not respect |
| 8 | إِلًّا | *'Illa* | Kinship |
| 8 | ذِمَّةً | *Dhimmah* | Covenant |
| 9 | ثَمَنًا قَلِيلًا | *Thamanan qalila* | Miserable price |
| 10 | لَا يَرْقُبُونَ | *La yarqabun* | They do not respect |
| 12 | نَكَثُوا أَيْمَانَهُمْ | *Nakathu 'ay-ma-nahum* | They violated their oaths |
| 15 | غَيْظَ | *Ghayz* | Indignation |
| 16 | وَلِيجَةً | *Walijah* | Friend and protector |
| 17 | مَسَاجِدَ اللَّهِ | *Masajidal-lah* | The mosques of Allah |
| 19 | سِقَايَةَ الْحَاجِّ | *Siqa-yatal-Hajj* | Giving drink to the pilgrims |
| 23 | اسْتَحَبُّوا الْكُفْرَ | *Is-tahabbul-kufr* | They loved infidelity |
| 24 | اقْتَرَفْتُمُوهَا | *Iq-taraf-tumuha* | *pl.* You gained it |
| 24 | كَسَادَ | *Kasad* | Decline (of commerce) |
| 24 | تَرَبَّصُوا | *Tarab-basu* | *im. pl.* Wait |
| 25 | رَحُبَتْ | *Rahu-bat* | Became wide |
| 26 | سَكِينَتَهُ | *Sa-kina-tah* | His calm |
| 28 | الْمُشْرِكُونَ نَجَسٌ | *Al-mushri-kuna najas* | Pagans are unclean |
| 28 | خِفْتُمْ عَيْلَةً | *Khiftum 'ay-la* | *pl.* You feared poverty |
| 29 | يُعْطُوا الْجِزْيَةَ | *Yu'-tul-Jizya* | They pay the tax |

| V. | WORD | TR. | MEANING |
|---|---|---|---|
| 29 | عَنْ يَدٍ | *'any-yad* | With their hands (i.e., with willing submission) |
| 29 | هُمْ صَاغِرُونَ | *Hum saghi-run* | They feel themselves subdued |
| 30 | يُضَاهِئُونَ | *Yudahi-'un* | They imitate |
| 31 | أَحْبَارَهُمْ | *'Ahba-rahum* | Their priests |
| 31 | رُهْبَانَهُمْ | *Ruhba-nahum* | Their anchorites |
| 31 | أَرْبَابًا | *'Ar-baba* | Lords |
| 33 | يُظْهِرَهُ | *Yuzhi-rah* | Causes it to prevail |
| 36 | أَرْبَعَةٌ حُرُمٌ | *'Arba-'atun hurum* | Four are sacred |
| 36 | الدِّينُ الْقَيِّمُ | *Ad-Dinul-Qay-yim* | The right religion |
| 37 | النَّسِيءُ | *An-nasi'* | Transposing |
| 37 | يُوَاطِئُوا | *Yuwati-'u* | They make it agree |
| 38 | انفِرُوا | *Unfiru* | *im. pl.* Go forth |
| 38 | اثَّاقَلْتُمْ | *Ath-thaqal-tum* | *pl.* You became heavy |
| 40 | فِي الْغَارِ | *Fil-ghar* | In the cave |
| 40 | صَاحِبِهِ | *Sahi-bih* | His companion |
| 41 | خِفَافًا | *Khifafa* | Lightly |
| 41 | ثِقَالًا | *Thiqala* | Heavily |
| 42 | عَرَضًا قَرِيبًا | *'Aradan-qari-ba* | Immediate gain (in sight) |
| 42 | شُقَّةُ | *Shuqqah* | Distance |
| 46 | انْبِعَاثَهُمْ | *In-bi-'athahum* | Their being sent forth |

| V. | WORD | TR. | MEANING |
|---|---|---|---|
| 46 | ثَبَّطَهُمْ | *Thabba-tahum* | He made them lag behind |
| 47 | خَبَالًا | *Khaba-la* | Corruption, disorder |
| 47 | لَأَوْضَعُوا | *La-'awda-'u* | They would have hurried to and fro |
| 47 | خِلَالَكُمْ | *Khila-lakum* | Among you |
| 47 | يَبْغُونَكُمُ الْفِتْنَةَ | *Yabghuna-kumul-fitna* | They sow sedition among you |
| 48 | قَلَّبُوا لَكَ الْأُمُورَ | *Qallabu lakal-'umur* | They upset Matters for you |
| 49 | ائْذَنْ لِي | *I'dhanl-li* | *im.* Grant me exemption |
| 49 | لَا تَفْتِنِّي | *La taf-tinni* | *ni.* Draw me not into trail |
| 52 | حُسْنَيَيْنِ | *Husna-yayn* | Two glorious things (martyrdom or victory) |
| 55 | تَزْهَقَ أَنفُسُهُمْ | *Tazhaqa 'anfusu-hum* | Their souls (shall) depart (die) |
| 56 | قَوْمٌ يَفْرَقُونَ | *Qawmuny-yafraqun* | They are a people who are afraid (of you) |
| 57 | مَلْجَأً | *Malja'* | Place to flee to |
| 57 | مَغَارَاتٍ | *Magharat* | Caves |
| 57 | مُدَّخَلًا | *Mudda-khala* | A place of entering, a place of retreat |
| 57 | يَجْمَحُونَ | *Yajma-hun* | They turn straightway |
| 58 | يَلْمِزُكَ | *Yal-mizuk* | Slanders you |
| 59 | حَسْبُنَا اللَّهُ | *Hasbu-nallah* | Allah is Sufficient for us |
| 60 | عَامِلِينَ | *'Amilin* | *ap.* Those who are |

| V. | WORD | TR. | MEANING |
|---|---|---|---|
| | | | employed |
| 60 | رِقَابِ | *Riqab* | Necks, those in bondage |
| 60 | غَارِمِين | *Gharimin* | Those in debt |
| 60 | فِي سَبِيلِ اللَّهِ | *Fi Sabi-lillah* | In the cause of Allah |
| 60 | ابْنِ السَّبِيلِ | *Ibnis-sabil* | Wayfarer |
| 61 | هُوَ أُذُنٌ | *Huwa 'udhun* | He is (all) ear (i.e., he listens to everybody) |
| 61 | أُذُنُ خَيْرٍ لَكُمْ | *'Udhunu khay-rillakum* | He listens to what is best for you |
| 63 | يُحَادِدْ | *Yuhad-id* | Opposes |
| 65 | نَخُوضُ وَنَلْعَبُ | *Nakhudu wa nal-'ab* | We talk idly and play |
| 67 | يَقْبِضُونَ أَيْدِيَهُمْ | *Yaqbi-duna 'aydi-yahum* | They close their hands [from giving (spending in Allah's Cause) alms, etc.] |
| 67 | نَسِيَهُمْ | *Nasi-yahum* | He forgot them |
| 69 | خُضْتُمْ | *Khudtum* | *pl.* You indulged in idle talk |
| 70 | مُؤْتَفِكَاتِ | *Mu'-tafi-kat* | Overthrown cities (i.e., the people to whom Lut عليه السلام preached) |
| 73 | اغْلُظْ عَلَيْهِمْ | *Agh-luz 'alayhim* | *im.* Be firm against them |
| 74 | نَقَمُوا | *Naqamu* | They disliked |
| 78 | يَعْلَمُ سِرَّهُمْ | *Ya'-lamu sirra-hum* | He knows their secret |

| V. | WORD | TR. | MEANING |
|---|---|---|---|
| 78 | نَجْوَاهُمْ | *Naj-wahum* | Their secret counsels |
| 79 | سَخِرَ | *Sakhir* | Mocked |
| 81 | خِلَافَ رَسُولِ اللَّهِ | *Khilafa Rasu-lillah* | Behind the Messenger of Allah صلى الله عليه وسلم |
| 81 | لَا تَنفِرُوا | *La tanfiru* | *ni. pl.* Do not go forth |
| 83 | خَالِفِينَ | *Khalifin* | *ap.* Those who remain behind |
| 86 | أُولُوا الطَّوْلِ مِنْهُمْ | *'Ulut-tawli minhum* | Those with wealth and influence among them |
| 87 | خَوَالِفِ | *Khawa-lif* | Those (Women) who remain behind in case of war |
| 90 | مُعَذِّرُونَ | *Mu-'adh-dhirun* | Those who make excuses |
| 92 | تَفِيضُ | *Tafid* | Streams |
| 92 | دَمْعِ | *Dam'* | Tears |
| 97 | أَجْدَرُ | *Ajdar* | More fitting |
| 98 | يَتَرَبَّصُ بِكُمُ الدَّوَائِرَ | *Yatarabbasu bikumud-da-wa-'ir* | Watches for disasters for you |
| 98 | عَلَيْهِمْ دَائِرَةُ السَّوْءِ | *'Alay-him da-'iratus-suw'* | On them be the disaster of evil |
| 99 | صَلَوَاتِ الرَّسُولِ | *Salawatir-Rasul* | The prayers of the Messenger صلى الله عليه وسلم |
| 101 | مَرَدُوا عَلَى النِّفَاقِ | *Maradu 'alan-nifaq* | They persisted in hypocrisy |
| 103 | صل عليهم | *Salli 'alay-him* | *im.* Pray for them |

| V. | WORD | TR. | MEANING |
|---|---|---|---|
| 103 | سَكَنٌ لَهُمْ | *Sakanul-lahum* | (Source of) security for them |
| 104 | يَأْخُذُ | *Ya'-khudh* | Receives |
| 104 | صَدَقَات | *Sada-qat* | Gifts of charity |
| 106 | مُرْجَوْنَ | *Murjawn* | Those held in suspense, those who are made to wait |
| 107 | ضِرَارًا | *Dirara* | Harm |
| 107 | إِرْصَادًا | *'Irsada* | Means of preparation, outpost |
| 109 | شَفَا | *Shafa* | Brink |
| 109 | جُرُف | *Juruf* | Precipice |
| 109 | هَارٍ | *Harr* | That which is ready to crumble to pieces |
| 110 | رِيبَةً فِي قُلُوبِهِمْ | *Ribatan-fi qulu-bihim* | Doubt and hypocrisy in their hearts |
| 110 | تَقَطَّعَ قُلُوبُهُمْ | *Taqatta-'a qulubu-hum* | Their hearts are cut to pieces |
| 112 | سَائِحُونَ | *Sa-'ihun* | Those who wonder in devotion to Cause of Allah, those who fast |
| 114 | أَوَّاهٌ | *'Awwah* | Tender-hearted |
| 117 | سَاعَةِ الْعُسْرَةِ | *Sa-'atil-'usra* | Hour of hardship, time of distress |
| 120 | يَرْغَبُوا بِأَنفُسِهِمْ | *Yarghabu bi-'anfusihim* | They prefer their own lives |
| 120 | نَصَبٌ | *Nasab* | Fatigue |

| V. | WORD | TR. | MEANING |
|---|---|---|---|
| 120 | مَخْمَصَةٌ | *Makh-masa* | Hunger |
| 120 | يَغِيظُ الْكُفَّارَ | *Ya ghi-zul-kuffar* | Raises the ire of the unbelievers |
| 120 | نَيْلًا | *Nayla* | To gain |
| 123 | غِلْظَةً | *Ghilzah* | Harshness |
| 125 | رِجْسًا | *Rijsa* | Doubt, hypocrisy, disbelief |
| 126 | يُفْتَنُونَ | *Yufta-nun* | *pv.* They are tried |
| 128 | عَزِيزٌ عَلَيْهِ | *'Azizun 'alayh* | Grieves him |
| 128 | عَنِتُّمْ | *'Anit-tum* | *pl.* You are made to suffer |

# سُورَةُ يُونس

## [10] SURAT YUNUS

## JONAH

| V. | WORD | TR. | MEANING |
|---|---|---|---|
| 2 | قَدَم صدق | *Qadama Sidq* | Good actions |
| 4 | حَميم | *Hamim* | Boiling fluids |
| 5 | قَدَّر | *Qaddar* | Measured |
| 5 | مَنَازِل | *Manazil* | Stages |
| 7 | لَا يَرْجُونَ | *La yar-jun* | They do not expect / hope |
| 10 | دَعْوَاهُمْ | *Da'-wa-hum* | Their prayer |
| 11 | لَقُضِيَ إِلَيْهِمْ أَجَلُهُمْ | *Laqu-diya 'ilay-him 'ajalu-him* | Their respite would be settled at once (i.e., Their doom would be sealed at once) |
| 11 | فِي طُغْيَانِهِمْ | *Fi tughya-nihim* | In their trespasses |
| 12 | ضُرٌّ | *Durr* | Trouble |
| 12 | دَعَانَا لِجَنْبِهِ | *Da-'ana lijam-bih* | He cried unto Us (in all postures)-lying down on his side |
| 12 | قَاعِداً | *Qa-'ida* | Sitting |
| 12 | قَآئماً | *Qa-'ima* | Standing |
| 12 | مَرَّ | *Marr* | Passed |
| 15 | بَدِّلْهُ | *Bad-dilh* | Change it |
| 16 | أَدْرَاكُمْ بِهِ | *'Adra-kum-bih* | He made it known to you |
| 17 | لَا يُفْلِحُ الْمُجْرِمُونَ | *La yuflihul-mujri-mun* | Sinners will never prosper |

| V. | WORD | TR. | MEANING |
|---|---|---|---|
| 21 | ضَرَّاءَ مَسَّتْهُمْ | *Dar-ra-'a massat-hum* | Adversity touched them |
| 21 | مَكْرٌ | *Makr* | Plot |
| 21 | اللَّهُ أَسْرَعُ مَكْرًا | *Allahu 'asra-'u makra* | Allah is Swifter in planning |
| 22 | رِيحٍ طَيِّبَةٍ | *Rihin tayyi-ba* | Favourable wind |
| 22 | رِيحٌ عَاصِفٌ | *Rihun 'asif* | Stormy wind |
| 23 | يَبْغُونَ | *Yab-ghun* | They transgress |
| 24 | زُخْرُفَهَا | *Zukh-rufaha* | Its ornaments / adornments |
| 24 | أَمْرُنَا | *'Amruna* | Our Command |
| 24 | حَصِيدًا | *Hasida* | Clean-mown harvest |
| 24 | لَمْ تَغْنَ | *Lam taghn* | It had not flourished |
| 26 | حُسْنَى | *Husna* | Happy state (i.e., Paradise) |
| 26 | زِيَادَةٌ | *Zi-adah* | More |
| 26 | لَا يَرْهَقُ وُجُوهَهُمْ | *La yar-haqu wujuha-hum* | Will not cover their faces |
| 26 | قَتَرٌ | *Qatar* | Black dust, darkness |
| 26 | ذِلَّةٌ | *Dhillah* | Abasement |
| 27 | عَاصِمٍ | *'Asim* | *ap.* Defender |
| 27 | أُغْشِيَتْ وُجُوهُهُمْ | *'Ughshi-yat wuju-huhum* | Their faces are covered |
| 28 | مَكَانَكُمْ | *Maka-nakum* | (Remain in) your place |
| 28 | زَيَّلْنَا بَيْنَهُمْ | *Zayyalna bay-nahum* | We separated them |
| 32 | رَبُّكُمْ الْحَقُّ | *Rab-bukumul-Haqq* | *pl.* Your true Lord |

| V. | WORD | TR. | MEANING |
|---|---|---|---|
| 32 | فَأَنَّا تُصْرَفُونَ | *Fa-'anna tus-rafun* | How then are you turned away? |
| 33 | حَقَّتْ | *Ḥaqqat* | Proved true |
| 34 | فَأَنَّا تُؤْفَكُونَ | *Fa-'anna tu'-fakun* | Then how are you deluded away (from the truth)? |
| 35 | لَا يَهِدِّي | *La yahiddi* | Cannot find guidance |
| 39 | يَأْتِهِمْ تَأْوِيلُهُ | *Ya' ti-him ta'willuh* | Its interpretation comes unto them |
| 43 | يَنْظُرُ إِلَيْكَ | *Y-yanzuru 'ilayk* | Looks at you |
| 50 | بَيَاتًا | *Ba-yata* | By night |
| 51 | أَلْآنَ | *'A al-'an* | What!Now? |
| 53 | يَسْتَنْبِئُونَكَ | *Yas-tambi-unak* | They seek information from you |
| 53 | إِي وَرَبِّي | *'Ii wa Rabbi* | Yes! By my Lord |
| 54 | نَدَامَةَ | *Nadama* | Regret |
| 59 | اللهُ أَذِنَ لَكُمْ | *Allahu 'adhina lakum* | Allah permitted you |
| 61 | وَمَا تَكُونُ فِي شَأْنٍ | *Wa ma takunu fi sha'-n* | Whatever you may be doing |
| 61 | تُفِيضُونَ فِيهِ | *Tufi-duna fih* | *pl.* You start doing it |
| 61 | مَا يَعْزُبُ | *Ma ya'-zub* | Not hidden |
| 65 | الْعِزَّةَ لِلَّهِ | *Al-'izzata lillah* | All power and honour belong to Allah |
| 66 | يَخْرُصُونَ | *Yakh-rusun* | They guess / tell lies |
| 71 | كَبُرَ عَلَيْكُمْ | *Kabura 'alay-kum* | Became hard on you |

| V. | WORD | TR. | MEANING |
|---|---|---|---|
| 71 | مَقَامِي | *Maqa-mi* | My staying |
| 71 | فَأَجْمِعُوا أَمْرَكُمْ | *Fa-'ajmi-'u 'amrakum* | *im. pl.* So devise your plot |
| 71 | غُمَّةً | *Ghumma* | Dubious |
| 71 | اقْضُوا إِلَيَّ | *Aqdu 'ilay-y* | *im. pl.* Pass your sentence on me |
| 71 | لَا تُنْظِرُونِي | *La tunzi-runi* | *im. pl.* Give me no respite |
| 78 | لِتَلْفِتَنَا | *Lital-fitana* | To turn us away |
| 85 | لَا تَجْعَلْنَا فِتْنَةً | *La taj-'alna fitna* | *ni.* Make us not a trial |
| 87 | تَبَوَّآ | *Ta-bawwa-'a* | *im. dl.* (You both) provide dwellings |
| 88 | اطْمِسْ عَلَى أَمْوَالِهِمْ | *Atmis 'ala 'amwa-lihim* | *im.* Destroy their wealth |
| 88 | اشْدُدْ عَلَى قُلُوبِهِمْ | *Ash-dud 'ala qulu-bihim* | *im.* Harden their hearts |
| 90 | بَغْيًا وَعَدْوًا | *Bagh-yanw wa 'ad-wa* | In insolence and spite |
| 93 | مُبَوَّأَ صِدْقٍ | *Mu-bawwa-'a sidq* | Honourable dwelling-place |
| 98 | عَذَابَ الْخِزْيِ | *'Adha-bal-khizy* | The Chastisement of Ignominy |
| 100 | يَجْعَلُ الرِّجْسَ | *Yaj-'alur rijs* | Places abomination |
| 105 | أَقِمْ وَجْهَكَ لِلدِّينِ | *'Aqim waj-haka lid-Din* | *im.* Set your face towards Religion |

| V. | WORD | TR. | MEANING |
|---|---|---|---|

## سُورَةُ هُودْ

## [11] SURAT HUD

### THE PROPHET HUD

| V. | WORD | TR. | MEANING |
|---|---|---|---|
| 1 | أُحْكِمَتْ | *'Uh-kimat* | *pv.* Perfected, Guarded |
| 1 | فُصِّلَتْ | *Fussi-lat* | *pv.* Explained in detail |
| 1 | مِن لَّدُنْ | *Milla-dun* | From before, from the presence of, from |
| 1 | حَكِيمٍ | *Hakim* | Wise |
| 1 | خَبِيرٍ | *Khabir* | Well-Acquainted |
| 2 | نَذِيرٌ | *Nadhir* | Warner |
| 2 | بَشِيرٌ | *Bashir* | Bringer of glad tidings |
| 5 | يَثْنُونَ | *Yath-nun* | They fold up |
| 5 | صُدُورَهُمْ | *Sudura-hum* | Their hearts (*lit.* breast) |
| 5 | يَسْتَخْفُوا مِنْهُ | *Yas-takh-fu minh* | They lie hid from him |
| 5 | يَسْتَغْشُونَ ثِيَابَهُمْ | *Yas-tagh-shuna Thi-yaba-hum* | They cover themselves with their garments |
| 6 | يَعْلَمُ مُسْتَقَرَّهَا | *Ya'-lamu musta-qarra-ha* | He knows its resting place |
| 6 | مُسْتَوْدَعَهَا | *Mus-tawda-'aha* | Its temporary deposit |
| 7 | أَحْسَنُ عَمَلًا | *'Ahsanu 'amala* | Best in deed |
| 8 | أُمَّةٍ مَعْدُودَةٍ | *'Umma-tim-ma'duda* | Definite term |
| 9 | إِنَّهُ لَيَئُوسٌ | *'Innahu laya-'us* | He is despairing |

| V. | WORD | TR. | MEANING |
|---|---|---|---|
| 9 | كَفُورٌ | *Kafur* | Ungrateful |
| 10 | إِنَّهُ لَفَرِحٌ | *'Innahu lafarih* | He is exultant |
| 10 | فَخُورٌ | *Fakhur* | Prideful |
| 15 | لَا يُبْخَسُونَ | *La yub-kha-sun* | They will not have diminution |
| 17 | بَيِّنَةٍ | *Bayyi-na* | Clear sign |
| 17 | مِرْيَةٍ | *Mir-ya* | Doubt |
| 20 | مُعْجِزِينَ | *Mu'-jizin* | Those who escape from Allah's Torment |
| 22 | لَا جَرَمَ | *La jaram* | Certainly, without a doubt |
| 23 | أَخْبَتُوا إِلَى رَبِّهِمْ | *'Akh-batu 'ila Rabbi-him* | They humbled themselves before their Lord |
| 27 | بَادِيَ الرَّأْيِ | *Badi-yar-ra'y* | At first thought, apparently |
| 28 | فَعُمِّيَتْ عَلَيْكُمْ | *Fa-'ummi-yat 'alay-kum* | It was obscured from your sight |
| 31 | تَزْدَرِي أَعْيُنُكُمْ | *Taz-dari 'a'-yunu-kum* | (Those whom) your eyes look down upon |
| 35 | فَعَلَيَّ إِجْرَامِي | *Fa-'alay-ya 'ijrami* | Upon me be my crime |
| 36 | لَا تَبْتَئِسْ | *La tabta-'is* | *im.* Do not grieve |
| 37 | بِأَعْيُنِنَا | *Bi-'a'-yunina* | Under our eyes |
| 39 | يُخْزِيهِ | *Yukh-zih* | Covers him with shame |
| 39 | يَحِلُّ | *Yahill* | Will fall / unloose |
| 40 | فَارَ التَّنُّورُ | *Farat-tan-nur* | The oven gushed forth |

| V. | WORD | TR. | MEANING |
|---|---|---|---|
| 41 | مَجْرَاهَا | *Maj-ra-ha* | Its moving course |
| 41 | مُرْسَاهَا | *Mursa-ha* | Its resting anchorage |
| 43 | سَآوِي | *Sa-'awi* | I will betake myself |
| 43 | لَا عَاصِمَ | *La 'a-sim* | (There is) no saviour |
| 44 | أَقْلِعِي | *'Aqli-'i* | *im.* Withhold |
| 44 | غِيضَ | *Ghiz* | Abated |
| 44 | اسْتَوَتْ عَلَى الْجُودِيِّ | *Asta-wat 'alal-Ju-diyy* | It (the ship) rested on Mount Judi |
| 44 | بُعْدًا | *Bu'-da* | Be away |
| 48 | بَرَكَات | *Bara-kat* | Blessings |
| 52 | مِدْرَارًا | *Mid-rara* | Abundant rain |
| 54 | اعْتَرَاكَ | *A'-tarak* | Seized you |
| 56 | بِنَاصِيَتِهَا | *Bi-nasi-yatiha* | Its fore-lock |
| 58 | غَلِيظٍ | *Ghaliz* | Severe |
| 59 | جَبَّارٍ | *Jabbar* | Proud |
| 59 | عَنِيدٍ | *'Anid* | Obstinate transgressor (oppressor of the truth) |
| 60 | بُعْدًا لِعَادٍ | *Bu'-dal-li-'Ad* | Away with 'Ad |
| 61 | اسْتَعْمَرَكُمْ | *Asta'-marakum* | (He) settled you |
| 63 | تَخْسِيرٍ | *Takh-sir* | Perdition, loss |
| 67 | صَيْحَةُ | *Sayha* | (Mighty) blast |
| 67 | جَاثِمِينَ | *Jathi-min* | *ap.* Those lying on their breast |
| 69 | عِجْلٍ حَنِيذٍ | *'Ijlin-hanidh* | Roasted calf |

| V. | WORD | TR. | MEANING |
|---|---|---|---|
| 70 | نَكِرَهُمْ | *Naki-rahum* | He felt mistrust of them |
| 70 | أَوْجَسَ مِنْهُمْ خِيفَةً | *'Awjasa minhum khi-fah* | He conceived a fear of them |
| 72 | يَاوَيْلَتَا | *Ya-way-lata* | Woe unto me |
| 73 | مَجِيدٌ | *Majid* | All-Glorious |
| 74 | رَوْعُ | *Raw'* | Fear |
| 75 | حَلِيمٌ | *Hali-m* | Forbearing, patient |
| 75 | مُنِيبٌ | *Munib* | One who turns to Allah again and again |
| 77 | سِيءَ بِهِمْ | *Si-'a bihim* | He was grieved on their account |
| 77 | ضَاقَ بِهِمْ ذَرْعًا | *Daqa bihim dhar-'a* | He felt himself powerless to protect them |
| 77 | يَوْمٌ عَصِيبٌ | *Yaw-mun 'asib* | Distressful day |
| 78 | يُهْرَعُونَ إِلَيْهِ | *Yuhra-'una 'ilayh* | They came rushing towards him |
| 78 | لَا تُخْزُونِي | *La tukh-zuni* | *ni.* Cover me not with disgrace |
| 79 | حَقٍّ | *Haqq* | Need |
| 80 | رُكْنٍ | *Rukn* | Support |
| 81 | قِطْعٍ مِنْ اللَّيْلِ | *Qit-'im-minal-layl* | Part of the night |
| 82 | سِجِّيلٍ | *Sijjil* | Baked clay |
| 82 | مَنْضُودٍ | *Mandud* | *pp.* Piled up (in order) |
| 84 | أَرَاكُمْ بِخَيْرٍ | *'Ara-kum-bi-khayr* | I see you in prosperity |
| 85 | لَا تَبْخَسُوا | *La tab-khasu* | *ni. pl.* Do not reduce |

| V. | WORD | TR. | MEANING |
|---|---|---|---|
| 85 | لَا تَعْثَوْا | *La ta'-thaw* | *ni. pl.* Do not commit evil |
| 86 | بَقِيَّةُ اللَّهِ | *Ba-qiyya-tullah* | That which is left by Allah |
| 91 | رَهْطُكَ | *Rahtuk* | Your family |
| 92 | وَرَاءَكُمْ ظِهْرِيًّا | *Wara-'akum zih-riyya* | Away behind your backs |
| 93 | مَكَانَتِكُمْ | *Maka-natikum* | *pl.* Your ability |
| 93 | ارْتَقِبُوا | *Arta-qibu* | *im. pl.* Watch, wait |
| 95 | لَمْ يَغْنَوْا فِيهَا | *Lamyagh-naw fiha* | They had never dwelt and flourished there |
| 98 | يَقْدُمُ قَوْمَهُ | *Yaq-dumu qaw-mah* | He will go ahead of his people |
| 98 | أَوْرَدَهُمُ النَّارَ | *'Awrada-humun-Nar* | He led them into the Fire |
| 98 | وِرْدُ | *Wird* | Place of descent |
| 98 | مَوْرُودُ | *Maw-rud* | *pp.* Descended into |
| 99 | رِفْدُ | *Rifd* | Gift |
| 99 | مَرْفُودُ | *Marfud* | *pp.* Given |
| 100 | حَصِيدٌ | *Ha-sid* | Mown down |
| 101 | تَتْبِيب | *Tat-bib* | Perdition |
| 106 | زَفِيرٌ | *Zafir* | Sighing |
| 106 | شَهِيقٌ | *Shahiq* | Sobbing |
| 108 | غَيْرَ مَجْذُوذٍ | *Ghayra maj-dhudh* | Without break |
| 110 | مُرِيب | *Murib* | Suspicious |
| 112 | لَا تَطْغَوْا | *La tat-ghaw* | *ni. pl.* Transgress not |

| V. | WORD | TR. | MEANING |
|---|---|---|---|
| 113 | لَا تَرْكَنُوا | *La tar-kanu* | *ni. pl.* Incline not |
| 114 | زُلَفًا مِنَ اللَّيْلِ | *Zulafam-minal-layl* | Approaches of the night |
| 114 | ذِكْرَى لِلذَّاكِرِينَ | *Thikra lidh-dha-kirin* | A reminder (an advice) for the mindful (those who accept advice) |
| 116 | أُولُوا بَقِيَّةٍ | *'Ulu-ba-qiyya* | Men of righteousness |
| 116 | أُتْرِفُوا | *'Ut-rifu* | *pv.* They were given the enjoyment of the good things of this life |
| 119 | تَمَّتْ | *Tammat* | Fulfilled |

| V. | WORD | TR. | MEANING |
|---|---|---|---|

## سُورَةُ يُوسُفَ

## [12] SURAT YUSUF

## JOSEPH

| | | | |
|---|---|---|---|
| 1 | الكِتَابِ المُبِينِ | *Al-Kitbil-Mubin* | The Perspicuous Book (i.e., the Holy Qûr'an) |
| 2 | لَعَلَّكُمْ تَعْقِلُونَ | *La-'allakum ta'-qilun* | In order that you may learn wisdom |
| 3 | نَقُصُّ عَلَيْكَ | *Naqussu 'alayk* | We relate unto you (Muhammad صلى الله عليه وسلم) |
| 6 | يَجْتَبِيكَ | *Yajta-bik* | Chooses you |
| 6 | تَأْوِيلِ | *Ta'-wil* | Interpretation |
| 6 | أَحَادِيثِ | *'Aha-dith* | Dreams, stories, events |
| 8 | نَحْنُ عُصْبَةٌ | *Nahnu 'usbah* | We are a strong body |
| 9 | اطْرَحُوهُ أَرْضًا | *Itrahu-hu 'arda* | *im. pl.* Cast him out to some (unknown) land |
| 9 | يَخْلُ لَكُمْ وَجْهُ أَبِيكُمْ | *Yakhlu lakum wajhu 'abi-kum* | The favour of your father may be given to you alone |
| 10 | غَيَابَةِ | *Gha-ya-ba* | Dark depth, bottom |
| 10 | جُبِّ | *Jubb* | Well |
| 10 | سَيَّارَةِ | *Say-yara* | Caravan of travellers |
| 12 | يَرْتَعْ | *Yar-ta'* | Enjoys |
| 12 | يَلْعَبْ | *Yal-'ab* | Plays |
| 15 | أَجْمَعُوا | *'Ajma-'u* | They (all) agreed |

| V. | WORD | TR. | MEANING |
|---|---|---|---|
| 17 | نَسْتَبِقُ | *Nasta-biq* | We race |
| 18 | سَوَّلَتْ | *Saw-walat* | Made up |
| 18 | فَصَبْرٌ جَمِيلٌ | *Fa-sabrun-jamil* | So patience is most fitting |
| 19 | وَارِدَهُمْ | *Wari-dahum* | Their water-carrier / drawer |
| 19 | أَدْلَى | *'Adla* | Let down |
| 19 | دَلْوَهُ | *Dalwah* | His bucket |
| 19 | أَسَرُّوهُ | *'Asar-ruh* | They concealed him |
| 19 | بِضَاعَةً | *Bida-'ah* | Merchandise |
| 20 | شَرَوْهُ | *Sha-rawh* | They sold him |
| 20 | ثَمَنٍ | *Thaman* | Price |
| 20 | بَخْسٍ | *Bakhs* | Low |
| 21 | أَكْرِمِي مَثْوَاهُ | *'Akrimi math-wah* | *im.* Make his stay honourable |
| 21 | اللهُ غَالِبٌ عَلَى أَمْرِهِ | *Allahu gha-libun 'ala 'amrih* | Allah has full power and control over His affairs |
| 22 | بَلَغَ أَشُدَّهُ | *Balagha 'a-shud-dah* | He attained his full manhood |
| 23 | رَاوَدَتْهُ | *Ra-wadat-h* | She sought to seduce him |
| 23 | هَيْتَ لَكَ | *Hay-ta lak* | Come on, O you |
| 23 | مَعَاذَ اللَّهِ | *Ma-'adhal-lah* | I seek refuge in Allah, Allah forbid! |
| 24 | مُخْلَصِينَ | *Mukh-lasin* | *pp.* Chosen |
| 25 | اسْتَبَقَا الْبَابَ | *Asta-baqal-bab* | They both raced each other to the door |

| V. | WORD | TR. | MEANING |
|---|---|---|---|
| 25 | قَدَّتْ | *Qaddat* | *fg*. Tore |
| 25 | قَمِيصَهُ | *Qami-sah* | His shirt |
| 25 | أَلْفَيَا سَيِّدَهَا | *'Alfa-ya sayyi-daha* | They both found her lord (i.e., her husband) |
| 26 | شَهِدَ | *Shahid* | Bore witness |
| 30 | شَغَفَهَا حُبًّا | *Shaghafa-ha huba* | He inspired her with violent love |
| 31 | مُتَّكَأً | *Muttaka-'a* | A place where any one reclines (i.e., banquet) |
| 31 | أَكْبَرْنَهُ | *'Akbar-nah* | They exalted him |
| 31 | قَطَّعْنَ أَيْدِيَهُنَّ | *Qatta'-na 'aydiya-hun* | They cut their hands |
| 31 | حَاشَ لِلَّهِ | *Hasha lillah* | How Perfect is Allah, Allah forbid! |
| 32 | اسْتَعْصَمَ | *Ista'-sam* | Refused |
| 33 | أَصْبُ إِلَيْهِنَّ | *'Asbu 'ilay-hinn* | I will fell inclined towards them |
| 36 | أَعْصِرُ خَمْرًا | *'A'-siru khamra* | I press wine |
| 43 | عِجَافٌ | *'Ijaf* | *pl.* Lean |
| 43 | تَعْبُرُونَ | *Ta'-burun* | *pl.* You interpret |
| 44 | أَضْغَاثُ أَحْلَامٍ | *'Ad-ghathu 'ahlam* | A confused medley of dreams |
| 45 | ادَّكَرَ بَعْدَ أُمَّةٍ | *Adda-kara ba'-da 'um-ma* | He remembered after long time |
| 47 | دَأَبًا | *Da-'aba* | As usual |
| 48 | تُحْصِنُونَ | *Tuh-sinun* | *pl.* You guard (store) |
| 49 | يُغَاثُ النَّاسُ | *Yugha-thun-nas* | The people will have abundant |

| V. | WORD | TR. | MEANING |
|---|---|---|---|
| | | | water |
| 49 | يَعْصِرُونَ | *Ya'-sirun* | They will press |
| 50 | مَا بَالُ النِّسْوَةِ | *Ma balun-niswa* | What was the matter with the ladies? |
| 51 | مَا خَطْبُكُنَّ | *Ma khat-bukunn* | What was your affair? |
| 51 | حَصْحَصَ | *Has-has* | Became manifest, came to light |
| 54 | مَكِينٌ | *Maki-n* | One whose standing is high |
| 56 | يَتَبَوَّأُ | *Yata-baw-wa'* | Takes possession |
| 59 | جَهَّزَهُمْ بِجَهَازِهِمْ | *Jahha-zahum-bi-jaha-zihim* | He furnished them forth with provisions |
| 62 | بِضَاعَتَهُمْ | *Bida-'atahum* | Their money |
| 62 | رِحَالِهِمْ | *Riha-lihim* | Their saddle-bags |
| 65 | مَتَاعَهُمْ | *Mata-'ahum* | Their baggage |
| 65 | مَا نَبْغِي | *Ma nabghi* | What more can we desire? |
| 65 | نَمِيرُ أَهْلَنَا | *Namiru 'ahlana* | We shall get (more) food for our family |
| 66 | مَوْثِقًا | *Maw-thiqa* | Solemn oath |
| 69 | آوَى إِلَيْهِ أَخَاهُ | *'A-wa 'ilayhi 'akhah* | He (Yusuf عليه السلام) betook his brother (Binyamin) to him |
| 70 | سِقَايَةَ | *Siqa-ya* | Drinking cup |
| 70 | عِيرُ | *'Ir* | Caravan |
| 72 | صُوَاعَ الْمَلِكِ | *Suwa-'al-malik* | The drinking cup of the king |
| 72 | زَعِيمٌ | *Za-'im* | Bound |

| V. | WORD | TR. | MEANING |
|---|---|---|---|
| 76 | كِدْنَا لِيُوسُفَ | *Kid-na li-Yusuf* | We planned for Yusuf |
| 76 | دِينِ الْمَلِكِ | *Dinil-malik* | The law of the king |
| 80 | اسْتَيْئَسُوا مِنْهُ | *As-tay-'asu minh* | They despaired of him |
| 80 | خَلَصُوا نَجِيًّا | *Khalasu na-jiyya* | They held a conference in private |
| 80 | فَرَّطتُمْ | *Farrat-tum* | *pl.* You failed |
| 84 | يَاأَسَفَى | *Ya-'asafa* | Alas, my grief ! |
| 84 | ابْيَضَّتْ عَيْنَاهُ | *Abyad-dat 'ay-nah* | His eyes became white(i.e., he lost his sight) |
| 84 | كَظِيمٌ | *Kazim* | Filled with silent sorrow |
| 85 | تَفْتَأُ تَذْكُرُ | *Tafta-'u tadhkur* | You will never cease remembering |
| 85 | تَكُونَ حَرَضًا | *Taku-na harda* | You reach the last extremity of illness |
| 86 | بَثِّي | *Baththi* | My grief |
| 87 | تَحَسَّسُوا مِنْ يُوسُفَ | *Tahassa-su miny-Yusuf* | *im. pl.* Enquire about Yusuf عليه السلام |
| 87 | رَوْحِ اللَّهِ | *Raw-hillah* | The Soothing Mercy of Allah |
| 88 | ضُرُّ | *Durr* | Famine |
| 88 | بِضَاعَةٍ مُزْجَاة | *Bida-'atim-muz-jat* | Scanty capital |
| 91 | آثَرَكَ اللَّهُ عَلَيْنَا | *'A-thara-kallahu 'alay-na* | Allah preferred you above us |
| 92 | لَا تَثْرِيبَ عَلَيْكُمْ | *La that-riba 'alay-kum* | No reproach on you |

| V. | WORD | TR. | MEANING |
|---|---|---|---|
| 93 | يَأْتِ بَصِيرًا | *Ya'ti basira* | He will come to see (clearly) |
| 94 | تُفَنِّدُونِ | *Tufanni-dun* | *pl.* You think me a dotard (a person who has weakness of mind because of old age) |
| 100 | بَدْوِ | *Badw* | Desert |
| 100 | نَزَغَ الشَّيْطَانُ | *Nazaghash-shay-tan* | Satan sowed enmity |
| 107 | غَاشِيَةٌ | *Ghashi-ya* | Covering veil |
| 110 | اسْتَيْئَسَ الرُّسُلُ | *As-tay-'asar-rusul* | The messengers gave up hold |
| 111 | عِبْرَةٌ | *'Ibra* | Lesson |

| V. | WORD | TR. | MEANING |
|---|---|---|---|

# سُورَةُ الرَّعْد

## [13] SURAT AR-R‘AD

## THUNDER

| V. | WORD | TR. | MEANING |
|---|---|---|---|
| 2 | بِغَيْرِ عَمَدٍ | *Bi-ghayri ‘amad* | Without any pillars |
| 2 | يُدَبِّرُ الْأَمْرَ | *Yudab-birul-’amr* | Regulates all affairs |
| 3 | مَدَّ الْأَرْضَ | *Maddal-’ard* | Spread out the earth |
| 3 | رَوَاسِيَ | *Rawa-siy* | Mountains |
| 4 | قِطَعٌ | *Qita‘* | Different tracts |
| 4 | نَخِيلٌ صِنْوَانٌ | *Nakhilun-sin-wan* | Palm trees having one roots |
| 4 | أُكُلِ | *’Ukul* | Whatever is eaten |
| 5 | أَغْلَالُ | *’Aghlal* | Yokes |
| 6 | مَثُلَاتُ | *Mathu-lat* | Exemplary punishments |
| 8 | تَغِيضُ | *Taghi-d* | Fall short |
| 9 | الْكَبِيرُ | *Al-Kabir* | The Most Great |
| 9 | الْمُتَعَالِ | *Al-Muta-‘al* | The Most High |
| 10 | سَارِبٌ | *Sarib* | One who walks |
| 11 | مُعَقِّبَاتٌ | *Mu-‘aqqi-bat* | Angels who succeed each other |
| 11 | مِنْ أَمْرِ اللَّهِ | *Min ’amrillah* | By command of Allah |
| 11 | وَالٍ | *Wal* | Protector |
| 12 | سَحَابَ | *Sahab* | *pl.* Clouds |
| 12 | ثِقَالَ | *Thiqal* | *pl.* Heavy |
| 13 | شَدِيدُ الْمِحَالِ | *Shadidul-mihal* | Mighty in Power, Severe in |

| V. | WORD | TR. | MEANING |
|---|---|---|---|
| | | | punishment |
| 14 | لَهُ دَعْوَةُ الْحَقِّ | *Lahu da'-watul-Haqq* | For Him (Alone) is the Word of Truth (i.e., none has the right to be worshipped but Allah) |
| 15 | لِلَّهِ يَسْجُدُ | *Lillahi yas-jud* | Unto Allah (Alone) falls in prostration |
| 15 | ظِلَالُهُمْ | *Zilalu-hum* | Their shadows |
| 17 | زَبَدًا | *Zabada* | Foam |
| 17 | رَابِيًا | *Rabi-ya* | Mounting up to the surface (of the water), floating on the surface (of the water) |
| 17 | جُفَاءً | *Jufa'* | Forth |
| 22 | يَدْرَءُونَ | *Yad-ra-'un* | They ward off |
| 22 | عُقْبَى الدَّارِ | *'Uqbad-Dar* | The final attainment of the (Eternal) Home (i.e., Paradise) |
| 25 | سُوءُ الدَّارِ | *Su-'ud-Dar* | The terrible Home (i.e., Hell) |
| 26 | مَتَاعٌ | *Mata'* | Brief passing enjoyment |
| 27 | أَنَابَ | *'Anab* | Turned (to Allah) in penitence |
| 29 | طُوبَى | *Tuba* | Blessedness |
| 29 | حُسْنُ مَآبٍ | *Husnu ma-'ab* | A beautiful place of (final) return |
| 30 | إِلَيْهِ مَتَابِ | *'Ilay-hi matab* | To Him will be my return with |

| V. | WORD | TR. | MEANING |
|---|---|---|---|
| | | | repentance |
| 31 | يَيْئَسْ | *Yay-'as* | Know |
| 31 | قَارِعَةٌ | *Qari-'a* | Disaster |
| 32 | أَمْلَيْتُ | *'Amlayt* | I granted respite |
| 34 | وَاقٍ | *Waq* | Defender, protector |
| 35 | أُكُلُهَا دَائِمٌ | *'Uku-luha da-'im* | Its fruits is eternal |
| 36 | إِلَيْهِ مَآبِ | *'Ilay-hi ma-'ab* | To Him are my return |
| 38 | لِكُلِّ أَجَلٍ | *Li-kulli 'ajal* | For each period |
| 38 | كِتَابٌ | *Kitab* | A low decreed, a decree established |
| 39 | أُمُّ الْكِتَابِ | *'Ummul-Kitab* | The Mother of the Book (Al-Lauh Al-Mahfuz) |
| 41 | لَا مُعَقِّبَ لِحُكْمِهِ | *La mu-'aqqiba li Hukmih* | There is none to put back His command |

| V. | WORD | TR. | MEANING |
|---|---|---|---|

# سُورَةُ إِبْرَاهِيم

## [14] SURAT IBRAHIM

## ABRAHAM

| V. | WORD | TR. | MEANING |
|---|---|---|---|
| 1 | بِإِذْنِ رَبِّهِمْ | *Bi-'idhni Rabbi-him* | By the leave of their Lord |
| 1 | الْعَزِيزِ | *Al-'Aziz* | The All-Mighty |
| 1 | الْحَمِيدِ | *Al-Hamid* | The Owner of all Praise |
| 2 | وَيْلٌ | *Wayl* | Great misfortune |
| 3 | يَسْتَحِبُّونَ | *Yasta-hibbun* | They prefer |
| 5 | أَيَّامِ اللَّهِ | *'Ayya-millah* | The Days of Allah |
| 7 | تَأَذَّنَ رَبُّكُمْ | *Ta-'adhdhana Rabbu-kum* | Your Lord caused to be declared (publicly) |
| 9 | رَدُّوا أَيْدِيَهُمْ فِي أَفْوَاهِهِمْ | *Raddu 'ay-diyahum fi 'afwa-hihim* | They put their hands in their mouths (biting them in anger) |
| 14 | مَنْ خَافَ مَقَامِي | *Man khafa Maqa-mi* | One who fears standing before Me (on the Day of Resurrection) |
| 15 | اسْتَفْتَحُوا | *Istaf-tahu* | They (the messengers) sought victory and help (from Allah) |
| 15 | خَابَ | *Khab* | Frustrated |
| 15 | كُلُّ جَبَّارٍ | *Kullu jabbar* | Every powerful obstinate |
| 15 | عَنِيدٍ | *'Anid* | Arrogant dictator (who refuses to believe in the |

| V. | WORD | TR. | MEANING |
|---|---|---|---|
| | | | Oneness of Allah) |
| 16 | صَدِيدٍ | *Sadid* | Pus |
| 17 | يَتَجَرَّعُهُ | *Yatajarra-'uh* | He sips it in gulps |
| 17 | لَا يَكَادُ | *La Yakad* | He will not be near |
| 17 | يُسِيغُهُ | *Yusi-ghuh* | Swallows it (down his throat) |
| 18 | يَوْمٍ عَاصِفٍ | *Yaw-min 'asif* | Stormy day |
| 21 | بَرَزُوا | *Barazu* | They appeared |
| 21 | مُغْنُونَ عَنَّا | *Mugh-nuna 'anna* | *pl.* You can avail us |
| 21 | مَحِيصٍ | *Mahis* | Way of escape |
| 22 | مُصْرِخٍ | *Musrikh* | Helper |
| 24 | كَلِمَةً طَيِّبَةً | *Kalimatan-Tayyi-ba* | Goodly word |
| 25 | تُؤْتِي أُكُلَهَا | *Tu'ti 'ukulaha* | It brings forth its fruit |
| 26 | كَلِمَةٍ خَبِيثَةٍ | *Kalimatin khabi-tha* | Evil word |
| 26 | اجْتُثَّتْ | *Ij-tuththat* | Uprooted |
| 28 | دَارَ الْبَوَارِ | *Daral-Bawar* | The House of Perdition |
| 29 | يَصْلَوْنَهَا | *Yaslaw-naha* | They will burn/enter |
| 31 | خِلَالٌ | *Khilal* | Friendship |
| 33 | دَائِبَيْنِ | *Da-'ibayn* | Both of whom diligently perform their work |
| 35 | اجْنُبْنِي | *Aj-nubni* | *im.* Preserve me, keep me away |
| 37 | تَهْوِي إِلَيْهِمْ | *Tahwi 'ilay-him* | Incline towards them |

| V. | WORD | TR. | MEANING |
|---|---|---|---|
| 42 | تَشْخَصُ | *Tash-khas* | Stare in horror |
| 43 | مُهْطِعِينَ | *Muhti-'in* | They hasten with extended necks |
| 43 | مُقْنِعِي رُءُوسِهِمْ | *Muqni-'i ru-'usihim* | Their heads uplifted |
| 43 | أَفْئِدَتُهُمْ هَوَاءٌ | *'Af-'idatuhum hawa'* | Their hearts empty |
| 49 | مُقَرَّنِينَ | *Muqar-ranin* | *pp.* Those bound together |
| 50 | سَرَابِيلُهُمْ | *Sara-biluhum* | Their garments / shirts |
| 52 | بَلَاغٌ لِلنَّاسِ | *Bala-ghul-linnas* | A message for mankind |

| V. | WORD | TR. | MEANING |
|---|---|---|---|

## سُورَةُ الحِجْر

## [15] SURAT AL-HIJR
## THE ROCKY TRACT

| | | | |
|---|---|---|---|
| 2 | رُبَمَا | *Rubama* | Often, perhaps |
| 3 | ذَرْهُمْ | *Dhar-hum* | *Im.* Leave them |
| 7 | لَوْ مَا | *Law ma* | Why not |
| 7 | تَأْتِينَا | *Ta'-tina* | You bring to us |
| 9 | الذِّكْرَ | *Adh-dhikr* | The Message (i.e., the Holy Qûr'an) |
| 10 | شِيَعِ الْأَوَّلِينَ | *Shiya-'il-'awwa-lin* | Sects (communities) of old |
| 12 | نَسْلُكُهُ | *Naslukuh* | We let it enter |
| 14 | يَعْرُجُونَ | *Ya'-rujun* | They ascend |
| 15 | سُكِّرَتْ أَبْصَارُنَا | *Suk-ki-rat 'absa-runa* | Our eyes have been intoxicated |
| 15 | مَسْحُورُونَ | *Mas-hurun* | *pp.* These who are bewitched |
| 16 | بُرُوجًا | *Buru-ja* | Constellations |
| 18 | اسْتَرَقَ السَّمْعَ | *Is-taraqas-sam-'* | Listened by stealth |
| 18 | شِهَابٌ | *Shihab* | Fiery comet |
| 19 | مَدَدْنَا | *Madad-na* | We spread out |
| 19 | رَوَاسِيَ | *Rawa-siy* | Mountains |
| 19 | مَوْزُونٍ | *Maw-zun.* | In due balance |
| 20 | مَعَايِشَ | *Ma-'ayish* | Means of subsistence |
| 21 | عِنْدَنَا خَزَائِنُهُ | *'Indana khaza-'inuh* | With Us are its (sources and) treasures |

| V. | WORD | TR. | MEANING |
|---|---|---|---|
| 22 | رِيَاحَ | *Riyah* | Winds |
| 22 | لَوَاقِحَ | *Lawa-qih* | *ap.* That (winds) which fecundate |
| 23 | نَحْنُ الْوَارِثُونَ | *Nahnul-wari-thun* | We who remain inheritors |
| 26 | صَلْصَالِ | *Sal-sal* | Sounding clay |
| 26 | حَمَإٍ مَسْنُونٍ | *Hama-'im-masnun* | Altered black smooth mud |
| 27 | نَارِ السَّمُومِ | *Naris-samum* | Fire of a scorching wind |
| 31 | أَبَى | *'Aba* | Refused |
| 32 | مَا لَكَ | *Ma lak* | What is your reason? |
| 34 | رَجِيمٌ | *Rajim* | Rejected, stoned, accursed |
| 35 | اللَّعْنَةَ | *Al-la'-na* | Curse |
| 38 | يَومِ الْوَقْتِ الْمَعْلُومِ | *Yawmil-Waqtil-Ma'-lum* | The Day of the Time Appointed |
| 39 | لَأُغْوِيَنَّهُمْ | *La-'ughwi-yan-nahum* | I will put them in the wrong |
| 44 | جُزْءٌ | *Juz'* | Class |
| 47 | غِلٍّ | *Ghill* | Hidden enmity, grudge |
| 48 | نَصَبٌ | *Nasab* | Fatigue |
| 51 | ضَيْفِ إِبْرَاهِيمَ | *Dayfi 'Ibrahim* | *sr.* and *pl.* The guests of Ibrahim |
| 52 | وَجِلُونَ | *Wajilun* | Those who are afraid |
| 55 | قَانِطِينَ | *Qa-nitin* | Those who despair |
| 57 | فَمَا خَطْبُكُمْ | *Fama khatbu-kum* | What then is the business on which you (have come)? |

| V. | WORD | TR. | MEANING |
|---|---|---|---|
| 60 | قَدَّرْنَا | *Qaddar-na* | We ascertained / decreed |
| 62 | قَوْمٌ مُنْكَرُونَ | *Qawmum-munkarun* | Unknown people, uncommon people |
| 63 | يَمْتَرُونَ | *Yamtarun* | They doubt |
| 65 | اتَّبِعْ أَدْبَارَهُمْ | *Wattabi' 'adbarahum* | *im.* Go behind them |
| 66 | دَابِرَ هَؤُلَاءِ | *Dabira ha-'ula'* | The last remnants of those (sinners) |
| 66 | مُصْبِحِينَ | *Musbi-hin* | Those who enter upon the morning |
| 70 | عَالَمِينَ | *Al-'alamin* | Foreigners, strangers, people |
| 72 | لَعَمْرُكَ | *La-'amruk* | By your life (O Muhammad صلى الله عليه وسلم) |
| 72 | سَكْرَتِهِمْ | *Sakrati-him* | Their wild intoxication / error |
| 73 | مُشْرِقِينَ | *Mushri-qin* | *ap.* Those on whom the sun has risen |
| 75 | مُتَوَسِّمِينَ | *Muta-wasimin* | Those who know a thing by its outward signs |
| 76 | سَبِيلٍ مُقِيمٍ | *Sabilim-muqim* | Highway |
| 78 | أَصْحَابُ الْأَيْكَةِ | *'As-habul-'Ayka* | The companions of the wood<br>The inhabitants of a wood (near Midian to whom the Prophet Shu'aib عليه السلام was sent ) |
| 79 | إِمَامٍ مُبِينٍ | *'Imamim-mubin* | Open highway, plain to see |

| V. | WORD | TR. | MEANING |
|---|---|---|---|
| 80 | الْحِجْرِ | *Al-Hijr* | The Rocky Tract (i.e., the country inhabited by the tribe of Thamud) |
| 87 | سَبْعًا | *Sab-'a* | Seven |
| 87 | مَثَانِي | *Mathani* | Oft-repeated (verses) |
| 88 | أَزْوَاجًا مِنْهُمْ | *'Azwajam-minhum* | Certain classes of them (the disbelievers) |
| 88 | اخْفِضْ جَنَاحَكَ | *Akhfid janahak* | *im.* Lower your wing (behave with humility) |
| 90 | مُقْتَسِمِينَ | *Muqtasi-min* | Those who divide (i.e., the people of the Book) |
| 91 | عِضِينَ | *'Idin* | Parts |
| 94 | اصْدَعْ بِمَا تُؤْمَرُ | *Asda' bima tu'mar* | *im.* Proclaim openly that which you are commanded |
| 99 | يَقِينُ | *Yaqin* | Certainty (i.e., death) |

| V. | WORD | TR. | MEANING |
|---|---|---|---|

# سُورَةُ النَّحْلِ

## [16] SURAT AN-NAHL

## THE BEE

| | | | |
|---|---|---|---|
| 2 | بِالرُّوحِ | *Bir-ruh* | With inspiration |
| 4 | خَصِيمٌ | *Khasim* | Disputer |
| 5 | دِفْءٌ | *Dif-'* | Warmth, warm clothing |
| 6 | جَمَالٌ | *Jamal* | Beauty |
| 6 | تُرِيحُونَ | *Turihun* | *pl.* You drive them back to home in the evening |
| 6 | تَسْرَحُونَ | *Tas-rahun* | *pl.* You lead them forth to pasture in the morning |
| 7 | تَحْمِلُ أَثْقَالَكُمْ | *Tahmilu 'athqa-lakum* | They carry your heavy loads |
| 7 | بِشِقِّ الْأَنفُسِ | *Bi-shiqqil-'anfus* | With great difficulty |
| 9 | قَصْدُ السَّبِيلِ | *Qasdus-Sabil* | The right path |
| 9 | جَائِرٌ | *Ja-'ir* | That which turns aside |
| 10 | تُسِيمُونَ | *Tusimun* | *pl.* You pasture (your) cattle |
| 13 | ذَرَأَ لَكُمْ | *Dhara-'a lakum* | Created for you |
| 14 | تَسْتَخْرِجُوا | *Tastakh-riju* | *pl.* You extract |
| 14 | مَوَاخِرَ | *Mawakhir* | Those (ships) which plough the waves with a dashing noise |
| 15 | تَمِيدَ | *Tamid* | Shakes |

| V. | WORD | TR. | MEANING |
|---|---|---|---|
| 16 | عَلَامَاتٍ | *'Alamat* | Sign-posts, land-marks |
| 23 | لَا جَرَمَ | *La jaram* | Undoubtedly, most certainly |
| 26 | قَوَاعِدِ | *Qawa-'id* | Foundations |
| 27 | تُشَاقُّونَ | *Tushaq-qun* | *pl.* You dispute |
| 28 | أَلْقَوُا السَّلَمَ | *'Alqa-wus-salam* | They made (false) submission |
| 32 | طَيِّبِينَ | *Tayyi-bin* | Those who are in a state of purity |
| 34 | حَاقَ بِهِمْ | *Haqa bihim* | Surrounded them |
| 36 | حَقَّتْ | *Haqqat* | Became obligatory |
| 41 | نُبَوِّئَنَّهُمْ | *Nu-bawwi-'annahum* | We give them home |
| 44 | بَيِّنَاتٍ | *Bayyi-nat* | Clear signs |
| 45 | يَخْسِفَ | *Yyakh-sif* | Causes (the earth) to swallow |
| 47 | تَخَوُّفٍ | *Takhaw-wuf* | Slow wastage |
| 48 | يَتَفَيَّأُ ظِلَالُهُ | *Yatafayya-'u zilaluh* | Their shadows incline / turn round |
| 48 | دَاخِرُونَ | *Dakhi-run* | *pl.* Humblest manner |
| 52 | وَاصِبًا | *Wasiba* | Always |
| 53 | تَجْأَرُونَ | *Taj-'arun* | *pl.* You cry with groans for help |
| 58 | هُوَ كَظِيمٌ | *Huwa Kazim* | He is filled with inward grief |
| 59 | يَتَوَارَى | *Yata-wara* | Hides himself |
| 59 | هُونٍ | *Hun* | Contempt |
| 59 | يَدُسُّهُ | *Yadussuh* | Buries it |

| V. | WORD | TR. | MEANING |
|---|---|---|---|
| 60 | مَثَلُ السَّوْءِ | *Mathalus-saw* | Similitude of evil |
| 62 | مُفْرَطُونَ | *Mufratun* | Those who will be hastened on (into the Fire) |
| 66 | فَرْثٌ | *Farth* | Excretions |
| 67 | سَكَرًا | *Sakara* | Strong drinks |
| 68 | يَعْرِشُونَ | *Ya'-ri-shun* | They construct |
| 69 | ذُلُلًا | *Dhulula* | Smooth |
| 70 | أَرْذَلِ الْعُمُرِ | *'Ardhalil-'umur* | Feeble age |
| 71 | سَوَاءٌ | *Sawa'* | Equal |
| 72 | حَفَدَةً | *Hafada* | Grandchildren |
| 76 | أَبْكَمُ | *'Abkam* | Dumb |
| 76 | هُوَ كَلٌّ | *Huwa kall* | He is a burden |
| 77 | لَمْحِ الْبَصَرِ | *Lamhil-basar* | Twinkling of an eye |
| 80 | تَسْتَخِفُّونَ | *Tastakhif-fun* | *pl.* You find light in weight |
| 80 | ظَعْنِكُمْ | *Za'-nikum* | *pl.* You travel |
| 80 | أَثَاثًا | *Atha-tha* | Household stuff |
| 80 | مَتَاعًا | *Mata-'a* | Articles of convenience |
| 81 | أَكْنَانًا | *'Aknana* | Shelters, places of refuge |
| 81 | تَقِيكُمْ بَأْسَكُمْ | *Taqikum ba'-sakum* | Protect you from your (mutual) violence |
| 84 | لَا هُمْ يُسْتَعْتَبُونَ | *La hum yusta'-tabun* | They will not be allowed to make amends |

| V. | WORD | TR. | MEANING |
|---|---|---|---|
| 87 | سَلَمَ | *Salam* | Submission |
| 90 | إِحْسَانِ | *'Ihsan* | Doing good |
| 90 | فَحْشَاءِ | *Fahsha-'* | Indecent deeds |
| 90 | بَغْيِ | *Baghy* | All kinds of oppression |
| 91 | كَفِيلًا | *Kafila* | Surety |
| 92 | أَنكَاثًا | *'Ankatha* | Untwisted strands |
| 92 | أَرْبَى | *'Arba* | More numerous |
| 94 | تَزِلَّ | *Tazill* | Slips |
| 96 | يَنفَدُ | *Yanfad* | Vanishes |
| 98 | اسْتَعِذْ بِاللَّهِ | *Ista-'idh billah* | *im.* Seek refuge with Allah |
| 100 | يَتَوَلَّوْنَهُ | *Yata-wallaw-nah* | They take him as patron |
| 103 | يُلْحِدُونَ | *Yulhidun* | They wickedly incline towards, they wickedly point to |
| 107 | اسْتَحَبُّوا | *Is-tahabbu* | They chose / loved |
| 110 | لِلَّذِينَ هَاجَرُوا | *Lilladhina hajaru* | To those who left their homes (emigrated) |
| 110 | فُتِنُوا | *Futinu* | *pv.* They are put to trail |
| 112 | رَغَدًا | *Raghada* | Abundantly |
| 120 | كَانَ أُمَّةً | *Kana 'umma* | He was a model |
| 120 | قَانِتًا لِلَّهِ | *Qanital-lillah* | Obedient to Allah |
| 123 | مِلَّةَ إِبْرَاهِيمَ | *Millata 'Ibrahim* | The ways of Ibrahim عليه السلام |

| V. | WORD | TR. | MEANING |
|---|---|---|---|

# سُورَةُ الإِسْرَاء

## [17] SURAT AL-ISRA'

## THE JOURNEY BY NIGHT

| | | | |
|---|---|---|---|
| 1 | أَسْرَى بِعَبْدِهِ | *Asra bi-'Abdih* | Took His Servant for a journey |
| 1 | نُرِيَهُ | *Nuriyah* | We show him |
| 3 | ذُرِّيَّة | *Dhurriyya* | Offspring |
| 4 | قَضَيْنَا إِلَى بَنِي إِسْرَائِيل | *Qadhayna 'lla Bani 'Isra-'il* | We decreed for the Children of Israel |
| 4 | لَتَعْلُنَّ | *Lata'-lunn* | *pl.* You will verily be elated (i.e., you will become tyrants) |
| 5 | بَأْس شَدِيد | *Ba'-sin-shadid* | Terrible warfare |
| 5 | جَاسُوا | *Jasu* | They entered |
| 5 | خِلَالَ الدِّيَارِ | *Khilalad-diyar* | The very inmost parts of homes |
| 6 | كَرَّة | *Al-karra* | Return, turn of luck |
| 6 | أَكْثَرَ نَفِيرًا | *'Akthara nafira* | More numerous in man-power |
| 7 | لِيَسُوءُوا وُجُوهَكُمْ | *Li-yasu-'u wujuhakum* | To disfigure your faces |
| 7 | يُتَبِّرُوا | *Yutab-biru* | They will destroy |
| 7 | مَا عَلَوْا | *Ma 'alaw* | That which fell in their hands |
| 7 | تَتْبِيرًا | *Tatbira* | Utter destruction |
| 8 | حَصِيرًا | *Hasira* | Prison |
| 9 | أَقْوَم | *'Aqwam* | Most right |
| 12 | مَحَوْنَا آيَةَ اللَّيْل | *Mahawna* | We have made dark |

| V. | WORD | TR. | MEANING |
|---|---|---|---|
| | | *'Ayatal-Layl* | the sign of the night |
| 12 | مُبْصِرَةً | *Mubsira* | Bright |
| 13 | أَلْزَمْنَا | *'Alzam-na* | We fastened |
| 13 | طَائِرَ | *Ta-'ir* | Fate, deeds |
| 14 | حَسِيبًا | *Hasiba* | One who takes an account |
| 15 | لَا تَزِرُ | *La tazir* | Can not bear |
| 15 | وَازِرَةٌ | *Wazira* | Bearer of burden |
| 16 | أَمَرْنَا | *'Amarna* | We commanded |
| 16 | دَمَّرْنَاهَا | *Dammar-naha* | We destroyed it |
| 17 | قُرُونِ | *Qurun* | Generations (past nations) |
| 18 | يَصْلَاهَا | *Yaslaha* | Will burn therein |
| 18 | مَذْمُومًا | *Madhmuma* | *pp.* Disgraced |
| 18 | مَدْحُورًا | *Mad-hura* | *pp.* Driven away, rejected |
| 20 | نُمِدُّ | *Numidd* | We bestow |
| 20 | مَحْظُورًا | *Mahzura* | *pp.* Hindered, forbidden |
| 22 | مَخْذُولًا | *Makhdhula* | *pp.* Destitute |
| 23 | أُفٍّ | *'Uff* | A word of contempt |
| 23 | لَا تَنْهَرْهُمَا | *La tanharhuma* | *ni.* Do not repel them |
| 23 | قَوْلًا كَرِيمًا | *Qawlan-karima* | Terms of honour |
| 25 | أَوَّابِينَ | *'Awwabin* | Sincere penitent, those who turn to Allah in true penitence again and |

| V. | WORD | TR. | MEANING |
|---|---|---|---|
| | | | again |
| 29 | لا تجعل يَدَكَ مَغْلُولَةً | *La taj-'al yadaka magh-lula* | *ni.* Make not your hand tied (like a niggard) |
| 29 | تَبْسُطْهَا كُلَّ الْبَسْطِ | *Tabsut-ha kullal-bast* | You stretch it forth to its utmost reach (like a spendthrift) |
| 29 | مَحْسُورًا | *Mahsura* | *pp.* Destitute |
| 31 | خَشْيَةَ إِمْلَاقٍ | *Khashyata 'imlaq* | Fear of want |
| 31 | خِطْئًا كَبِيرًا | *Khit-'an-kabira* | Great sin |
| 35 | قِسْطَاس | *Qistas* | Balance |
| 35 | مُسْتَقِيم | *Mustaqim* | Straight |
| 35 | أَحْسَنُ تَأْوِيلًا | *Ahsanu ta'wila* | Better in the final determination |
| 36 | لَا تَقْفُ | *La taqf* | *ni.* Pursue not, follow not |
| 37 | مَرَحًا | *Maraha* | With insolence |
| 40 | أَفَأَصْفَاكُمْ رَبُّكُمْ | *'Afa-'asfakum Rabbukum* | Has then your Lord (O pagans) preferred you? |
| 41 | صَرَّفْنَا | *Sarrafna* | We explained (in various ways) |
| 41 | نُفُورًا | *Nufura* | Flight (from the truth) |
| 42 | إِبْتَغَوْا | *Ib-taghaw* | They sought |
| 42 | سَبِيلًا | *Sabila* | Way |
| 45 | حِجَابًا مَسْتُورًا | *Hijabam-mastu-ra* | Invisible veil |
| 47 | وَإِذْ هُمْ نَجْوَى | *Wa 'idh hum najwa* | And when they meet in private |
| 47 | مَسْحُورًا | *Mas-hura* | *pp.* Bewitched |

| V. | WORD | TR. | MEANING |
|---|---|---|---|
| 49 | رُفَاتًا | *Rufata* | Fragments, dust |
| 51 | سَيُنْغِضُونَ | *Sa-yun-ghidun* | They will shake (their heads) |
| 53 | يَنزَغُ بَيْنَهُمْ | *Yanzaghu baynahum* | Sows dissensions among them |
| 56 | تَحْوِيلًا | *Tahwila* | Shift, change |
| 57 | وَسِيلَةَ | *Wasila* | Means of access |
| 59 | مُبْصِرَةً | *Mubsira* | Visible Sign |
| 59 | ظَلَمُوا بِهَا | *Zalamu biha* | They treated her wrongfully |
| 60 | الشَّجَرَةَ الْمَلْعُونَةَ | *Ash-Shajaratal-Mal'una* | The Cursed Tree (i.e., the tree of Zaqqum) |
| 62 | لَأَحْتَنِكَنَّ ذُرِّيَّتَهُ | *La-'ahtani-kanna dhurriyyatah* | I will surely seize and mislead his offspring |
| 64 | اسْتَفْزِزْ | *Astafziz* | *im.* Arouse |
| 64 | أَجْلِبْ عَلَيْهِمْ | *'Ajlib 'alayhim* | *im.* Make assaults on them |
| 64 | خَيْلِكَ وَرَجِلِكَ | *Khaylika wa rajilik* | Your cavalry and your infantry |
| 66 | يُزْجِي | *Yuzji* | Makes it go smoothly, drives |
| 68 | يَخْسِفَ بِكُمْ | *Yakhsifa bikum* | Causes the earth to swallow you up |
| 68 | حَاصِبًا | *Hasiba* | Violent tornado |
| 69 | قَاصِفًا | *Qasifa* | Heavy gale |
| 69 | تَبِيعًا | *Tabi-'a* | Helper |
| 73 | يَفْتِنُونَكَ | *Yaftinu-nak* | They tempt you |
| 73 | لِتَفْتَرِيَ عَلَيْنَا | *Li-taftariya 'alayna* | To substitute in Our name |

| V. | WORD | TR. | MEANING |
|---|---|---|---|
| 74 | تَرْكَنُ إِلَيْهِمْ | *Tarkanu 'ilayhim* | You incline to them |
| 75 | ضِعْفَ الْحَيَاة | *Di '-fal-hayat* | Double portion (of punishment) in this life |
| 78 | دُلُوك الشَّمْسِ | *Dulu-kish-shams* | The declining of the sun from the meridian |
| 78 | غَسَق اللَّيْلِ | *Ghasaqil-layl* | The darkness of the night |
| 78 | وقُرْآنَ الْفَجْرِ | *Wa Qur-'anal-Fajr* | *im.* And recite the Qûr'an in the early dawn (i.e., the morning prayer) |
| 79 | تَهَجَّدْ | *Tahajjud* | *im.* Keep awake, perform Tahajjud |
| 79 | نَافِلَةً لَك | *Nafilatal-lak* | An additional prayer for you |
| 79 | مَقَامًا مَحْمُودًا | *Maqamam-Mahmuda* | Station of Praise and Glory |
| 80 | مُدْخَلَ صِدْقٍ | *Mudkhala Sidq* | Gate of Truth and Honour |
| 81 | زَهَقَ | *Zahaq* | Perished |
| 81 | بَاطِلُ | *Batil* | Falsehood |
| 82 | خَسَارًا | *Khasara* | Loss |
| 83 | نَأَى | *Na-'a* | Became remote/arrogant |
| 83 | جَانِبِه | *Janibih* | His side |
| 83 | يَئُوسًا | *Ya-'usa* | Desperate |
| 84 | شَاكِلَة | *Shakila* | Disposition, way |
| 88 | ظَهِيرًا | *Zahira* | Helper |
| 89 | كُلِّ مَثَلٍ | *Kulli mathal* | Every kind of similitude |

| V. | WORD | TR. | MEANING |
|---|---|---|---|
| 89 | كُفُوراً | *Kufura* | Ungrateful |
| 90 | يَنْبُوعًا | *Yambu-'a* | Spring |
| 92 | كِسَفًا | *Kisa-fa* | In pieces |
| 92 | قَبِيلًا | *Qabila* | Face to face |
| 93 | زُخْرُف | *Zukhruf* | Gold |
| 97 | خَبَتْ | *Khabat* | Abated |
| 97 | سَعِيرًا | *Sa'ira* | Burning flame |
| 100 | قَتُوراً | *Qatura* | Niggardly |
| 102 | مَثْبُوراً | *Mathbura* | *pp.* Doomed to destruction |
| 104 | لَفِيفًا | *Lafifa* | Mingled crowed |
| 106 | فَرَقْنَا | *Faraqna* | We divided (into parts) |
| 106 | عَلَى مُكْثٍ | *'Ala mukth* | Slowly and deliberately |
| 110 | لَا تُخَافِتْ بِهَا | *La tukhafit biha* | *ni.* Do not speak it in a low tone |

| V. | WORD | TR. | MEANING |
|---|---|---|---|

## سُورَةُ الكَهْف

## [18] SURAT AL-KAHF

## THE CAVE

| | | | |
|---|---|---|---|
| 1 | لَمْ يَجْعَلْ لَهُ عِوَجًا | *Lam yaj-'al-lahu 'iwaja* | He has not placed therein any crookedness |
| 2 | قَيِّمًا | *Qayyima* | Straight |
| 5 | كَبُرَتْ كَلِمَةً | *Kaburat kalima* | How odious a word |
| 6 | بَاخِعٌ | *Bakhi'* | *ap.* One who frets himself to death |
| 6 | أَسَفًا | *'Asafa* | In grief |
| 8 | صَعِيدًا جُرُزًا | *Sa'idan-juruza* | Dust and dry soil (without growth or herbage) |
| 9 | أَمْ حَسِبْتَ | *'Am hasibt* | Do you think ? |
| 9 | أَصْحَابَ الْكَهْفِ | *'As-habal-Kahf* | The Companions of the Cave |
| 9 | رَقِيمِ | *Raqim* | Inscription |
| 10 | أَوَى الْفِتْيَةُ | *'Awal-fitya* | The youths betook themselves |
| 10 | رَشَدًا | *Rashada* | Right way |
| 11 | فَضَرَبْنَا عَلَى آذَانِهِمْ | *Fadarabna 'ala 'adha-nihim* | Then we draw (a veil) over their ears |
| 12 | بَعَثْنَاهُمْ | *Ba-'athnahum* | We roused them |
| 12 | أَمَدًا | *'Amada* | Term, time period |
| 14 | رَبَطْنَا | *Rabatna* | We gave strength |
| 14 | شَطَطًا. | *Shatata* | Enormity in disbelief |

| V. | WORD | TR. | MEANING |
|---|---|---|---|
| 16 | مِرفَقًا | *Mirfaqa* | Comfort and ease |
| 17 | تَقْرِضُهُمْ | *Taqri-duhum* | Turns away from them |
| 17 | فَجْوَةٍ | *Fajwa* | Clean open space |
| 18 | وَصِيدِ | *Wasid* | Threshold |
| 19 | وَرِقِكُمْ | *Wariqikum* | *pl.* Your money |
| 19 | أَزْكَى طَعَامًا | *'Az-ka ta-'amma* | The purest and best food |
| 20 | يَظْهَرُوا عَلَيْكُمْ | *Yazharu 'alaykum* | They come to know of you, They come upon you |
| 21 | أَعْثَرْنَا عَلَيْهِمْ | *'A'-tharna 'alay-him* | We made their case known to the people |
| 22 | رَجْمًا بِالْغَيْبِ | *Rajmam-bil-ghayb* | Doubtfully guessing at the unknown |
| 22 | لَا تُمَارِ فِيهِمْ | *La tumari fi-him* | *ni.* Debate not (about their number and matter) |
| 22 | إِلَّا مِرَاءً ظَاهِرًا | *'Illa mira-'an-zahira* | Except with the clear proof (which We have revealed to you) |
| 24 | رَشَدًا | *Rashada* | Right course |
| 26 | أَبْصِرْ بِهِ | *'Absir bih* | How clearly He sees |
| 27 | مُلْتَحَدًا | *Multa-hada* | Refuge |
| 28 | اصْبِرْ نَفْسَكَ | *Asbir nafsak* | *im.* Keep yourself content |
| 28 | لَا تَعْدُ عَيْنَاكَ عَنْهُمْ | *La ta'-du 'aynaka 'an-hum* | *ni.* Let not your eyes pass beyond them |

| V. | WORD | TR. | MEANING |
|---|---|---|---|
| 28 | أَغْفَلْنَا قَلْبَهُ | *'Aghfalna qalbah* | We made his heart heedless |
| 28 | فُرُطًا | *Furuta* | Excess |
| 29 | سُرَادِقُ | *Suradiq* | Walls and roof of a tent |
| 29 | مُهْلِ | *Muhl* | Melted brass, boiling oil |
| 29 | مُرْتَفَقًا | *Murtafaqa* | Couch, resting place |
| 31 | جَنَّاتُ عَدْنٍ | *Jannatu 'And* | Gardens of Eternity |
| 31 | سُنْدُسٍ | *Sundus* | Fine silk |
| 31 | إِسْتَبْرَقٍ | *'Istabraq* | Silk of a thick texture, heavy brocade |
| 31 | أَرَائِكِ | *'Ara-'ik* | Raised thrones |
| 32 | جَنَّتَيْنِ | *Jannatayn* | Two gardens |
| 32 | حَفَفْنَاهُمَا | *Hafaf-nahum* | We surrounded them |
| 33 | وَلَمْ تَظْلِمْ مِنْهُ شَيْئًا | *Wa lam tazlim-minhu shay-'a* | Nor did they fail in any of it |
| 33 | فَجَّرْنَا | *Fajjarna* | We caused (a river) to flow |
| 33 | خِلَالَهُمَا | *Khi-lalahuma* | In the midst of them (i.e., between the two gardens) |
| 34 | ثَمَرٌ | *Thamar* | Property, fruit |
| 34 | أَعَزُّ نَفَرًا | *'A-'azzu nafara* | Stronger in respect of men |
| 35 | تَبِيدَ | *Tabid* | Perishes |
| 36 | مُنْقَلَبًا | *Munqalaba* | *pp.* That which is exchanged |
| 40 | حُسْبَانًا | *Husbana* | Thunderbolts (by |

| V. | WORD | TR. | MEANING |
|---|---|---|---|
| | | | way of reckoning) |
| 40 | صَعِيدًا زَلَقًا | *Sa-'idan-zalaqa* | Slippery sand |
| 41 | غَوْرًا | *Ghawra* | (Water) running away underground |
| 42 | أُحِيطَ بِثَمَرِهِ | *'Uhita bi-thamarih* | His fruits were encompassed (with ruin) |
| 42 | يُقَلِّبُ كَفَّيْهِ | *Yuqallibu kaffayh* | He turns his hands upside down |
| 44 | الْوَلَايَةُ لِلَّهِ | *Al-walayatu lillah* | The (only) protection comes from Allah |
| 44 | خَيْرٌ عُقْبًا | *Khayrun 'uqba* | The best to give success |
| 45 | هَشِيمًا | *Hashima* | Dry stubble |
| 45 | تَذْرُوهُ الرِّيَاحُ | *Tadhruhur-riyah* | The winds scatter it |
| 47 | بَارِزَةً | *Bariza* | *ap.* Levelled plain |
| 48 | مَوْعِدًا | *Maw-'ida* | Appointment |
| 49 | وُضِعَ الْكِتَابُ | *Wudi-'al-Kitab* | The Book (of Deeds) will be placed |
| 49 | مُشْفِقِينَ | *Mushfiqin* | *ap. pl.* Fearful |
| 49 | يَاوَيْلَتَنَا | *Ya-waylatana* | Woe to us |
| 49 | لَا يُغَادِرُ | *La yu-ghadir* | Does not leave out (anything) |
| 49 | أَحْصَاهَا | *'Ahsaha* | Takes an account of it |
| 51 | عَضُدًا | *'Aduda* | Helpers |
| 52 | مَوْبِقًا | *Mawbiqa* | A place of common perdition (i.e., the Fire) |

| V. | WORD | TR. | MEANING |
|---|---|---|---|
| 53 | مُّوَاقِعُوا | *Muwaqi'u* | Those who fall into |
| 53 | مَصْرِفًا | *Masrifa* | Place to turn to |
| 55 | سُنَّةُ الْأَوَّلِينَ | *Sunatul-'awwalin* | The ways of the ancients |
| 55 | قُبُلًا | *Qubula* | Face to face |
| 56 | يُدْحِضُوا | *Yud-hidu* | They refute / weaken |
| 58 | مَوْئِلًا | *Maw-'ila* | Refuge |
| 59 | مَهْلِكِهِمْ | *Mahlikihim* | Their destruction |
| 60 | فَتَاهُ | *Fatah* | His boy-servant (i.e., Yusha' bin Nun) |
| 60 | مَجْمَعَ الْبَحْرَيْنِ | *Majma-'al-bahrayn* | The junction of the two seas |
| 60 | أَمْضِيَ | *'Amdiy* | I will go on (travel) |
| 60 | حُقُبًا | *Huquba* | A long space of time, space of eighty years |
| 61 | سَرَبًا | *Saraba* | As in a tunnel |
| 62 | نَصَبًا | *Nasaba* | Fatigue |
| 63 | أَوَيْنَا | *'Away-na* | We betook ourselves |
| 63 | عَجَبًا | *'Ajaba* | Marvellous (way) |
| 64 | فَارْتَدَّا عَلَى آثَارِهِمَا | *Fartadda 'ala 'athari-hima* | So they went back on their footsteps |
| 64 | قَصَصًا | *Qasasa* | Following, retracing |
| 65 | عَبْدًا | *'Abda* | A servant (i.e., Al-Khidr عليه السلام) |
| 68 | خُبْرًا | *Khubra* | Knowledge |

| V. | WORD | TR. | MEANING |
|---|---|---|---|
| 71 | شَيْئًا إِمْرًا | *Shay-'an 'imra* | Strange thing, Dreadful thing |
| 73 | لَا تُرْهِقْنِي | *La turhiqni* | *im.* Do not overburden me |
| 73 | عُسْرًا | *'Usra* | Difficulty |
| 74 | شَيْئًا نُكْرًا | *Shay-'an-nukra* | A great prohibited thing |
| 77 | أَبَوْا | *'Abaw* | They refused |
| 77 | يَنقَضَّ | *Yanqadd* | Falls down |
| 79 | غَصْبًا | *Ghasba* | By force |
| 80 | يُرْهِقَهُمَا | *Yurhi-qahuma* | He oppresses (both of) them |
| 81 | زَكَاةً | *Zakat* | Purity |
| 81 | أَقْرَبَ رُحْمًا | *'Aqraba ruhma* | Closer in affection |
| 82 | يَبْلُغَا أَشُدَّهُمَا | *Yablugha 'ashuddahuma* | *dl.* They attain their age of full strength |
| 84 | سَبَبًا | *Sababa* | Way, means |
| 86 | عَيْنٍ | *'Ayn* | Spring |
| 86 | حَمِئَةٍ | *Hami-'a* | Black mud, murky water |
| 87 | عَذَابًا نُكْرًا | *'Adhaban-nukra* | Terrible torment |
| 90 | سِتْرًا | *Sitra* | Covering, shelter |
| 93 | سَدَّيْنِ | *Saddayn* | Two mountains |
| 94 | يَأْجُوجَ وَمَأْجُوجَ | *Ya'-juja wa Ma'-juj* | Names of two tribes of barbarians |
| 94 | خَرْجًا | *Kharaja* | Tribute |
| 94 | سَدًّا | *Sadda* | Barrier |
| 95 | رَدْمًا | *Radma* | Strong barrier |

| V. | WORD | TR. | MEANING |
|---|---|---|---|
| 96 | زُبَرَ الْحَدِيدِ | *Zubaral-hadiḍ* | Blocks of iron |
| 96 | صَدَفَيْنِ | *Sadafayn* | Two steep mountain-sides |
| 96 | قِطْرًا | *Qitra* | Molten brass |
| 97 | يَظْهَرُوهُ | *Yaz-haruh* | They scale it |
| 97 | نَقْبًا | *Naqba* | The act of digging through |
| 98 | جَعَلَهُ دَكَّاءَ | *Ja-'alahu dak-ka'* | He will make it into dust |
| 99 | يَمُوجُ | *Yamuj* | Surges |
| 101 | غِطَاءِ | *Ghita'* | Veil |
| 102 | نُزُلًا | *Nuzula* | Entertainment |
| 105 | وَزْنًا | *Wazna* | Weight |
| 107 | فِرْدَوْسِ | *Firdaws* | Paradise |
| 108 | حِوَلًا | *Hiwala* | Change, removal |
| 109 | مِدَادًا | *Midada* | Ink |
| 109 | نَفِدَ | *Nafid* | Exhausted |
| 109 | بَحْرُ | *Bahr* | Sea |
| 109 | مَدَدًا | *Madada* | Additional help |

| V. | WORD | TR. | MEANING |
|---|---|---|---|

# سُورَةُ مَرْيَم

## [19] SURAT MARYAM

## MARY

| | | | |
|---|---|---|---|
| 3 | نِدَاءً | *Nida'* | Call |
| 3 | خَفِيًّا | *Khafiyya* | In secret |
| 3 | وَهَنَ | *Wahan* | Weakened, fainted |
| 4 | عَظْمُ | *'Azm* | Bone |
| 4 | شَقِيًّا | *Shaqiyya* | Disappointed |
| 5 | خِفْتُ الْمَوَالِيَ | *Khiftul-mawa-liy* | I fear my relatives |
| 5 | وَلِيًّا | *Waliyya* | Heir |
| 6 | رَضِيًّا | *Radiyya* | Well-pleased |
| 8 | عِتِيًّا | *'Itiyya* | Decrepit (old man) |
| 10 | سَوِيًّا | *Sa-wiyya* | Being in sound health |
| 11 | مِحْرَابِ | *Mihrab* | Chamber |
| 13 | حَنَانًا | *Hanana* | Mercy |
| 13 | زَكَاةً | *Zakah* | Purity |
| 13 | كَانَ تَقِيًّا | *Kana taqiyya* | He was devout |
| 14 | بَرًّا بِوَالِدَيْهِ | *Barram-bi-walidayh* | Kind to his parents |
| 14 | جَبَّارًا | *Jabbara* | Overbearing |
| 14 | عَصِيًّا | *'Asiyya* | Rebellious |
| 16 | انتَبَذَتْ | *'Intabadhat* | *fg.* Went aside |
| 17 | بَشَرًا سَوِيًّا | *Basharan-sawiyya* | A man in all respects |
| 19 | غُلَامًا زَكِيًّا | *Ghulaman-zakiyya* | Pure son |

| V. | WORD | TR. | MEANING |
|---|---|---|---|
| 20 | بَغِيًّا | *Baghiyya* | Unchaste |
| 22 | مَكَانًا قَصِيًّا | *Makanan-qasiyya* | Remote place |
| 23 | فَأَجَاءَهَا الْمَخَاضُ | *Fa-'aja-'ahal-makhad* | And the pains of childbirth drove her |
| 23 | نَسْيًا مَنْسِيًّا | *Nasyam-mansiyya* | Forgotten thing |
| 24 | نَادَاهَا | *Nadaha* | Cried to her |
| 24 | سَرِيًّا | *Sariyya* | Rivulet, stream |
| 25 | رُطَبًا جَنِيًّا | *Ruta-ban-janiyya* | Fresh ripe dates |
| 26 | قَرِّي عَيْنًا | *Qarri 'ayna* | *im.fg.* Cool your eye (i.e., comfort yourself and be glad) |
| 27 | شَيْئًا فَرِيًّا | *Shay-'an-fariyya* | Strange thing |
| 29 | مَهْدِ | *Mahd* | Cradle |
| 32 | بَرًّا بِوَالِدَتِي | *Barram-bi-walidati* | Kind to my mother |
| 34 | قَوْلَ الْحَقِّ | *Qawlal-haqq* | Statement of truth |
| 34 | يَمْتَرُونَ | *Yamtarun* | They (vainly) dispute |
| 38 | أَسْمِعْ بِهِمْ وَأَبْصِرْ | *'Asmi 'bihim wa 'absir* | How plainly will they see and hear |
| 39 | يَوْمَ الْحَسْرَةِ | *Yawmal-Hasra* | The Day of Distress |
| 44 | عَصِيًّا | *'Asiyya* | Rebel |
| 46 | اهْجُرْنِي مَلِيًّا | *Ahjurni maliyya* | *im.* Get away from me for a good long while |
| 47 | حَفِيًّا | *Hafiyya* | Most Gracious |
| 50 | لِسَانَ صِدْقٍ | *Lisana sidq* | Tongue of truth |

| V. | WORD | TR. | MEANING |
|---|---|---|---|
| 51 | كَانَ مُخْلَصًا | *Kana mukh-lasa* | He was (specially) chosen |
| 52 | قَرَّبْنَاهُ نَجِيًّا | *Qar-rabnahu najiyya* | We made him draw near to Us, for converse in secret |
| 58 | بُكِيًّا | *Bukiyya* | Weeping |
| 59 | خَلَفَ | *Khalaf* | Succeeded |
| 59 | يَلْقَوْنَ غَيًّا | *Yalqawna ghayya* | They face destruction |
| 61 | مَأْتِيًّا | *Ma'-tiyya* | Must come to pass |
| 62 | لَغْوًا | *Laghwa* | Vain discourse |
| 68 | جِثِيًّا | *Jithiyya* | On knees |
| 70 | صِلِيًّا | *Siliyya* | Being burned there in the Fire |
| 73 | نَدِيًّا | *Nadiyya* | Assembly |
| 74 | أَحْسَنُ أَثَاثًا | *'Ahsanu 'athatha* | Better in goods |
| 74 | رِئْيًا | *Ri'-ya* | Outward appearance |
| 75 | يَمْدُدْ | *Yamdud* | Extends |
| 75 | أَضْعَفُ جُنْدًا | *'Ad-'afu junda* | Weaker in forces |
| 76 | خَيْرٌ مَرَدًّا | *Khayrum-maradda* | Better for resort |
| 78 | أَاطَّلَعَ الْغَيْبَ | *A'attala-'al Ghayb* | Has he known the unseen ? |
| 81 | عِزًّا | *'Izza* | Exalted rank, glory, power |
| 82 | ضِدًّا | *Didda* | Adversary |
| 85 | وَفْدًا | *Wafda* | Delegation |
| 86 | وِرْدًا | *Wirda* | In a thirsty state |

| V. | WORD | TR. | MEANING |
|---|---|---|---|
| 89 | شَيْئًا إِدًّا | *Shay-'an 'idda* | Monstrous thing |
| 90 | تَخِرُّ الْجِبَالُ هَدًّا | *Takhirrul-jibalu hadda* | The mountains fall in ruins |
| 96 | وُدًّا | *Wudda* | Love |
| 97 | قَوْمًا لُدًّا | *Qawmal-ludda* | Quarrelsome people |
| 98 | تُحِسُّ | *Tuhiss* | Finds |
| 98 | رِكْزًا | *Rikza* | Whisper |

| V. | WORD | TR. | MEANING |
|---|---|---|---|

# سُورَةُ طه

## [20] SURAT TA-HA

### TA-HA

| | | | |
|---|---|---|---|
| 2 | تَشْقَى | *Tashqa* | You fall into distress |
| 6 | مَا تَحْتَ الثَّرَى | *Ma tahtath-thara* | That which is beneath the soil |
| 10 | آنَسْتُ نَارًا | *'Anastu nara* | I have seen a fire |
| 10 | قَبَس | *Qabas* | Burning brand |
| 10 | هُدًى | *Huda* | Guidance |
| 12 | طُوًى | *Tuwa* | Name of a sacred valley near Mount Sinai, where Prophet Musa عليه السلام received the Torah |
| 15 | أَكَادُ أُخْفِيهَا | *'Akadu 'ukhfiha* | I have almost kept it hidden |
| 16 | تَرْدَى | *Tarda* | You perish |
| 18 | أَتَوَكَّأُ عَلَيْهَا | *'Ata-wakka-'u 'alayha* | I lean on it |
| 18 | أَهُشُّ | *'Ahush* | I beat down the leaves (as food) |
| 18 | مَآرِبُ أُخْرَى | *Ma-'aribu 'ukhra* | Other uses |
| 20 | حَيَّةٌ | *Hayya* | Snake, serpent |
| 20 | تَسْعَى | *Tas-'a* | Moves quickly |
| 21 | سِيرَتَهَا الْأُولَى | *Siratahal-'ula* | Its former condition |
| 22 | جَنَاحِكَ | *Janahik* | Your (left) side |
| 22 | بَيْضَاءَ | *Bayda'* | White (and |

| V. | WORD | TR. | MEANING |
|---|---|---|---|
| | | | shining) |
| 22 | مِن غَيْرِ سُوءٍ | *Min ghayri su'* | Without harm (or stain) |
| 24 | طَغَى | *Tagha* | Transgressed all bounds |
| 29 | وَزِيرًا | *Wazira* | Minister, helper |
| 31 | أَزْرِي | *'Azri* | My strength |
| 36 | أُوتِيتَ سُؤْلَكَ | *'Utita su'-lak* | You are granted your request |
| 39 | اقْذِفِيهِ فِي الْيَمِّ | *Iqdhifihi fil-yamm* | *im.* Throw it (the chest) into the river (Nile) |
| 39 | لِتُصْنَعَ عَلَى عَيْنِي | *Li-tusna-'a 'ala 'ayni* | In order that you may be brought up under My Eye |
| 40 | يَكْفُلُهُ | *Yakfuluh* | Nurses and rears him |
| 40 | كي تَقَرَّ عَيْنُهَا | *Kay taqarra 'aynuha* | So that her eye might be cool (i.e., that she might rejoice) |
| 40 | فَتَنَّاكَ فُتُونًا | *Fatannaka futuna* | We tried you in various ways |
| 40 | جِئْتَ عَلَى قَدَرٍ | *Ji'-ta 'ala qadar* | You came (here) according to a fixed term |
| 41 | اصْطَنَعْتُكَ لِنَفْسِي | *Istana'-tuka li-nafsi* | I have chosen you for Myself (for service) |
| 42 | لَا تَنِيَا | *La taniya* | *ni. dl.* Do not slacken |
| 45 | يَفْرُطَ عَلَيْنَا | *Yafruta 'alayna* | Hastens to punish us |
| 45 | يَطْغَى | *Yatgha* | Transgresses all |

| V. | WORD | TR. | MEANING |
|---|---|---|---|
| | | | bounds |
| 50 | خَلْقَهُ | *Khalaqah* | Its form |
| 51 | مَا بَالُ | *Ma bal* | What condition, what state |
| 53 | مَهْدًا | *Mahda* | Bed (spread out) |
| 53 | أَزْوَاجًا | *'Azwaja* | Pairs |
| 53 | شَتَّى | *Shatta* | Diverse |
| 54 | أُولِي النُّهَى | *'Ulin-nuha* | Men of understanding |
| 58 | مَكَانًا سُوًى | *Makanan-suwa* | In an equal place |
| 59 | يَوْمُ الزِّينَةِ | *Yawmuz-zina* | The Day of the Festival |
| 61 | يُسْحِتَكُمْ | *Yus-hitakum* | Destroys you |
| 63 | طَرِيقَتِكُمُ الْمُثْلَى | *Tari-qati-kumul-muthla* | *pl.* Your most cherished way |
| 64 | أَجْمِعُوا كَيْدَكُمْ | *'Ajmi'u kaydakum* | *im. pl.* Concert your plan |
| 64 | أَفْلَحَ | *'Aflah* | Won |
| 67 | أَوْجَسَ | *'Awjas* | Conceived |
| 69 | تَلْقَفْ | *Talqaf* | Swallows up quickly |
| 77 | أَسْرِ بِعِبَادِي | *'Asri bi-'ibadi* | *im.* Travel by night with My servants |
| 77 | يَبَسًا | *Yabasa* | Dry |
| 77 | لَا تَخَافُ دَرَكًا | *La takhafu daraka* | *ni.* Do not fear of being overtaken (by Pharaoh) |
| 77 | لَا تَخْشَى | *La takhsha* | *ni.* Do not be afraid (of drawing in the sea) |
| 78 | غَشِيَهُمْ | *Ghashiyahum* | Overwhelmed them |

| V. | WORD | TR. | MEANING |
|---|---|---|---|
| | | | and covered them up |
| 81 | يَحِلَّ عَلَيْكُمْ | *Yahilla 'alaykum* | Descends on you |
| 81 | هَوٰى | *Hawa* | Perished |
| 83 | مَا أَعْجَلَكَ | *Ma 'a'-jalak* | What made you hasten? |
| 85 | فَتَنَّا قَوْمَكَ | *Fatan-na qawmak* | We have tried your people |
| 86 | أَسِفًا | *'Asifa* | In a state of sorrow |
| 86 | مَوْعِدِي | *Maw-'idi* | *pl.* Your promise to me |
| 87 | مَلْكِنَا | *Malkina* | Our power |
| 87 | أَوْزَارًا | *'Awzara* | Burthens, heavy weights |
| 87 | زِينَةِ الْقَوْمِ | *Zinatil-Qawm* | The ornaments of the (Pharaoh's) people |
| 88 | عِجْلًا جَسَدًا | *'Ijlan-jasada* | Image of a calf |
| 88 | خُوَارٌ | *Khuwar* | Lowing |
| 92 | مَا مَنَعَكَ | *Ma mana-'ak* | What stopped you? |
| 96 | بَصُرْتُ | *Basurt* | I saw |
| 96 | أَثَرِ الرَّسُولِ | *'Atharir-Rasul* | The hoof print of the messenger (Jibril's horse) |
| 96 | نَبَذْتُهَا | *Nabadhtuha* | I threw it |
| 97 | لَا مِسَاسَ | *La Misas* | Touch me not |
| 97 | نَنسِفَنَّهُ | *Nansifan-nah* | We scatter it |
| 102 | زُرْقًا | *Zurqa* | Blear-eyed with terror |
| 103 | يَتَخَافَتُونَ | *Yatakha-fatun* | They converse in a |

| V. | WORD | TR. | MEANING |
|---|---|---|---|
| | | | low tone |
| 104 | أَمْثَلُهُمْ طَرِيقَةً | *'Am-thaluhum Tariqa* | The best of them in knowledge |
| 106 | قَاعًا | *Qa'a* | Plain |
| 106 | صَفْصَفًا | *Safsafa* | Smooth and level |
| 107 | عِوَجًا | *'Iwaja* | Crookedness |
| 107 | أَمْتًا | *'Amta* | Height, elevated place |
| 108 | هَمْسًا | *Hamsa* | Low voice of footsteps |
| 111 | عَنَتْ | *'Anat* | Humbled |
| 111 | حَمَلَ ظُلْمًا | *Hamala zulma* | Carried (a burden of) wrongdoing |
| 112 | هَضْمًا | *Hamda* | Curtailment (of one's reward) |
| 114 | قبل أَنْ يُقْضَى إِلَيْكَ | *Qabli 'anyyuqda 'ilayk* | Before its revelation to you is completed |
| 118 | لَا تَجُوعَ | *La taju'* | You will not be hungry |
| 118 | لَا تَعْرَى | *La ta'-ra* | You will not be naked |
| 119 | لَا تَظْمَؤُ | *La tadmu'* | You will not be thirsty |
| 119 | لَا تَضْحَى | *La tadha* | You will not suffer from the sun's heat |
| 120 | مُلْكٍ لَا يَبْلَى | *Mulkil-la yabla* | A Kingdom that never decays |
| 121 | سَوْآتُهُمَا | *Saw-'atuhuma* | *dl.* Their private parts |
| 121 | طَفِقَا يَخْصِفَانِ | *Tafiqa yakhsifan* | *dl.* They began to stick |
| 121 | غَوَى | *Ghawa* | Went astray |

| V. | WORD | TR. | MEANING |
|---|---|---|---|
| 124 | مَعِيشَةً ضَنكًا | *Ma-'ishatan-danka* | A life of narrowness |
| 128 | أُولِي النُّهَى | *'Ulinnuha* | Men of understanding |
| 129 | لِزَامًا | *Lizama* | Unavoidable, inevitable |
| 130 | سَبِّحْ بِحَمْدِ رَبِّكَ | *Sabbih bi-Hamdi Rabbik* | *im.* Celebrate the praises of your Lord |
| 131 | أَزْوَاجًا مِنْهُمْ | *'Azwajam-minhum* | Parties of them (polytheists and disbelievers) |
| 131 | زَهْرَةَ الْحَيَاةِ الدُّنيَا | *Zahra-tal-hayatid-dunya* | The splendour of the life of this world |
| 135 | مُتَرَبِّصٌ | *Mutarabbis* | *ap.* One who waits |

| V. | WORD | TR. | MEANING |
|---|---|---|---|

# سُورَةُ الأَنْبِيَاء

## [21] SURAT AL-ANBIYA'

## THE PROPHETS

| | | | |
|---|---|---|---|
| 1 | اقْتَرَبَ | *'Iqtarab* | Drew near |
| 2 | مُحْدَثٍ | *Muhdath* | *pp.* That which is newly revealed |
| 5 | أَضْغَاثُ أَحْلَامٍ | *'Adghathu 'ahlam* | Medleys of dreams |
| 10 | فِيهِ | *Fih* | In it (the Holy Qûr'an) |
| 10 | ذِكْرُكُمْ | *Dhikrukum* | *pl.* Your eminence |
| 11 | قَصَمْنَا | *Qasamna* | We (utterly) destroyed |
| 12 | أَحَسُّوا بَأْسَنَا | *'Ahassu ba-sana* | They felt Our Punishment |
| 12 | يَرْكُضُونَ | *Yarkudun* | They flee |
| 13 | أُتْرِفْتُمْ | *Utriftum* | *pl.* You enjoyed the good things of this life |
| 15 | حَصِيدًا | *Hasida* | Harvest, mown, down |
| 15 | خَامِدِينَ | *Khamidin* | *ap. pl.* Extinct, dead |
| 17 | نَتَّخِذَ لَهْوًا | *Natta-khidha lahwa* | We take a pastime |
| 18 | نَقْذِفُ بِالْحَقِّ | *Naqdhifu bil-Haqq* | We hurl the Truth |
| 18 | يَدْمَغُهُ | *Yadmaghuh* | Destroys it |
| 18 | زَاهِقٌ | *Zahiq* | That which vanishes away |
| 19 | لَا يَسْتَحْسِرُونَ | *La yastahsi-run* | They weary not (of Allah's service) |

| V. | WORD | TR. | MEANING |
|---|---|---|---|
| 20 | لَا يَفْتُرُونَ | *La yafturun* | They flay not / intermit not |
| 22 | فَسَدَتَا | *Fasadata* | *dl.* They ruined |
| 26 | وَلَدًا | *Walada* | Son |
| 28 | مُشْفِقُونَ | *Mushfiqun* | *ap.* Those who are afraid (or in terror) |
| 30 | كَانَتَا رَتْقًا | *Kanata ratqa* | *dl.* They were joined together |
| 30 | فَتَقْنَا | *Fataqna* | We cloved / parted |
| 31 | أَنْ تَمِيدَ بِهِمْ | *'An-tamida bihim* | Lest it should shake with them |
| 31 | فِجَاجًا | *Fijaja* | Broad ways |
| 32 | سَقْفًا | *Saqfa* | Roof, canopy |
| 32 | مَحْفُوظًا | *Mahfuda* | *pp.* Well guarded |
| 33 | فَلَكٍ | *Falak* | The orbit of a celestial body |
| 33 | يَسْبَحُونَ | *Yasbahun* | They float / swim |
| 39 | لَا يَكُفُّونَ | *La yakuffuna* | They will not be able to ward off |
| 40 | تَبْهَتُهُمْ | *Tab-hatu-hum* | (Will) confound them |
| 42 | يَكْلَؤُكُمْ | *Yakla-'ukum* | Keeps you safe |
| 43 | يُصْحَبُونَ | *Yus-habun* | *pv.* They will be defended / protected |
| 46 | نَفْحَةٌ | *Nafha* | Breath |
| 47 | قِسْطَ | *Qist* | Justice |
| 52 | تَمَاثِيلُ | *Tamathil* | Images |
| 58 | جُذَاذًا | *Judhadha* | Pieces |

| V. | WORD | TR. | MEANING |
|---|---|---|---|
| 61 | عَلَى أَعْيُنِ النَّاسِ | *'ala 'a'-yunin-nas* | Before the eyes of the people |
| 65 | نُكِسُوا عَلَى رُءُوسِهِمْ | *Nukisu 'ala ru-usihim* | *lit.* They were turned upside down upon their heads (i.e., they relapsed into idolatry) |
| 71 | إِلَى الْأَرْضِ | *'Ilal-'ardh* | To the land (of Syria) |
| 72 | نَافِلَةً | *Nafilah* | An additional gift |
| 78 | نَفَشَتْ | *Nafashat* | Pastured at night |
| 80 | صَنْعَةَ | *San-'a* | (Art of) making |
| 80 | لَبُوسٍ | *Labus* | Metal coats of mail (for battles) |
| 80 | تُحْصِنَكُمْ | *Tuhsinakum* | Protects you |
| 81 | عَاصِفَةً | *'Asifa* | Violent, strongly raging |
| 82 | يَغُوصُونَ | *Yaghusun* | They dive |
| 85 | ذَا الْكِفْلِ | *Dhal-kifl* | *lit.* "Possessor of, or giving, a double requital or portion". (perhaps it is the title of Ilyas عليه السلام) |
| 87 | ذَا النُّونِ | *Dhan-nun* | The man of the fish or the whale (i.e., the title of Prophet Yunus عليه السلام) |
| 87 | مُغَاضِبًا | *Mughadiba* | Being angry |
| 90 | رَغَبًا وَرَهَبًا | *Raghabanw wa rahaba* | With hope and fear |
| 91 | أَحْصَنَتْ فَرْجَهَا | *'Ahsanat farjaha* | *fg.* Guarded her |

| V. | WORD | TR. | MEANING |
|---|---|---|---|
| | | | chastity |
| 93 | تَقَطَّعُوا أَمْرَهُمْ | *Taqatta-'u 'amra-hum* | They broke and divided their religion |
| 95 | أَنَّهُمْ لَا يَرجِعُونَ | *'Annahum la yarji-'un* | They shall not return |
| 96 | حَدَب | *Hadab* | Hill, mound |
| 96 | يَنسِلُونَ | *Yansilun* | They swiftly swarm |
| 97 | الْوَعْدُ الْحَقُّ | *Al-Wa'-dul-Haq* | The True Promise (i.e., the Day of Resurrection) |
| 98 | حَصَبُ جَهَنَّمَ | *Hasabu Jahannam* | Fuel for Hell |
| 98 | لَهَا وَارِدُونَ | *Laha wa-ridun* | Those who will enter it |
| 100 | زَفِيرٌ | *Zafir* | A deep breath |
| 102 | حَسِيسَهَا | *Hasisaha* | Its slightest sound |
| 103 | الْفَزَعُ الْأَكْبَرُ | *Al-Faza-'ul-'Akbar* | The Great terror (on the Day of Resurrection) |
| 105 | الذِّكْرِ | *Adh-dhikr* | The Message [i.e., Al-Lauh Al-Mahfuz (the Book, that is in the heaven with Allah) ] |
| 109 | آذَنْتُكُمْ | *'Adhantukum* | I have proclaimed the Message to you |
| 109 | إِنْ أَدْرِي | *'In 'adri* | I know not |

| V. | WORD | TR. | MEANING |
|---|---|---|---|

## سُورَةُ الحَجِّ

## [22]SURAT AL-HAJJ
## THE PILGRIMAGE

| | | | |
|---|---|---|---|
| 1 | زَلْزَلَةَ السَّاعَةِ | *Zalzalatas-Sa-'a* | The convulsion of the Hour (of Judgement) |
| 2 | تَذْهَلُ | *Tadhhal* | Will forget |
| 3 | مَرِيدٍ | *Marid* | Obstinate in rebellion |
| 4 | تَوَلَّاهُ | *Tawallah* | Turns to him for friendship |
| 5 | نُطْفَةٍ | *Nutfa* | Sperm |
| 5 | عَلَقَةٍ | *'Alaqa* | Clot (a piece of thick coagulated blood) |
| 5 | مُضْغَةٍ | *Mudgha* | A morsel of flesh |
| 5 | مُخَلَّقَةٍ | *Mukhallaqa* | *pp.* (Partly) formed |
| 5 | تَبْلُغُوا أَشُدَّكُمْ | *Tablughu 'ashuddakum* | *pl.* You (may) reach your age of full strength |
| 5 | أَرْذَلِ الْعُمُرِ | *'Ardhalil-'umur* | The feeblest old age |
| 5 | هَامِدَةً | *Hamida* | Barren and lifeless |
| 5 | اهْتَزَّتْ | *'Ihtazzat* | Stirred |
| 5 | رَبَتْ | *Rabat* | Swelled |
| 5 | زَوْجٍ بَهِيجٍ | *Zawjim-bahij* | Beautiful pairs |
| 9 | ثَانِيَ عِطْفِهِ | *Thaniya 'itfih* | A turner of his side (i.e., proud) |
| 11 | عَلَى حَرْفٍ | *'Ala harf* | On the verge (i.e., in doubt) |

| V. | WORD | TR. | MEANING |
|---|---|---|---|
| 13 | عَشِيرُ | *'Ashir* | Companion |
| 15 | سَبَب | *Sabab* | Rope |
| 15 | يَقْطَعْ | *Yaqta'* | Cuts |
| 15 | كَيْدُه | *Kayduh* | His plan |
| 19 | خَصْمَانِ | *Khasman* | Two antagonists / opponents |
| 20 | يُصْهَرُ | *Yashar* | *pv.* Will be melted |
| 21 | مَقَامِعُ | *Maqami'* | Maces, hooked rods |
| 21 | حديد | *Hadid* | Iron |
| 25 | عَاكِفُ | *'Akif* | Dweller |
| 25 | بَادِ | *Bad* | Visitor |
| 25 | إِلْحَادِ | *'Ilhad* | Profanity |
| 26 | بَوَّأْنَا لِإِبْرَاهِيمَ | *Bawwa'-na li-'Ibrahim* | We showed Ibrahim عليه السلام |
| 27 | رِجَالًا | *Rijala* | (They) come on feet |
| 27 | ضَامِرِ | *Damir* | Lean camel |
| 27 | فَجٍّ عَمِيق | *Fajjin 'amiq* | Distant mountain highway |
| 28 | بَهِيمَةِ الْأَنْعَامِ | *Bahimatil-'an-'am* | The best of cattle |
| 29 | يَقْضُوا | *Yaqdu* | They bring an end / complete |
| 29 | تَفَثَهُمْ | *Tafathahum* | Their filth |
| 30 | حُرُمَاتِ اللَّهِ | *Hurumatillah* | The sacred rites of Allah |
| 30 | قَوْلَ الزُّورِ | *Qawlaz-zur* | Lying speech (i.e., false statements) |

| V. | WORD | TR. | MEANING |
|---|---|---|---|
| 31 | تَهْوِي | *Tahwi* | Throws, sweeps off |
| 31 | مَكَانٍ سَحِيقٍ | *Makanin-sahiq* | A far-distant place |
| 33 | مَحِلُّهَا | *Mahilluha* | Their place |
| 33 | الْبَيْتِ الْعَتِيقِ | *Al-Baytil-'Atiq* | The Ancient House (the *Haram*- sacred territory of Makka city) |
| 34 | بَشِّرِ الْمُخْبِتِينَ | *Bash-shiril-Mukhbitin* | *im.* Give glad tidings to those who humble themselves |
| 36 | بُدْنَ | *Budn* | Camels |
| 36 | صَوَافَّ | *Sawaff* | (Camels) Standing with their fore-feet in line |
| 36 | وَجَبَتْ | *Wajabat* | Fell down |
| 36 | جُنُوبُهَا | *Junubuha* | Their sides |
| 36 | قَانِعَ | *Qani'* | *ap.* One who asks humbly, one who is content |
| 36 | مُعْتَرَّ | *Mu'-tarr* | One who does not beg, though poor |
| 38 | خَوَّانٍ | *Khaw-wan* | Perfidious person |
| 38 | كَفُورٍ | *Kafur* | Ungrateful |
| 40 | صَوَامِعُ | *Sawami'* | Monasteries |
| 40 | بِيَعٌ | *Biya'* | Churches |
| 40 | صَلَوَاتٌ | *Salawat* | Synagogues |
| 40 | مَسَاجِدُ | *Masajid* | Mosques |
| 44 | أَمْلَيْتُ لِلْكَافِرِينَ | *'Amlaytu lil-kafirin* | I granted respite to the unbelievers |

| V. | WORD | TR. | MEANING |
|---|---|---|---|
| 44 | نكير | *Nakir* | Denial, reprobation, punishment |
| 45 | قَصْرٍ | *Qasr* | Castles |
| 45 | مَشِيدٍ | *Mashid* | Lofty and well-built |
| 51 | مُعَاجِزِينَ | *Mu-'ajizin* | *ap.* Those who frustrate or weaken |
| 52 | تَمَنَّى | *Taman-na* | Desired |
| 54 | تُخْبِتَ لَهُ | *Tukhbita lah* | Submit to it with humility |
| 55 | يَوْمٍ عَقِيمٍ | *Yawmin 'Aqim* | A barren day (i.e., the Day of Resurrection) |
| 59 | مُدْخَلًا | *Mud-khala* | Entrance |
| 72 | مُنْكَرَ | *Munkar* | A denial ( of something stated or pointed out) |
| 72 | يَسْطُونَ | *Yas-tun* | They attack |
| 78 | حَرَجٍ | *Haraj* | Difficulty, hardship |

| V. | WORD | TR. | MEANING |
|---|---|---|---|

## سُورَةُ المُؤمِنُون

## [23] SURAT AL-MU'MINUN
## THE BELIEVERS

| | | | |
|---|---|---|---|
| 3 | لَغْوِ | *Laghw* | Vain talk |
| 7 | عَادُونَ | *'Adun* | Transgressors |
| 11 | فِرْدَوْسَ | *Firdaws* | Paradise |
| 12 | سُلَالَةٍ | *Sulala* | Extract |
| 13 | قَرَارٍ مَكِينٍ | *Qararim-makin* | Place of rest (womb of the women) |
| 14 | تَبَارَكَ اللَّهُ | *Tabarakallah* | Blessed be Allah |
| 14 | أَحْسَنُ الْخَالِقِينَ | *'Ahsanul-khaliqin* | The Best of creators |
| 17 | سَبْعَ طَرَائِقَ | *Sab-'a tara-'iq* | Seven tracts (i.e., seven heavens) |
| 20 | دُهْنِ | *Duhn* | Oil |
| 20 | صِبْغٍ لِلْآكِلِينَ | *Sibghil-lil-'akilin* | Relish for the eaters |
| 24 | يَتَفَضَّلَ عَلَيْكُمْ | *Y-yata-faddala 'alaykum* | Asserts his superiority over you |
| 29 | مُنْزَلًا | *Munzala* | Landing-place |
| 33 | أَتْرَفْنَاهُمْ | *'Atrafnahum* | We had bestowed on them |
| 36 | هَيْهَاتَ | *Hay-hat* | Far, very far |
| 41 | فَجَعَلْنَاهُمْ غُثَاءً | *Faja-'alnahum ghutha'* | We made them as rubbish of dead leaves / scum floating on a torrent |
| 44 | تَتْرَى | *Tatra* | In succession |

| V. | WORD | TR. | MEANING |
|---|---|---|---|
| 44 | جَعَلْنَاهُمْ أَحَادِيثَ | *Ja-'alnahum 'ahadith* | We made them as a tale (that is told) |
| 46 | قَوْمًا عَالِينَ | *Qawman 'alin* | Arrogant people |
| 50 | آوَيْنَاهُمَا | *'Away-nahuma* | We gave them both shelter |
| 50 | رَبْوَةٍ | *Rab-wa* | High ground |
| 50 | مَعِينٍ | *Ma-'in* | Spring, flowing stream |
| 53 | زُبُرًا | *Zubura* | Sects |
| 60 | يُؤْتُونَ مَا آتَوا | *Yu'-tuna ma 'atawwa* | They give that ( their charity) which they give |
| 60 | قُلُوبُهُمْ وَجِلَةٌ | *Qulubuhum wajila* | Their hearts full of fear |
| 63 | غَمْرَةٍ | *Gham-ra* | Confused ignorance |
| 64 | يَجْأَرُونَ | *Yaj-'arun* | They groan in supplication |
| 66 | تَنكِصُونَ | *Tankisun* | *pl.* You tern back on your heels |
| 67 | مُسْتَكْبِرِينَ | *Mustak-birin* | *ap.* Those who are proud and haughty |
| 67 | سَامِرًا | *Samira* | Telling fables by night |
| 67 | تَهْجُرُونَ | *Tahjurun* | *pl.* You talk nonsense |
| 71 | ذِكْرِهِمْ | *Dhikrihim* | Their admonition / reminder |
| 72 | خَرْجًا | *Kharja* | Wage |
| 74 | نَاكِبُونَ | *Nakibun* | Those deviating for astray (from the Path of Truth) |
| 75 | لَجُّوا | *Lajju* | They persisted |

| V. | WORD | TR. | MEANING |
|---|---|---|---|
| | | | obstinately |
| 76 | مَا اسْتَكَانُوا | *Mastakanu* | They humbled not themselves |
| 76 | مَا يَتَضَرَّعُونَ | *Ma yatadarra-'un* | They do not invoke (Allah) with submission |
| 79 | ذَرَأَ | *Dhara'* | Created, multiplied |
| 88 | مَلَكُوتُ | *Mala-kut* | Sovereignty |
| 88 | هُوَ يُجِيرُ | *Huwa yujir* | He protects |
| 88 | لَا يُجَارُ عَلَيْهِ | *La yujaru 'alayh* | No protection is given against Him |
| 89 | فَأَنَّا تُسْحَرُونَ | *Fa-'anna tus-harun* | Then how are you deluded ? |
| 97 | أَعُوذُ بِكَ | *'A-'udhu bik* | I seek refuge with You |
| 97 | هَمَزَاتِ الشَّيَاطِينِ | *Hamazatish-shayatin* | The suggestions of the Satans |
| 100 | وَرَائِهِمْ | *Wwara-'ihim* | Before them |
| 100 | بَرْزَخٌ | *Barzakh* | Partition |
| 104 | تَلْفَحُ | *Talfah* | Burns |
| 104 | كَالِحُونَ | *Kali-hun* | Those who grin, with their lips displaced |
| 106 | غَلَبَتْ عَلَيْنَا | *Ghalabat 'alayna* | Overwhelmed us |
| 106 | شِقْوَتُنَا | *Shiqwatuna* | Our misfortune |
| 108 | اخْسَئُوا فِيهَا | *Ikhsa-'u fiha* | *im. pl.* Remain you in it with ignominy |
| 110 | سِخْرِيًّا | *Sikhriyya* | Ridicule |

| V. | WORD | TR. | MEANING |
|---|---|---|---|

## سُورَةُ النُّور

## [24] SURAT AN-NUR

## THE LIGHT

| | | | |
|---|---|---|---|
| 1 | فَرَضْنَاهَا | *Faradnaha* | We ordained it |
| 4 | يَرْمُونَ الْمُحْصَنَاتِ | *Yarmunal-muh-sanat* | They launch a charge against chaste women |
| 8 | يَدْرَأُ عَنْهَا الْعَذَابَ | *Yadra-'u-'anhul-'adhab* | Will avert the punishment from her |
| 11 | إِفْكِ | *'Ifk* | Falsehood, slander, lie |
| 11 | عُصْبَةٌ مِنْكُمْ | *'Usbatum-minkum* | A group among you |
| 11 | تَوَلَّى كِبْرَهُ منهم | *Tawalla kibrahu minhum* | Took on himself the lead among them |
| 14 | أَفَضْتُمْ | *'Afadtum* | *pl.* You spoke extensively |
| 15 | هَيِّنًا | *Hayyina* | Light matter, little thing |
| 16 | سُبْحَانَكَ | *Subhanak* | Glory to You (O Allah) |
| 16 | بُهْتَانٌ | *Buhtan* | Slander, lie |
| 22 | لَا يَأْتَلِ | *La ya'-tal* | *ni.* (Let them) swear not |
| 22 | أُولُوا الْفَضْلِ | *'Ulul-fadl* | Those who are endued with grace |
| 22 | سَعَةِ | *Sa-'a* | Wealth |
| 25 | دِينَهُمُ الْحَقَّ | *Dinahumul-haqq* | Their just dues |
| 27 | تَسْتَأْنِسُوا | *Tas-ta'-nisu* | *pl.* You ask permission |

| V. | WORD | TR. | MEANING |
|---|---|---|---|
| 28 | أَزْكَى | *'Azka* | Purer |
| 29 | جُنَاحٌ | *Junah* | Sin |
| 30 | مَتَاعٌ | *Mata-'* | Use, interest |
| 31 | يَغُضُّوا مِنْ أَبْصَارِهِمْ | *Yaghud-du min 'absarihim* | Lower their gaze (from looking at forbidden things) |
| 31 | زِينَتَهُنَّ | *Zinatahunn* | Their beauty and ornaments |
| 31 | لْيَضْرِبْنَ | *Lyad-ribn* | Let them draw |
| 31 | خُمُرِهِنَّ | *Khumurihinn* | Their veils |
| 31 | عَلَى جُيُوبِهِنَّ | *'Ala juyubihinn* | Over their bosoms |
| 31 | بُعُولَتِهِنَّ | *Bu-'ulatihinn* | Their husbands |
| 31 | غير أُوْلِي الْإِرْبَةِ | *Ghayri 'ulil-'irba* | Who have no need (of women) |
| 31 | لَمْ يَظْهَرُوا | *Lam yazharu* | Those who have no carnal knowledge (of women) |
| 32 | أَنكِحُوا الْأَيَامَى | *'Ankihul-ayama* | *im. pl.* Marry those who are single (unmarried, divorced or widowed) |
| 33 | يَبْتَغُونَ الْكِتَابَ | *Yabtaghunal-Ki-tab* | They seek a writing (of emancipation) |
| 33 | فَتَيَاتِكُمْ | *Fatayatikum* | *pl.* Your slave girls |
| 33 | بِغَاءِ | *Bigha'* | Prostitution |
| 33 | تَحَصُّنًا | *Tahassuna* | Chastity |
| 35 | مِشْكَاة | *Mishkat* | Niche |
| 35 | مِصْبَاحٌ | *Misbah* | Lamp |

| V. | WORD | TR. | MEANING |
|---|---|---|---|
| 35 | زُجَاجَةٍ | *Zuja-jah* | Glass |
| 35 | كَوْكَبٌ دُرِّيٌّ | *Kawkabun durriyy* | Brilliant star |
| 36 | بُيُوتٍ | *Buyut* | Houses (mosques) |
| 36 | تُرْفَعَ | *Turfa'* | *pv.* Be raised, exalted |
| 38 | بِغَيْرِ حِسَابٍ | *Bighayri hisab* | Without measure |
| 39 | سَرَابٍ | *Sarab* | Mirage |
| 39 | قِيعَةٍ | *Bi-qi-'a* | Level plain (desert) |
| 40 | بَحْرٍ لُجِّيٍّ | *Bahril-lujjiyy* | Vast deep sea |
| 40 | سَحَابٌ | *Sahab* | Clouds |
| 41 | صَافَّاتٍ | *Saffat* | *ap.* Extending their wings |
| 43 | يُزْجِي سَحَابًا | *Yuzji sahaba* | Makes the clouds more gently |
| 43 | يَجْعَلُهُ رُكَامًا | *Yaj-'aluhu rukama* | Makes them into a heap of layers |
| 43 | وَدْقَ | *Wadq* | Rain |
| 43 | خِلَالِ | *Khilal* | Midst, between |
| 43 | سَنَا بَرْقِهِ | *Sana barqih* | The vivid flash of its lightning |
| 49 | مُذْعِنِينَ | *Mudh-'inin* | *ap.* Those who are submissive |
| 50 | يَحِيفَ | *Yahif* | Will deal unjustly |
| 53 | طَاعَةٌ مَعْرُوفَةٌ | *Ta-'atum-ma'-rufah* | (Your) obedience is known (to be false) |
| 57 | مُعْجِزِينَ | *Mu'-jizin* | *ap.* Those who can escape |
| 60 | الْقَوَاعِدُ مِنْ النساء | *Al-Qawa-'idu minan-nisa'* | Elderly women |

| V. | WORD | TR. | MEANING |
|---|---|---|---|
| 60 | مُتَبَرِّجَاتٍ بِزِينَةٍ | *Mutabarri-ja-tim-bizinah* | (Women) who make a wanton display of their adornment |
| 61 | أَشْتَاتًا | *'Ashtata* | Separately |
| 62 | أَمْرٍ جَامِعٍ | *'Amrin-jami'* | (Important) matter requiring collective action |
| 63 | يَتَسَلَّلُونَ | *Yatasallalun* | They slip away |
| 63 | لِوَاذًا | *Liwa-dha* | Under shelter |
| 63 | يُخَالِفُونَ عَنْ أَمْرِهِ | *Yukhali-funa 'an 'amrih* | They appose his command |

| V. | WORD | TR. | MEANING |
|---|---|---|---|

# سُورَةُ الفُرقَان

## [25] SURAT AL-FURQAN
## THE CRITERION

| | | | |
|---|---|---|---|
| 3 | نُشُورًا | *Nushura* | Resurrection |
| 8 | جَنَّةٌ يَأْكُلُ مِنْهَا | *Jannatuny-ya'-kulu minha* | A garden whereof he may eat |
| 11 | سَعِيرًا | *Sa-'ira* | Blazing Fire |
| 12 | تَغَيُّظًا | *Taghayyuza* | Fury |
| 12 | زَفِيرًا | *Zafira* | Roaring |
| 13 | مُقَرَّنِينَ | *Muqarra-nin* | *pp. pl.* Bound together, chained together |
| 13 | ثُبُورًا | *Thubu-ra* | Destruction |
| 18 | بُورًا | *Bura* | Destroyed |
| 19 | صَرْفًا | *Sarfa* | Averting |
| 21 | عُتُوًّا | *'Utuwwa* | Insolence, pride |
| 22 | حِجْرًا | *Hijra* | Barrier |
| 22 | مَحْجُورًا | *Mahjura* | *pp.* Forbidden |
| 23 | هَبَاءً | *Haba'* | Dust floating in the air |
| 23 | مَنْثُورًا | *Manthura* | *pp.* Scattered |
| 24 | مَقِيلًا | *Maqila* | Place of repose at noon |
| 29 | خَذُولًا | *Khadhula* | Traitor |
| 30 | مَهْجُورًا | *Mahjura* | *pp.* Deserted |
| 32 | رَتَّلْنَاهُ | *Rattalnah* | We rehearsed it |
| 33 | أَحْسَنَ تَفْسِيرًا | *'Ahsana tafsira* | Better explanation |

| V. | WORD | TR. | MEANING |
|---|---|---|---|
| 38 | أَصْحَابَ الرَّسِّ | *'As-habar-Rass* | The Companions of the Rass |
| 40 | مَطَرَ السَّوْءِ | *Mataras-saw'* | Shower of evil (i.e., shower of brimstone) |
| 45 | ظِلَّ | *Zill* | Shadow |
| 47 | لِبَاسًا | *Libasa* | Covering |
| 47 | سُبَاتًا | *Subata* | Repose |
| 50 | صَرَّفْنَاهُ بَيْنَهُمْ | *Sarrafnahu baynahum* | We have distributed it among them |
| 53 | مَرَجَ الْبَحْرَيْنِ | *Marajal-baḥrayn* | (He has) let free the two seas |
| 53 | عَذْبٌ | *'Adhb* | Palatable |
| 53 | فُرَاتٌ | *Furat* | Sweet |
| 53 | مِلْحٌ | *Milh* | Salt |
| 53 | أُجَاجٌ | *'Ujaj* | Bitter |
| 54 | نَسَبًا | *Nasaba* | Relationship of lineage |
| 54 | صِهْرًا | *Sihra* | Relationship of marriage |
| 55 | عَلَى رَبِّهِ ظَهِيرًا | *'Ala Rabbihi zahira* | (One who is) a helper (of evil) against his own Lord |
| 60 | نُفُورًا | *Nufura* | Aversion |
| 61 | بُرُوجًا | *Buruja* | Constellations |
| 62 | خِلْفَةً | *Khil-fa* | Following one another |
| 63 | هَوْنًا | *Hawna* | In humility, modestly |

| V. | WORD | TR. | MEANING |
|---|---|---|---|
| 65 | غَرَامًا | *Gharama* | Continuous torment |
| 67 | يَقْتُرُوا | *Yaqturu* | They spend stingily / niggardly |
| 67 | قَوَامًا | *Qawama* | Medium, equity, right |
| 73 | يَخِرُّوا | *Yakhirru* | They fall down / droop down |
| 75 | يُجْزَوْنَ | *Yujzawn* | They will be rewarded |
| 75 | غُرْفَةَ | *Ghur-fa* | The highest place (in Paradise) |
| 77 | مَا يَعْبَأُ | *Ma ya'-ba'* | Concerns not |
| 77 | لِزَامًا | *Lizama* | Inseparable and permanent (punishment) |

## سُورَةُ الشُّعَرَاء

## [26] SURAT ASH-SHU'ARA'

### THE POETS

| V. | WORD | TR. | MEANING |
|---|---|---|---|
| 4 | أَعْنَاقُهُمْ | *'A '-naqahum* | Their necks |
| 22 | عَبَّدْتَ | *'Abbatt* | You enslaved |
| 33 | نَزَعَ يَدَهُ | *Naza-'a yadah* | He drew out his hand |
| 36 | أَرْجِهِ وَأَخَاهُ | *'Arjih wa 'akhah* | *im.* Put him off and his brother (for a while) |
| 36 | حَاشِرِينَ | *Hashi-rin* | *ap.* Those who assemble |
| 39 | هَلْ أَنْتُمْ مُجْتَمِعُونَ | *Hal 'antum-mujtami-'un* | Are you (now) assembled ? |
| 44 | بِعِزَّةِ فِرْعَوْنَ | *Bi-'izzati Fir-'awn* | By the might of Pharaoh |
| 51 | لَا ضَيْرَ | *La dayr* | No harm |
| 53 | إِنَّكُمْ مُتَّبَعُونَ | *'Innakum-muttaba-'un* | *pl.* You will be pursued |
| 55 | شِرْذِمَةٌ | *Shir-dhima* | Band |
| 57 | حَاذِرُونَ | *Hadhirun* | *ap.* Those who are cautious / provident |
| 61 | مُشْرِقِينَ | *Mushri-qin* | *ap.* Those on whom the sun has risen |
| 62 | تَرَاءَى الْجَمْعَانِ | *Tara-'aljam-'an* | The two bodies saw each other |
| 64 | انفَلَقَ | *Infalaq* | Divided, separated |
| 64 | طَوْدِ | *Tawd* | Mountain |
| 65 | أَزْلَفْنَا | *'Azlafna* | We brought near |
| 87 | لَا تُخْزِنِي | *La tukhzini* | *r.* Do not disgrace me |

| V. | WORD | TR. | MEANING |
|---|---|---|---|
| 90 | أُزْلِفَتْ | *'Uzlifat* | *pv.* Is brought near |
| 91 | بُرِّزَتْ | *Burrizat* | *pv.* Is placed in full view |
| 91 | غَاوِينَ | *Ghawin* | *ap.* Those who go astray |
| 94 | كُبْكِبُوا | *Kubkibu* | *pv.* (They will) be thrown headlong |
| 101 | صديق | *Sadiq* | Friend |
| 101 | حَمِيمٍ | *Hamim* | Close |
| 102 | كَرَّةً | *Kar-ra* | Chance of return |
| 111 | أَرْذَلُونَ | *'Ardhalun* | Those who are meanest |
| 118 | افْتَحْ | *Iftah* | *im.* Judge |
| 119 | مَشْحُونِ | *Mash-hun* | *pp.* Filled, loaded |
| 128 | رِيعٍ | *Ri-'* | High place |
| 128 | تَعْبَثُونَ | *Ta'-bathun* | *pl.* You amuse |
| 129 | مَصَانِعَ | *Masani'* | Palaces, fine buildings |
| 132 | أَمَدَّ | *'Amadd* | Bestowed, aided |
| 137 | خُلُقُ الْأَوَّلِينَ | *Khuluqul-'awwalin* | A customary device of the ancients |
| 148 | هَضِيمٌ | *Hazim* | Ripe dates, (spathes) near breaking |
| 149 | فَارِهِينَ | *Farihin* | *ap.* Those who are skillful |
| 168 | قَالِينَ | *Qalin* | *ap.* Those who abhor |
| 176 | أَصْحَابُ الْأَيْكَةِ | *'As-habul-'Ayka* | The Companions of the Wood (near |

| V. | WORD | TR. | MEANING |
|---|---|---|---|
| | | | Madyan) |
| 181 | مِنَ الْمُخْسِرِينَ | *Minal-mukhsirin* | *ap.* Those who give short measure |
| 184 | الْجِبِلَّةَ الْأَوَّلِينَ | *Al-jibillatal-'awwalin* | The former generations |
| 185 | مُسَحَّرِينَ | *Musahharin* | *pp. pl.* Bewitched |
| 187 | كِسَفًا | *Kisafa* | Piece |
| 196 | زُبُرِ الْأَوَّلِينَ | *Zubu-ril-'awwalin* | The revealed Books of former peoples |
| 203 | هَلْ نَحْنُ مُنظَرُونَ | *Hal nahnu munzarun* | Shall we be respited? |
| 219 | تَقَلُّبَكَ | *Taqallubak* | Your movements |

| V. | WORD | TR. | MEANING |
|---|---|---|---|

# سُورَةُ النَّمْل

## [27] SURAT AN-NAML
## THE ANTS

| | | | |
|---|---|---|---|
| 3 | يُوقِنُونَ | *Yuqinun* | They believe with certainty |
| 7 | آنَسْتُ نَارًا | *'Anastu nara* | I perceive a fire |
| 7 | شِهَابٍ قَبَسٍ | *Shihabbin-qabas* | Burning brand |
| 7 | تَصْطَلُونَ | *Tastalun* | *pl.* You may warm (yourselves) |
| 8 | بُورِكَ | *Burik* | *pv.* Is blessed |
| 10 | تَهْتَزُّ | *Tahtazz* | Moving |
| 10 | جَانٌّ | *Jann* | Snake |
| 10 | لَمْ يُعَقِّبْ | *Lam yu-'aqqib* | Did not retrace his steps, did not look back |
| 12 | فِي جَيْبِكَ | *Fi jay-bik* | Your bosom |
| 12 | مِنْ غَيْرِ سُوءٍ | *Min ghayri su'* | Without stain |
| 16 | مَنطِقَ | *Mantiq* | Speech, language |
| 17 | يُوزَعُونَ | *Yuza-'un* | *pv.* They were kept in order and ranks |
| 18 | لَا يَحْطِمَنَّكُمْ | *La Yahtimannakum* | Lest (they) crush you |
| 19 | أَوْزِعْنِي | *'Awzi'-ni* | *im.* Inspire me |
| 25 | يُخْرِجُ الْخَبْءَ | *Yukhrijul-khab'* | Brings forth what is hidden |
| 28 | تَوَلَّ عَنْهُمْ | *Tawalla 'anhum* | *im.* Draw back from them |
| 33 | أُولُوا بَأْسٍ | *'Ulu-ba'-s* | Those endued with strength |

| V. | WORD | TR. | MEANING |
|---|---|---|---|
| 37 | لَا قِبَلَ لَهُمْ | *La qibala lahum* | Against whom they will have no power |
| 40 | طَرْفُكَ | *Tarfuk* | Your glance |
| 41 | نَكِّرُوا | *Nakkiru* | *im. pl.* Disguise |
| 44 | ادْخُلِي | *Ad-khuli* | *im.* Enter |
| 44 | صَرْحَ | *Sarh* | Lofty palace |
| 44 | حَسِبَتْهُ | *Hasibath* | She thought |
| 44 | لُجَّةً | *Lujja* | Lake |
| 44 | مُمَرَّدٌ | *Mumarrad* | Smoothly paved |
| 44 | قَوَارِيرَ | *Qawarir* | Glasses |
| 48 | رَهْطٍ | *Raht* | Men |
| 49 | تَقَاسَمُوا بِاللَّهِ | *Taqasamu billah* | Swear one to another by Allah |
| 49 | نُبَيِّتَنَّهُ وَأَهْلَهُ | *Nubayyi-tannahu wa 'ahlah* | We shall make a secret night attack on him and his people |
| 49 | مَهْلِكَ أَهْلِهِ | *Mahlika 'ahlih* | The destruction of his people |
| 60 | حَدَائِقَ | *Hada-'iq* | Orchards, gardens |
| 60 | ذَاتَ بَهْجَةٍ | *Dhata bahjah* | Full of beauty and delight |
| 60 | قَوْمٌ يَعْدِلُونَ | *Qaw-muny-ya'-dilun* | People who swerve from justice |
| 61 | قَرَارًا | *Qarar* | Fixed abode |
| 61 | حَاجِزًا | *Hajiza* | Barrier |
| 63 | رَحْمَتِهِ | *Rahmatih* | His Mercy (rain) |
| 66 | ادَّارَكَ | *Addarak* | Comprehends |

| V. | WORD | TR. | MEANING |
|---|---|---|---|
| 72 | رَدِفَ | *Radif* | Close behind (in pursuit) |
| 74 | مَا تُكِنُّ صُدُورُهُمْ | *Ma tukinnu suduru-hum* | What their breasts conceal |
| 75 | غَائِبَةٍ | *Gha-'i-ba* | *ap. fg.* That which is hidden |
| 87 | فَزِعَ | *Fazi'* | Terrified, smitten |
| 87 | دَاخِرِينَ | *Da-khirin* | *pl.* In utter humility |
| 90 | كُبَّتْ وُجُوهُهُمْ | *Kubbat wujuhuhum* | Their faces will be cast down |

# سُورَةُ القَصَص

## [28] SURAT AL-QASAS

## THE NARRATION

| V. | WORD | TR. | MEANING |
|---|---|---|---|
| 4 | عَلَا فِي الْأَرْضِ | *'Ala fil-'ard* | Exalted himself in the land |
| 6 | يَحْذَرُون | *Yahdharun* | They fear |
| 8 | كَانُوا خَاطِئِينَ | *Kanu khati-'in* | (They) were sinners |
| 10 | فَارِغًا | *Farigha* | *ap.* Void, empty |
| 10 | تُبْدِي | *Tubdi* | Discloses |
| 10 | رَبَطْنَا | *Rabatna* | We strengthened |
| 11 | قُصِّيهِ | *Qussih* | *im. fg.* Trace him |
| 11 | عَنْ جُنُبٍ | *'An-junub* | From distance / for place |
| 15 | وَكَزَهُ مُوسَى | *Wakazahu Musa* | Musa struck him with his fist |
| 17 | ظَهِيرًا لِلْمُجْرِمِينَ | *Zahiral-lil-mujrimin* | Helper to sinners |
| 18 | يَتَرَقَّبُ | *Yataraqqab* | Vigilant, looking about |
| 18 | يَسْتَصْرِخُهُ | *Yastasrikhuh* | Calls aloud for his help, calls for his help |
| 18 | غَوِيٌّ | *Ghawiyy* | One who is in the wrong |
| 19 | يَبْطِشَ | *Yabtish* | Seizes by force, attacks with violence |
| 20 | يَأْتَمِرُونَ بِكَ | *Ya'-tamiruna bik* | They take counsel together about you |
| 22 | تِلْقَاءَ مَدْيَنَ | *Tilqa-'a Madyan* | Towards (the land of) Madyain |

| V. | WORD | TR. | MEANING |
|---|---|---|---|
| 23 | أُمَّةً مِنَ النَّاسِ | *'Ummatam-minan-nas* | Group of men |
| 23 | تَذُودَانِ | *Tadhudan* | *fg. dl.* They keep back |
| 23 | حَتَّى يُصْدِرَ الرِّعَاءُ | *Hatta yus-dirarri-'a'* | Till the shepherds take back (their flocks) |
| 27 | تَأْجُرَنِي | *Ta'-jurani* | You serve me |
| 27 | حِجَجٍ | *Hijaj* | Years |
| 34 | رِدْءًا | *Rid-an* | Helper |
| 35 | سَنَشُدُّ عَضُدَكَ | *Sanashuddu 'adudak* | We will strengthen your arm |
| 36 | مُفْتَرًى | *Muftara* | *pp.* Faked up, invented |
| 40 | فَنَبَذْنَاهُمْ فِي الْيَمِّ | *Fanabadhnahum fil-yam* | And We flung them into the sea |
| 42 | مَقْبُوحِينَ | *Maqbuhin* | *pp.* Those who are loathed / despised |
| 43 | بَصَائِرَ لِلنَّاسِ | *Basa-'ira linnas* | Enlightenment for mankind |
| 45 | ثَاوِيًا | *Tha-wiya* | *ap.* Dweller |
| 48 | سِحْرَانِ تَظَاهَرَا | *Sihrani tazahara* | Two kinds of sorcery, each assisting the other |
| 51 | وَصَّلْنَا | *Wassalna* | We caused (it) to reach |
| 54 | يَدْرَءُونَ | *Yadra-'un* | They drive off / avert |
| 57 | نُتَخَطَّفْ | *Nutakhattaf* | *pv.* We will be snatched away |
| 58 | بَطِرَتْ | *Batirat* | Exulted |
| 63 | أَغْوَيْنَا | *'Aghwayna* | We led astray |

| V. | WORD | TR. | MEANING |
|---|---|---|---|
| 66 | فَعَمِيَتْ عَلَيْهِمُ الْأَنْبَاءُ | *Fa-'amiyat 'alayhimul-'amba'* | Then the arguments will be obscure to them |
| 68 | خِيَرَةُ | *Khiyarah* | Choice |
| 71 | سَرْمَدًا | *Sar-mada* | Perpetually |
| 76 | تَنُوءُ | *Tanu'* | Weighs down |
| 76 | لَا تَفْرَحْ | *La tafrah* | *ni.* Do not be exultant / glad |
| 80 | لَا يُلَقَّاهَا | *La Yulaq-qaha* | No one shall be granted it |
| 82 | يَقْدِرُ | *Yaqdir* | Restricts |
| 85 | مَعَاد | *Ma-'ad* | Place of return |

| V. | WORD | TR. | MEANING |
|---|---|---|---|

# سُورَةُ العَنْكَبُوت

## [29] SURAT AL-'ANKABUT

## THE SPIDER

| | | | |
|---|---|---|---|
| 2 | لَا يُفْتَنُونَ | *La yuftanun* | They will not be tested |
| 5 | أَجَلَ اللَّهِ | *'Ajalallah* | The Term (appointed) by Allah |
| 8 | حُسْنًا | *Husna* | Kindness, goodness |
| 21 | إِلَيْهِ تُقْلَبُونَ | *'Ilayhi tuqlabun* | To Him you will be returned |
| 25 | مَوَدَّةَ | *Mawadda* | Love |
| 29 | تَقْطَعُونَ السَّبِيلَ | *Taqta-'unas-sabil* | *pl.* You cut off the highway |
| 29 | نَادِيكُمْ | *Nadikum* | *pl.* Your council |
| 34 | رِجْزًا | *Rijza* | Punishment |
| 36 | لَا تَعْثَوْا | *La ta'-thaw* | *ni. pl.* Do not commit mischief |
| 37 | أَخَذَتْهُمُ الرَّجْفَةُ | *'Akhadhat-humur-rajfa* | The earthquake seized them |
| 38 | كَانُوا مُسْتَبْصِرِينَ | *Kanu Mustabsirin* | They were keen-sighted / intelligent |
| 40 | حَاصِبًا | *Hasiba* | Violent tornado (with showers of stones) |
| 41 | عَنكَبُوت | *'Ankabut* | Spider |
| 55 | يَغْشَاهُمُ الْعَذَابُ | *Yughshahumul-'adhab* | The punishment shall cover them |
| 64 | لَهْوٌ وَلَعِبٌ | *Lahwunw-wa la-'ib* | Amusement and play |
| 64 | حَيَوَانُ | *Hayawan* | Life |

| V. | WORD | TR. | MEANING |
|---|---|---|---|

# سُورَةُ الرُّومِ

# [30] SURAT AR-RUM

## THE ROMANS

| | | | |
|---|---|---|---|
| 2 | غُلِبَتْ الرُّومُ | *Ghulibatir-Rum* | The Romans have been defeated |
| 3 | فِي أَدْنَى الْأَرْضِ | *Fi 'adnal-'ardh* | In the nearest parts of the earth |
| 3 | بَعْدِ غَلَبِهِمْ | *Ba'-di ghalabihim* | After their defeat / victory |
| 9 | أَثَارُوا | *'Atharu* | They tilled |
| 12 | يُبْلِسُ الْمُجْرِمُونَ | *Yublisul-mujrimun* | The sinners will be struck dumb with despair |
| 15 | يُحْبَرُونَ | *Yuhbarun* | *pv.* They will be made happy |
| 18 | تُظْهِرُونَ | *Tuzhirun* | *pl.* You enter on the period of noon |
| 20 | تَنتَشِرُونَ | *Tantashirun* | *pl.* You scatter yourselves |
| 26 | قَانِتُونَ | *Qanitun* | *ap.* Those who are obedient to Allah |
| 27 | لَهُ الْمَثَلُ الْأَعْلَى | *Lahul-Mathalul-'A'-la* | To Him belongs the loftiest similitude (i.e., He is above all comparison) |
| 31 | مُنِيبِينَ | *Munibin* | *ap.* Those who turn with repentance to Allah |
| 36 | فَرِحُوا | *Farihu* | They exulted / rejoiced |
| 36 | يَقْنَطُونَ | *Yaqnatun* | They despair |
| 39 | رِبًا | *Riba* | Usury |

| V. | WORD | TR. | MEANING |
|---|---|---|---|
| 39 | يَرْبُوَا | *Yarbuwa* | Increases |
| 39 | لَا يَرْبُوا | *La yarbu* | Does not increase |
| 39 | مُضْعِفُونَ | *Mud-'ifun* | Those who have manifold increase, those who make double |
| 43 | يَصَّدَّعُونَ | *Yas-sadda-'un* | They are divided [(in two groups), a group in Paradise and a group in Hell ] |
| 44 | يَمْهَدُونَ | *Yamhadun* | They prepare a good place (in Paradise) |
| 48 | تُثِيرُ سَحَابًا | *Tuthiru sahaba* | Raise clouds |
| 48 | يَجْعَلُهُ كِسَفًا | *Yaj-'aluhu kisafan* | Breaks them into fragments |
| 48 | وَدْقَ | *Wadq* | Rain |
| 51 | مُصْفَرًّا | *Musfarra* | Yellow |
| 54 | شَيْبَةً | *Shaybah* | Hoariness |
| 57 | وَ لَا هُمْ يُسْتَعْتَبُونَ | *Wala hum yusta'-ta-bun* | And they will not be allowed to return to seek Allah's Pleasure |
| 60 | لَا يَسْتَخِفَنَّكَ | *La yasta-khliffan-nak* | Let not them make you excited |

| V. | WORD | TR. | MEANING |
|---|---|---|---|

# سُورَةُ لُقْمَان

## [31] SURAT LUQMAN

## LUQMAN (THE WISE)

| | | | |
|---|---|---|---|
| 6 | لَهْوَ الْحَدِيثِ | *Lahwal-hadith* | Idle tale |
| 6 | هُزُوًا | *Huzuwwa* | Ridicule |
| 7 | وَلَّى مُسْتَكْبِرًا | *Walla mustakbiran* | Turned away in arrogance |
| 14 | وَهْنًا | *Wahna* | In weakness |
| 14 | فِصَالُهُ | *Fisaluh* | His weaning |
| 18 | لَا تُصَعِّرْ خَدَّكَ لِلنَّاسِ | *La tusa'-'ir khaddaka linnas* | *ni.* Swell not your cheek (for pride) at men |
| 18 | مَرَحًا | *Maraha* | In insolence |
| 18 | مُخْتَال | *Mukhtal* | Arrogant |
| 18 | فَخُور | *Fakhur* | Boaster |
| 19 | اقْصِدْ فِي مَشْيِكَ | *Aqsid fi mash-yika* | *im.* Be moderate in your pace |
| 19 | اغْضُضْ | *Aghdud* | *im.* Lower. |
| 20 | سَخَّرَ لَكُمْ | *Sakh-khara lakum* | Subjected to your (use) |
| 20 | أَسْبَغَ | *'Asbagh* | Completed and perfected |
| 22 | الْعُرْوَةِ الْوُثْقَى | *Al-'urwatil-wuthqa* | The firmest hand-hold |
| 32 | مُقْتَصِدٌ | *Muqtasid* | *ap.* One who halts between two opinions, one who keeps to the right path |
| 32 | خَتَّار | *Khattar* | Perfidious |

# سُورَةُ السَّجْدَة

## [32] SURAT AS-SAJDAH

## THE PROSTRATION

| | | | |
|---|---|---|---|
| 2 | تَنزِيلُ | *Tanzil* | Revelation |
| 4 | مِن دُونِهِ | *Min dunih* | Besides Him |
| 5 | يَعْرُجُ إِلَيْهِ | *Ya'-ruju 'ilayh* | Ascends unto Him |
| 8 | سُلَالَةٍ | *Sulala* | Quintessence |
| 9 | أَفْئِدَةَ | *'Af-'idah* | Hearts |
| 11 | وُكِّلَ | *Wukkil* | *pv.* Put in charge |
| 12 | صَالِحاً | *Saliha* | Righteousness |
| 12 | مُوقِنُونَ | *Muqinun* | *ap.* Those who believe firmly |
| 13 | حَقَّ الْقَوْلُ | *Haqqal-Qawl* | The Word (from Allah) took effect |
| 13 | جِنَّةِ | *Jinna* | Jinns |
| 14 | عَذَابَ الْخُلْدِ | *'Adhabal-khuld* | The chastisement of Eternity |
| 15 | خَرُّواْ | *Kharru* | They fell down |
| 16 | تَتَجَافَى جُنُوبُهُمْ عَنِ الْمَضَاجِعِ | *Tatajafa junubuhum 'anil-madaji'* | Their sides forsake their beds |
| 18 | فَاسِقاً | *Fasiqa* | Rebellious and wicked |
| 27 | الْأَرْضِ الْجُرُزِ | *Al-'ardil-juruz* | The dry land |
| 28 | فَتْحُ | *Fat-h* | Victory, decision |

| V. | WORD | TR. | MEANING |
|---|---|---|---|

## سُورَةُ الأَحْزَابِ

## [33] SURAT AL-AHZAB

## THE CONFEDERATES

| | | | |
|---|---|---|---|
| 1 | اتَّقِ اللَّهَ | *It-taqil-lah* | *im.* Fear Allah |
| 4 | تُظَاهِرُونَ مِنْهُنَّ أُمَّهَاتِكُمْ | *Tuzahiruna minhunna 'ummahatikum* | You declare them (your wives) to be like your mothers |
| 4 | أَدْعِيَاءَكُمْ | *'Ad-'iya-'akum* | *pl.* Your adopted sons |
| 5 | أَقْسَطُ | *'Aqsat* | Juster |
| 6 | أَوْلَى | *'Awla* | Closer |
| 6 | أُولُو الْأَرْحَامِ | *'Ulul-'arham* | Blood-relations |
| 9 | جُنُودٌ | *Junud* | Troops, hosts |
| 10 | زَاغَتْ | *Zaghat* | Swerved |
| 10 | بَلَغَتْ الْقُلُوبُ الْحَنَاجِرَ | *Balaghatil-qulubul-hanajir* | The hearts reached to the throats |
| 11 | ابْتُلِيَ | *Ibtuliy* | *pv.* Were / was tried |
| 11 | زُلْزِلُوا | *Zulzilu* | *pv.* They were shaken |
| 13 | يَثْرِبَ | *Yathrib* | The original name of Madina |
| 13 | لَا مُقَامَ لَكُمْ | *La muqama lakum* | There is no stand (possible) for you (against the enemy attack) |
| 13 | إِنَّ بُيُوتَنَا عَوْرَةٌ | *'Inna buyutana 'awrah* | Truly, our houses are bare and exposed (to the enemy) |
| 13 | فِرَارًا | *Firara* | Flight |

| V. | WORD | TR. | MEANING |
|---|---|---|---|
| 14 | أَقْطَارِهَا | *'Aqtariha* | Its sides |
| 14 | مَا تَلَبَّثُوا | *Ma talabbathu* | They did not tarry / remain |
| 18 | مُعَوِّقِينَ | *Mu-'awwiqin* | Those who keep back / hinder |
| 18 | هَلُمَّ إِلَيْنَا | *Halum-ma 'ilayna* | Come along to us |
| 19 | أَشِحَّةً | *'Ashih-hatan* | Covetous, grasping, niggardly |
| 19 | يُغْشَى عَلَيْهِ مِنَ الْمَوْتِ | *Yughsha 'alayhi minal-mawt* | (He) faints from death |
| 19 | سَلَقُوكُمْ | *Sala-qukum* | They will smite you |
| 19 | أَلْسِنَةٍ حِدَادٍ | *'Alsinatin hidad* | Sharp tongues |
| 20 | بَادُونَ | *Badun* | *ap.* Dwellers in the desert |
| 20 | أَعْرَابِ | *'A'-rab* | Bedouins |
| 21 | أُسْوَةٌ حَسَنَةٌ | *'Uswatun Hasana* | Good example |
| 23 | قَضَى نَحْبَهُ | *Qada nahbah* | He has fulfilled his vow (by offering up his life for the Faith) |
| 26 | الَّذِينَ ظَاهَرُوهُمْ | *Alladhina zaharu-hum* | Those who aided them (i.e., the Jewish tribe of the Banu Quraiza) |
| 26 | صَيَاصِيهِمْ | *Sayasihim* | Their strongholds / forts |
| 28 | أُمَتِّعْكُنَّ | *'Umat-ti'-kunn* | I will make a provision for you |
| 28 | أُسَرِّحْكُنَّ | *'Usarrih-kunn* | I will set you free |
| 28 | سَرَاحًا | *Saraha* | Dismissal (of a woman by |

| V. | WORD | TR. | MEANING |
|---|---|---|---|
| | | | divorce), release |
| 32 | لَا تَخْضَعْنَ بِالْقَوْلِ | *La Takhda'-na bil-qawl* | *ni. pl.* Be not too complaisant of speech |
| 33 | قَرْنَ فِي بُيُوتِكُنَّ | *Qarna fi buyutikunn* | *im. pl.* Stay quietly in your houses |
| 33 | لَا تَبَرَّجْنَ | *La tabarrajna* | *ni. pl.* Do not make a dazzling display |
| 36 | خِيَرَةُ | *Khiyarah* | Option, choice |
| 37 | وَطَرًا | *Watara* | A thing necessary to be done |
| 38 | قَدَرًا | *Qadara* | (Divine) decree |
| 38 | مَقْدُورًا | *Maqdura* | *pp.* Determined |
| 50 | آتَيْتَ أُجُورَهُنَّ | *'Atayta 'ujura-hunn* | You paid their dowers |
| 50 | أَفَاءَ | *'Afa'* | Returned, gave as booty |
| 51 | تُرْجِي | *Turji* | You may defer / postpone |
| 51 | تُؤْوِي | *Tu-'wi* | You may receive |
| 51 | عَزَلْتَ | *'Azalat* | You set aside |
| 51 | أَدْنَى | *'Adna* | Nigher |
| 53 | إِنَاهُ | *'Inah* | Its preparation |
| 56 | يُصَلُّونَ عَلَى النَّبِيِّ | *Yusalluna 'alan-Nabiyy* | They send blessings on the Prophet صلى الله عليه وسلم |
| 59 | يُدْنِينَ | *Yudnin* | *fg.* They draw near |
| 59 | جَلَابِيبِهِنَّ | *Jalabibihinn* | Their outer garments |
| 60 | مُرْجِفُونَ | *Murjifun* | Those who stir up |

| V. | WORD | TR. | MEANING |
|---|---|---|---|
| | | | sedition / spread false news |
| 60 | نُغْرِيَنَّكَ بِهِمْ | *Nugh-riyannaka bihim* | We shall let you overpower them |
| 61 | ثُقِفُوا | *Thuqifu* | They are found |
| 68 | ضِعْفَيْنِ | *Di'-fayn* | Double |
| 69 | وَجِيهًا | *Wajiha* | Honourable |
| 70 | سَدِيدًا | *Sadida* | Straight (to the goal), well-directed |
| 72 | أَمَانَةَ | *'Amana* | Trust |
| 72 | فَأَبَيْنَ | *Fa-'abayn* | But they refused |

| V. | WORD | TR. | MEANING |
|---|---|---|---|

## سُورَةُ سَبَأٍ

## [34] SURAT SABA'

## THE CITY OF SABA

| V. | WORD | TR. | MEANING |
|---|---|---|---|
| 2 | مَا يَلِجُ فِي الْأَرْضِ | *Ma yaliju fil-'ard* | That which goes into the earth |
| 2 | مَا يَعْرُجُ | *Ma ya'-ruj* | That which ascends |
| 3 | لَا يَعْزُبُ | *La ya'-zub* | Hidden not, escapes not |
| 5 | مُعَاجِزِينَ | *Mu-'ajizin* | Those who strive against (Allah's Signs) |
| 7 | مُزِّقْتُمْ | *Muzziq-tum* | You are scattered to pieces |
| 9 | نَخْسِفْ بِهِمُ الْأَرْضَ | *Nakhsif bihi-mul-'ard* | We shall cause the earth to swallow them up |
| 9 | كِسَفًا مِنَ السَّمَاءِ | *Kisafam-minas-sama'* | Piece of the sky |
| 9 | مُنِيبٍ | *Munib* | *ap.* One who turns with repentance to Allah |
| 10 | أَوِّبِي مَعَهُ | *'Awwibi ma-'ah* | *im.pl.* Echo back (the Praises of Allah) with him, glorify (Allah) with him |
| 11 | سَابِغَاتٍ | *Sabighat* | Coats of mail |
| 11 | سَرْدِ | *Sard* | Work made of rings woven together, as chain armour |
| 12 | غُدُوُّهَا | *Ghuduwwuha* | Its morning stride |

| V. | WORD | TR. | MEANING |
|---|---|---|---|
| 12 | رَوَاحُهَا | *Rawahuha* | Its evening stride |
| 12 | عَيْنَ الْقِطْرِ | *'Aynal-qitr* | Font of molten brass |
| 12 | يَزِغْ | *Yazigh* | Turns aside |
| 13 | مَحَارِيبَ | *Maharib* | Arches |
| 13 | تَمَاثِيلَ | *Tamathil* | Images |
| 13 | قُدُورٍ | *Qudur* | Cauldrons |
| 14 | دَابَّةُ الْأَرْضِ | *Dabbatul-'ard* | A little worm of the earth |
| 14 | مِنسَأَتَهُ | *Minsa-'atah* | His staff |
| 15 | سَبَإٍ | *Saba'* | Sheba ( a city in Yemen) |
| 16 | أَعْرَضُوا | *'A'-radu* | They turned away |
| 16 | سَيْلَ الْعَرِمِ | *Saylal-'Arim* | Flood released from the dams |
| 16 | أُكُلٍ خَمْطٍ | *'Ukulin khamt* | Bitter fruit |
| 16 | أَثْلٍ | *'Athl* | Tamarisks |
| 16 | سِدْرٍ | *Sidr* | Lote-tree |
| 19 | مَزَّقْنَاهُمْ | *Mazzaqna-hum* | We dispersed them |
| 23 | إِذَا فُزِّعَ عَنْ قُلُوبِهِمْ | *'Idha fuzzi-'a 'an-qulubihim* | When terror is removed from their hearts |
| 26 | هُوَ الْفَتَّاحُ | *Huwal-Fat-tah* | He is the Judge |
| 31 | مَوْقُوفُونَ | *Mawqufun* | *pp.* Those made to stand |
| 31 | يَرْجِعُ | *Yarji'* | Throw back (the word of blame) |
| 37 | جَزَاءُ الضِّعْفِ | *Jaza-'uddi'-f* | Multiplied reward |
| 37 | غُرُفَاتِ | *Ghurufat* | High dwellings, |

| V. | WORD | TR. | MEANING |
|---|---|---|---|
| | | | lofty apartments |
| 45 | مِعْشَارَ | *Mi'-shar* | One tenth (1/10$^{th}$) |
| 48 | يَقْذِفُ | *Yaqdhif* | Casts |
| 51 | إِذْ فَزِعُوا | *'Idh fazi-'u* | When they will be terrified |
| 51 | لَا فَوْتَ | *La fawt* | No escape |
| 51 | مَكَانٍ قَرِيبٍ | *Makanin-qarib* | Near place |
| 52 | تَنَاوُشُ | *Tana-wush* | The act of taking or receiving |
| 52 | مَكَانٍ بَعِيدٍ | *Makanim-ba-'id* | Far place |
| 54 | أَشْيَاعِهِمْ | *'Ashya-'ihim* | People of their kind, their partisans |

# سُورَةُ فَاطِر

## [35] SURAT FATIR

## THE ORIGINATOR OF CREATION

| | | | |
|---|---|---|---|
| 1 | فَاطِر | *Fatir* | Originator |
| 5 | الْغَرُور | *Al-Gharur* | The chief Deceiver (Satan) |
| 8 | لَا تَذْهَبْ نَفْسُكَ عَلَيْهِمْ حَسَرَات | *La tadh-hab nafsuka 'alayhim hasarat* | *ni.* Let not your soul be vested in regret for them |
| 9 | نُشُور | *Nushur* | Resurrection |
| 10 | عِزَّة | *'Izza* | Glory and power |
| 10 | الْكَلِمُ الطَّيِّبُ | *Al-Kalimut-Tay-yib* | The good word |
| 10 | الْعَمَلُ الصَّالِحُ | *Al-'Amalus-Salih* | The righteous deed |
| 10 | يَبُورُ | *Yabur* | Will be void, will perish |
| 11 | مُعَمَّر | *Mu-'ammar* | *pp.* One whose life is prolonged |
| 12 | عَذْبٌ | *'Adhb* | Palatable |
| 12 | فُرَاتٌ | *Furat* | Sweet |
| 12 | سَائِغٌ شَرَابُهُ | *Sa-'ighun-sharabuh* | Pleasant to drink |
| 12 | مِلْحٌ | *Milh* | Salt |
| 12 | أُجَاجٌ | *'Ujaj* | Bitter |
| 12 | مَوَاخِرَ | *Mawakhir* | Those (ships) which plough the wave with a dashing noise |
| 18 | لَا تَزِرُ وَازِرَةٌ وِزرَ أُخْرَى | *La taziru waziratunw-wizra* | And no bearer of burdens shall bear |

| V. | WORD | TR. | MEANING |
|---|---|---|---|
| | | *'ukhra* | another's burden |
| 18 | مُثْقَلَةٌ | *Muthqala* | *pp.* Heavily laden |
| 21 | حَرُورُ | *Harur* | Sun's heat |
| 27 | جُدَدٌ | *Judad* | Tracts, streaks |
| 27 | غَرَابِيبُ سُودٌ | *Gharabibu sud* | Very black |
| 29 | لَنْ تَبُورَ | *Lan-tabur* | Will never fail / perish |
| 32 | ظَالِمٌ لِنَفْسِهِ | *Zalimul-linafsih* | (He) wrongs his own soul |
| 32 | سَابِقٌ بِالْخَيْرَاتِ | *Sabiqum-bil-khayrat* | (One who is) foremost in good deeds |
| 34 | حَزَنَ | *Hazan* | Grief, sorrow |
| 35 | دَارَ الْمُقَامَةِ | *Daral-muqama* | The mansion of eternal abode (Paradise) |
| 35 | نَصَبٌ | *Nasab* | Toil |
| 35 | لُغُوبٌ | *Lughub* | Weariness |
| 37 | هُمْ يَصْطَرِخُونَ | *Hum yastarikhun* | They will cry aloud |
| 39 | مَقْتًا | *Maqta* | Odium, hatred, anger |
| 39 | خَسَارًا | *Kha-sara* | Loss |
| 42 | نُفُورًا | *Nufura* | Aversion |

# سُورَةُ يس

## [36] SURAT YA-SIN

### YA-SIN

| V. | WORD | TR. | MEANING |
|---|---|---|---|
| 6 | غَافِلُونَ | *Ghafilun* | *ap.* Those who are negligent or careless |
| 7 | لَقَدْ حَقَّ الْقَوْلُ | *Laqad haqqal-Qawl* | (Indeed) the Word (of punishment) is proved true |
| 8 | مُقْمَحُونَ | *Muqmahun* | Those whose heads are forced up so that they cannot see |
| 9 | أَغْشَيْنَاهُمْ | *'Aghshay-nahum* | We have covered them up |
| 11 | أَجْرٍ كَرِيمٍ | *'Aj-rin Karim* | Generous reward |
| 12 | آثَارَهُمْ | *'Atharahum* | What they left behind, their traces |
| 12 | أَحْصَيْنَا | *'Ah-sayna* | We have taken account |
| 12 | إِمَامٍ مُبِينٍ | *'Imamim-mubin* | Clear Book |
| 13 | قَرْيَةِ | *Qaryah* | City (Antioch) |
| 14 | عَزَّزْنَا بِثَالِثٍ | *'Azzazna bi-thalith* | We strengthened them with a third |
| 18 | لَنَرْجُمَنَّكُم | *Lanar-jumannakum* | We will certainly stone you |
| 19 | أَئِنْ ذُكِّرْتُمْ | *'A-'in dhukkirtum* | If you are admonished |
| 23 | لَا تُغْنِ عَنِّي | *La tughni 'anni* | (Their intercession will be) of no use for me |
| 27 | مُكْرَمِينَ | *Mukramin* | *pp.pl.* Honoured |
| 29 | خَامِدُونَ | *Kha-midun* | (They are) silent |

| V. | WORD | TR. | MEANING |
|---|---|---|---|
| | | | (like ashes) |
| 34 | فَجَّرْنَا فِيهَا من العُيُونِ | *Fajjarna fiha minal-'uyun* | We have caused springs (of water) to gush forth therein |
| 37 | نَسْلَخُ | *Naslakh* | We withdraw |
| 39 | مَنَازِلَ | *Manazil* | Stations |
| 39 | كَالْعُرْجُونِ الْقَدِيمِ | *Kal-'urjunil-qadim* | Like the old (and withered) lower part of a date-stalk |
| 40 | يَسْبَحُونَ | *Yasba-hun* | They swim / float |
| 41 | ذُرِّيَّتَهُمْ | *Dhurriyyatahum* | Their offspring / race |
| 41 | مَشْحُونِ | *Mash-hun* | *pp.* Loaded (a ship) |
| 43 | لَا صَرِيخَ لَهُمْ | *La sarikha lahum* | There will be no helper for them (to hear their cry) |
| 49 | هُمْ يَخِصِّمُونَ | *Hum yakhissi-mun* | They are disputing |
| 51 | أَجْدَاث | *'Ajdath* | Graves |
| 51 | يَنسِلُونَ | *Yansilun* | They will come out quickly |
| 55 | في شُغُلٍ | *Fi shughul* | Busy |
| 55 | فَاكِهُونَ | *Fakihun* | *ap.* Those who are very joyful / rejoice greatly |
| 56 | أرَائِك | *'Ara-'ik* | Raised couches |
| 59 | امْتَازُوا | *Amtazu* | *im. pl.* Be apart / separated |
| 62 | جِبِلًّا | *Jibilla* | Multitude, crowd |
| 64 | اصْلَوْهَا | *'Islaw-ha* | *im. pl.* Enter it, suffer of it |

| V. | WORD | TR. | MEANING |
|---|---|---|---|
| 66 | لَطَمَسْنَا | *Latamas-na* | We would (surely) have wiped out (blinded) |
| 68 | مَنْ نُعَمِّرْهُ | *Man-nu-'ammirh* | He whom We grant long life |
| 68 | نُنَكِّسْهُ فِي الْخَلْق | *Nunakkis-h* | We cause him to be reversed in nature |
| 72 | ذَلَّلْنَاهَا لَهُمْ | *Dhallalnaha lahum* | We have subjected them to their use |
| 78 | رَمِيمٌ | *Ramim* | Decomposed, rotten |
| 83 | مَلَكُوتُ | *Malakut* | Dominion |

| V. | WORD | TR. | MEANING |
|---|---|---|---|

# سُورَةُ الصَّافَّات

## [37]SURAT AS-SAFFAT
## THOSE RANGED IN RANKS

| V. | WORD | TR. | MEANING |
|---|---|---|---|
| 1 | وَالصَّافَّاتِ صَفًّا | *Was-saffati saffa* | By those who range themselves in ranks |
| 2 | فَالزَّاجِرَاتِ زَجْرًا | *Faz-zajirati zajra* | Those who so are strong in repelling (evil) |
| 3 | فَالتَّالِيَاتِ ذِكْرًا | *Fat-taliyati Dhikra* | Those who thus proclaim the Message (of Allah) |
| 4 | إِنَّ إِلَـٰهَكُمْ لَوَاحِدٌ | *'Inna 'Ilahakum la-Wahid* | Verily, your God is One |
| 7 | شَيْطَانٍ مَارِدٍ | *Shay-tanim-marid* | Rebellious Satan |
| 9 | دُحُوراً | *Duhura* | Repulsed |
| 9 | عَذَابٌ وَاصِبٌ | *'Adha-bunw-wasib* | Perpetual chastisement |
| 10 | شِهَابٌ | *Shihab* | Flaming fire |
| 10 | ثَاقِبٌ | *Thaqib* | *ap.* Piercing brightness |
| 11 | طِينٍ لَّازِبٍ | *Tinil-lazib* | Sticky clay |
| 18 | أَنْتُمْ دَاخِرُونَ | *'Antum da-khirun* | *pl.* You shall (then) be humiliated |
| 19 | زَجْرَةٌ وَاحِدَةٌ | *Zajra-tunw-wahida* | Single cry |
| 24 | قِفُوهُمْ | *Qifuhum* | *im. pl.* Stop them |
| 45 | كَأْسٍ | *Ka'-s* | Cup |
| 45 | مِنْ مَعِينٍ | *Mim-ma'in* | From a clear-flowing fountain |
| 47 | غَوْلٌ | *Ghawl* | Any kind of hurt, headache |

| V. | WORD | TR. | MEANING |
|---|---|---|---|
| 48 | قَاصِرَاتُ الطَّرْفِ | *Qasiratut-tarf* | Chaste women, restraining their glances (desiring none except their husbands) |
| 49 | بَيْضٌ | *Bayd* | (Delicate) eggs |
| 49 | مَكْنُونٌ | *Maknun* | Closely guarded |
| 53 | مَدِينُونَ | *Madinun* | Those who receive rewards or punishment |
| 55 | سَوَاءِ الْجَحِيمِ | *Sawa-'il-Jahim* | The midst of the Fire |
| 56 | إِنْ كِدْتَ لَتُرْدِينِ | *'In-kitta laturdin* | You was little short of bringing me to perdition |
| 57 | مُحْضَرِينَ | *Muhdarin* | *pp.* Those who are brought forward |
| 62 | خَيْرٌ نُزُلًا | *Khayrun-nuzula* | Better entertainment |
| 62 | شَجَرَةُ الزَّقُّومِ | *Shajaratuz-Zaqqum* | The tree of Zaqqum (a horrible tree in Hell) |
| 64 | أَصْلِ الْجَحِيمِ | *'Aslil-Jahim* | The bottom of Hell-Fire |
| 67 | شَوْبًا | *Shawba* | Mixture |
| 67 | حَمِيمٌ | *Hamim* | Boiling water |
| 70 | فَهُمْ عَلَى آثَارِهِمْ يُهْرَعُونَ | *Fahum 'ala 'atharihim yuhra-'un* | So they (too) were rushed down on their footsteps |
| 89 | إِنِّي سَقِيمٌ | *'Inni saqim* | I am indeed sick (at heart) |
| 91 | فَرَاغَ إِلَى آلِهَتِهِمْ | *Faragha 'ila 'alihatihim* | Then he turned to their gods |

| V. | WORD | TR. | MEANING |
|---|---|---|---|
| 93 | ضَرْبًا بِالْيَمِينِ | *Dharbam-bil-yamin* | Striking (their gods) with the right hand |
| 94 | يَزِفُّونَ | *Yazif-fun* | They (came) with hurried steps |
| 101 | غُلَامٍ حَلِيمٍ | *Ghulamin halim* | Forbearing son |
| 102 | فَلَمَّا بَلَغَ مَعَهُ السَّعْيَ | *Falamma balagha ma-'ahus-sa'-y* | When he (his son) reached the age of (serious) work with him |
| 103 | أَسْلَمَا | *'Aslama* | They both submitted (to Allah) |
| 103 | تَلَّهُ لِلْجَبِينِ | *Tallahu lil-jabin* | He laid him prostrate on his forehead (for sacrifice) |
| 106 | الْبَلَاءُ الْمُبِينُ | *Al-bala-'ul-mubin* | Clear trial |
| 107 | ذِبْحٍ | *Dhibh* | Sacrifice |
| 125 | بَعْلًا | *Ba'-la* | A name of an idol |
| 130 | إِلْ يَاسِينَ | *'Ilya-sin* | Elias |
| 140 | أَبَقَ | *'Abaq* | Ran away |
| 141 | سَاهَمَ | *Saham* | Cast lots |
| 141 | مُدْحَضِينَ | *Mudhadin* | Those who are rebutted / condemned |
| 142 | الْتَقَمَهُ الْحُوتُ | *Iltaqamahul-Hut* | The big fish swallowed him |
| 142 | مُلِيمٌ | *Mulim* | Deserving of blame |
| 143 | مُسَبِّحِينَ | *Musabbihin* | *ap.* Those who glorify Allah |

| V. | WORD | TR. | MEANING |
|---|---|---|---|
| 145 | نَبَذْنَاهُ بِالْعَرَاءِ | *Nabadhnahu bil-'ara-'* | We cast him forth on the naked shore |
| 146 | يَقْطِين | *Yaqtin* | Gourd |
| 162 | فَاتِنِينَ | *Fatinin* | *ap.* Those who lead into temptation |
| 163 | صَالِي الْجَحِيمِ | *Salil-Jahim* | One who is going to the blazing Fire |
| 165 | صَافُّونَ | *Saffun* | Those who are ranged in ranks |
| 177 | سَاحَتِهِمْ | *Sahati-him* | Their courtyard |
| 180 | رَبِّ الْعِزَّةِ | *Rabbika Rabbil-'Izza* | The Lord of Honour and Power |

| V. | WORD | TR. | MEANING |
|---|---|---|---|

# سُورَةُ ص

## [38] SURAT SAD

## SAD

| | | | |
|---|---|---|---|
| 2 | عِزَّةٍ | *'Izza* | Self-glory |
| 2 | شِقَاقٍ | *Shiqaq* | Apposition |
| 3 | لَاتَ حِينَ مَنَاصٍ | *Lata hina manas* | There was no longer time for escape |
| 5 | عُجَابٌ | *'Ujab* | Strange |
| 6 | امْشُوا | *Imshu* | *Im. pl.* Go on |
| 7 | الْمِلَّةِ الْآخِرَةِ | *Al-millatil-'akhirah* | The last religion |
| 7 | اخْتِلَاقٌ | *Ikh-tilaq* | Invention |
| 9 | الْوَهَّابِ | *Al-Wahhab* | The Grantor of Bounties without measure |
| 12 | ذُو الْأَوْتَادِ | *Dhul-'awtad* | The lord of stakes |
| 15 | فَوَاقٍ | *Fawaq* | Delay (i.e., the interval between one milking of a she-camel, and another) |
| 16 | قِطَّنَا | *Qittana* | Our sentence |
| 17 | ذَا الْأَيْدِ | *Dhal-'ayd* | The man of strength |
| 20 | شَدَدْنَا مُلْكَهُ | *Shadadna mulkah* | We strengthened his kingdom |
| 20 | آتَيْنَاهُ الْحِكْمَةَ | *'Aataynahul-hikma* | We gave him wisdom |
| 20 | فَصْلَ الْخِطَابِ | *Faslal-khitab* | Sound judgement in speech and |

| V. | WORD | TR. | MEANING |
|---|---|---|---|
| | | | decision |
| 21 | خَصْمِ | *Khasm* | *sr.* *dl.* and *pl.* Disputants |
| 21 | تَسَوَّرُوا الْمِحْرَابَ | *Tassawwarul-mihrab* | They climbed over the wall of the private chamber |
| 22 | لَا تُشْطِطْ | *La tush-tit* | *ni.* Be not unjust |
| 23 | أَكْفِلْنِيهَا | *'Akfilniha* | *im.* Commit her to my care |
| 23 | عَزَّنِي فِي الْخِطَابِ | *'Azzani fil-khitab* | (He) overcame me in the argument |
| 24 | خُلَطَاءِ | *Khulata'* | Partners |
| 24 | خَرَّ | *Kharr* | Fell down |
| 24 | أَنَابَ | *'Anab* | Turned (to Allah) in repentance |
| 25 | زُلْفَى | *Zulfa* | Near approach |
| 25 | حُسْنَ مَآبٍ | *Husna ma-'ab* | A good place of (final) return (i.e., Paradise) |
| 26 | هَوَى | *Hawa* | Desire, will, lust |
| 31 | بِالْعَشِيِّ | *Bil-'ashiy* | At eventide |
| 31 | الصَّافِنَاتُ الْجِيَادُ | *As-safinatul-jiyad* | Coursers of the highest breeding and swift of foot |
| 32 | أَحْبَبْتُ حُبَّ الْخَيْرِ | *'Ahbabtu hubbal-khayr* | I did love the good (the horses) |
| 32 | تَوَارَتْ بِالْحِجَابِ | *Tawarat bil-hijab* | (The sun) was hidden in the veil (of night) |
| 33 | رُدُّوهَا عَلَيَّ | *Rudduha 'alayy* | *im.* Bring them back to me |
| 33 | فَطَفِقَ مَسْحًا بِالسُّوقِ | *Fata-fiqamas-ham-bissuqi wal-* | Then he began to pass his hand over |

| V. | WORD | TR. | MEANING |
|---|---|---|---|
| | وَالْأَعْنَاقِ | *'a'-naq* | their legs and their necks |
| 36 | رُخَاءً | *Rukha'* | Gently |
| 36 | حَيْثُ أَصَابَ | *Haythu 'asab* | Whithersoever (he) willed |
| 37 | بَنَّاء | *Banna'* | Builder |
| 37 | غَوَّاص | *Ghawwas* | Diver |
| 41 | نُصْبٍ وَعَذَابٍ | *Nusbinw wa 'adhab* | Distress and suffering |
| 42 | ارْكُضْ بِرِجْلِكَ | *'Urkud birijlik* | *im.* Strike with your foot |
| 42 | مُغْتَسَلٌ | *Mughtasal* | Place for washing |
| 44 | ضِغْثًا | *Dightha* | Handful of green and dry grass (or other herbs) |
| 45 | أُولِي الْأَيْدِي | *'Ulil-'Aydi* | Owners of strength |
| 45 | أَبْصَارِ | *'Absar* | Religious understanding |
| 46 | إِنَّا أَخْلَصْنَاهُمْ بِخَالِصَةٍ | *'Inna 'akhlasna-hum-bi-khalisa* | Verily We did choose them for a special (purpose) |
| 47 | مُصْطَفَيْنَ | *Mustafayn* | *pp.pl.* Chosen |
| 47 | أَخْيَار | *'Akhyar* | Good ones |
| 52 | أَتْرَابٌ | *'Atrab* | Of equal age, of the same age |
| 54 | نَفَاد | *Nafad* | Exhaustion, failure |
| 57 | غَسَّاقٌ | *Ghassaq* | Corruption which flows from the bodies of the damned |
| 59 | فَوْجٌ | *Fawj* | Troop |

| V. | WORD | TR. | MEANING |
|---|---|---|---|
| 59 | مُقْتَحِمٌ | *Muqtahim* | *ap.* One who rushes or leaps headlong |
| 59 | لَا مَرْحَبًا بِهِمْ | *La marhabam-bihim* | No welcome for them |
| 63 | سِخْرِيًّا | *Sikhriyya* | Ridicule, mockery |
| 63 | زَاغَتْ عَنْهُمُ الْأَبْصَارُ | *Zaghat 'anhumul-'absar* | (Our) eyes have failed to perceive them |
| 69 | الْمَلَإِ الْأَعْلَى | *Al-mala-'il-'a'-la* | The Exalted chiefs (angels) |
| 75 | عَالِينَ | *'Alin* | Those who are high and mighty |
| 82 | بِعِزَّتِكَ | *Bi-'Izzatik* | By Your Power |
| 86 | مُتَكَلِّفِينَ | *Mutakallifin* | Pretenders |

| V. | WORD | TR. | MEANING |
|---|---|---|---|

## سُورَةُ الزُّمَر

## [39] SURAT AZ-ZUMAR

## THE GROUPS

| V. | WORD | TR. | MEANING |
|---|---|---|---|
| 2 | مُخْلِصًا لَهُ الدِّينَ | *Mukhlisal-lahud-din* | Offering Him sincere devotion |
| 5 | يُكَوِّرُ اللَّيْلَ عَلَى النَّهَارِ | *Yukawwirul-layla 'alan-nahar* | He makes the night overlap the day |
| 6 | ظُلُمَاتٍ ثَلَاثٍ | *Zulumatin thalath* | Three veils of darkness |
| 8 | إِذَا خَوَّلَهُ نِعْمَةً | *'Ida khawwalahu ni'-ma* | When He bestows a favour upon him |
| 9 | قَانِتٌ | *Qanit* | *ap.* One who is obedient to Allah |
| 9 | آنَاءَ اللَّيْلِ | *'Ana-'allayl* | The hours of the night |
| 16 | ظُلَلٌ مِنَ النَّارِ | *Zulalum-minan-Nar* | Layers of Fire |
| 21 | سَلَكَهُ يَنَابِيعَ | *Salakahu yanabi'* | He led it through springs |
| 21 | يَهِيجُ | *Yahij* | Withers |
| 21 | يَجْعَلُهُ حُطَامًا | *Yaj-'aluhu huta-ma* | He makes it dry up and crumble away |
| 23 | مُتَشَابِهًا | *Mutashabi-ha* | Consistent |
| 23 | مَثَانِيَ | *Mathaniy* | Oft-repeated |
| 23 | تَقْشَعِرُّ | *Taq-sha-'ir* | Trembles, shivers |
| 23 | تَلِينُ | *Talin* | Softens |
| 28 | عِوَجٍ | *'Iwaj* | Crookedness |
| 29' | مُتَشَاكِسُونَ | *Muta-shakisun* | *pl.* Quarrelling, at variance with each other |
| 29 | سَلَمًا | *Sala-ma* | Belonging entirely |

| V. | WORD | TR. | MEANING |
|---|---|---|---|
| 38 | حَسْبِيَ اللَّهُ | *Hasbi-yallah* | Allah is sufficient for me |
| 40 | يَحِلُّ عَلَيْهِ | *Yahillu 'alayh* | Descends on him |
| 42 | يَتَوَفَّى الْأَنْفُسَ | *Yatawaffal-'anfus* | Takes the souls |
| 44 | لِلَّهِ الشَّفَاعَةُ جَمِيعًا | *Lillahish-Shafa-'atu jami-'a* | To Allah belongs all intercession |
| 45 | اشْمَأَزَّتْ | *Ishma-'azzat* | Are filled with disgust |
| 47 | يَحْتَسِبُونَ | *Yahtasibun* | They reckon |
| 53 | أَسْرَفُوا | *'Asrafu* | They transgressed |
| 53 | لَا تَقْنَطُوا | *La taqnatu* | *ni. pl.* Do not despair |
| 56 | فَرَّطْتُ | *Farrattu* | I neglected |
| 56 | جَنْبِ اللَّهِ | *Jambillah* | Towards Allah |
| 61 | مَفَازَتِهِمْ | *Mafazatihim* | Their place or state of victory or achievement |
| 63 | مَقَالِيدُ | *Maqalid* | Keys |
| 67 | قَبْضَتُهُ | *Qabdatuh* | His handful |
| 67 | مَطْوِيَّاتٌ بِيَمِينِهِ | *Matwiy-yatum-biyaminih* | *pl.* Rolled up in His right hand |
| 69 | وُضِعَ الْكِتَابُ | *Wudi'-al-Kitab* | The Book (of deeds) will be placed (open) |
| 71 | زُمَرًا | *Zumara* | Groups |
| 73 | طِبْتُمْ | *Tibtum* | *pl.* You have done well |
| 74 | نَتَبَوَّأُ | *Natabaw wa'* | We (can) dwell |
| 75 | حَافِّينَ | *Haffin* | *pl.* Surrounding |

# سُورَةُ غَافِر

## [40] SURAT GHAFIR
## THE FORGIVER

| | | | |
|---|---|---|---|
| 3 | غَافِرِ الذَّنْبِ | *Ghafiridh-Dhamb* | One who forgives sin |
| 3 | قَابِلِ التَّوْبِ | *Qabilit-Tawb* | One who accepts repentance |
| 3 | ذِي الطَّوْلِ | *Dhit-Tawl* | One who is all-Bountiful |
| 3 | إِلَيْهِ الْمَصِيرُ | *'Ilayhil-Masir* | To Him is the final goal |
| 4 | تَقَلُّبُهُمْ | *Taqallubuhum* | Their strutting about |
| 7 | قِهِمْ عَذَابَ الْجَحِيمِ | *Qihim 'Adhabal-Jahim* | *im.* Preserve them from the chastisement of the blazing Fire |
| 10 | مَقْتُ اللَّهِ | *Maqtullah* | The aversion of Allah |
| 15 | رَفِيعُ الدَّرَجَاتِ | *Rafi-'ud-darajat* | Owner of High Ranks (Allah) |
| 15 | يُلْقِي الرُّوحَ | *Yulqir-ruh* | Sends the Inspiration |
| 15 | يَوْمَ التَّلَاقِي | *Yaw-mat-Talaq* | The Day of Mutual Meeting |
| 16 | هُمْ بَارِزُونَ | *Hum barizun* | They will (all) come forth |
| 17 | اللَّهَ سَرِيعُ الْحِسَابِ | *Allaha Sari-'ul-Hissab* | Allah is Swift in taking account |
| 18 | يَوْمَ الْآزِفَةِ | *Yawmal-'Aazifa* | The Day that is (ever) drawing near (i.e., the Day of Resurrection) |
| 18 | حَنَاجِرِ | *Hannajir* | Throats |

| V. | WORD | TR. | MEANING |
|---|---|---|---|
| 18 | كَاظِمِينَ | *Kazimin* | *ap.* Those who chokes or restrains |
| 18 | حَمِيمٍ | *Hamim* | Intimate friend |
| 19 | خَائِنَةَ الْأَعْيُنِ | *Kha-'inatal-'a'-yun* | Treachery of the eyes |
| 21 | وَاقٍ | *Waq* | *ap.* Defender, protector |
| 27 | عُذْتُ بِرَبِّي | *'Udhtu bi Rabbi* | I have sought refuge in my Lord |
| 29 | ظَاهِرِينَ | *Zahirin* | *ap.* Those who have the upper hand, those who are the uppermost |
| 31 | دَأْبِ قَوْمِ نُوحٍ | *Da'-bi Qawmi Nuh* | Like the fate of the people of Nuh |
| 32 | يَوْمَ التَّنَادِي | *Yawmat-Tanad* | The Day of mutual calling |
| 33 | عَاصِمٍ | *'Asim* | *ap.* Defender |
| 34 | مُرْتَابٌ | *Murtab* | *ap.* One who is in doubt |
| 35 | كَبُرَ مَقْتًا | *Kabura maqtan* | Very hateful |
| 37 | تَبَابٍ | *Tabab* | Perdition |
| 43 | لَا جَرَمَ | *La jaram* | No doubt |
| 43 | لَيْسَ لَهُ دَعْوَةٌ | *Laysa lahu da'-wa* | He has no claim to be called to |
| 43 | مَرَدَّنَا إِلَى اللَّهِ | *Marad-dana 'ilallah* | Our return will be to Allah |
| 44 | أُفَوِّضُ | *'Ufaw-wid* | I commit |
| 47 | مُغْنُونَ | *Mughnun* | *ap.* Those who suffice or stand in the place of others |
| 52 | مَعْذِرَتُهُمْ | *Ma'-dhiratuhum* | Their excuses |

| V. | WORD | TR. | MEANING |
|---|---|---|---|
| 63 | يُؤْفَكُ | *Yu'-fak* | *pv.* Are deluded |
| 69 | أَنَّى يُصْرَفُونَ | *Anna yusrafun* | How are they turned away (from the Reality)? |
| 72 | يُسْجَرُونَ | *Yusjarun* | *pv.* They are burned |
| 75 | تَفْرَحُونَ | *Tafrahun* | *pl.* You rejoice |
| 80 | حَاجَةً فِي صُدُورِكُمْ | *Hajatan-fi sudurikum* | A need in your hearts (*lit.* A need in your breasts) |

| V. | WORD | TR. | MEANING |
|---|---|---|---|

## سُورَةُ فُصِّلَتْ

## [41] SURAT FUSSILAT

### THEY ARE EXPLAINED IN DETAIL

| | | | |
|---|---|---|---|
| 3 | كِتَابٌ فُصِّلَتْ آيَاتُهُ | *Kitabun-fussilat 'Ayatuh* | A Book whereof the verses are explained in detail |
| 6 | فَاسْتَقِيمُوا إِلَيْهِ | *Fastaqi-mu 'ilayh* | *im.pl.* So take the straight path unto Him |
| 8 | غَيْرُ مَمْنُونٍ | *Ghayru mamnun* | Uninterrupted |
| 10 | بَارَكَ فِيهَا | *Baraka fiha* | Bestowed blessings on it |
| 10 | أَقْوَاتَهَا | *'Aqwataha* | Its sustenance |
| 10 | سَوَاءً | *Sawa'* | Equal |
| 11 | دُخَانٌ | *Dukhan* | Smoke |
| 11 | ائْتِيَا | *'Atayna* | *im.* Come both of you |
| 12 | فَقَضَاهُنَّ | *Faqadahunn* | So He completed them |
| 12 | حِفْظًا | *Hifza* | As a guard |
| 13 | أَنْذَرْتُكُمْ صَاعِقَةً | *'Andhartukum Sa-'iqata* | I have warned you of a thunderbolt |
| 16 | رِيحًا صَرْصَرًا | *Rihan sarsaran* | Furious wind |
| 16 | أَيَّامٍ نَحِسَاتٍ | *'Ayyamin-nahisat* | Days of evil omen / disaster |
| 17 | الْعَذَابِ الْهُونِ | *Al-'adhabil-hun* | The chastisement of humiliation |
| 19 | يُوزَعُونَ | *Yuza-'un* | (They will be) marched in ranks |
| 22 | تَسْتَتِرُونَ | *Tastati-run* | *pl.* You seek to hide yourselves |

| V. | WORD | TR. | MEANING |
|---|---|---|---|
| 22 | ظَنَنْتُمْ | *Zanantum* | *pl.* You thought |
| 23 | أَرْدَاكُمْ | *'Ardakum* | Brought you (all) to destruction |
| 24 | يَسْتَعْتِبُوا | *Yastạ'-tibu* | They beg for pardon |
| 24 | مُعْتَبِينَ | *Mu'-tabin* | Those who are pardoned |
| 25 | قَيَّضْنَا لَهُمْ | *Qay-yadhna lahum* | We have destined for them |
| 26 | الْغَوْا | *Alghaw* | *im. pl.* Talk at random, use vain words |
| 29 | أَسْفَلِينَ | *'Asfalin* | Those who are the vilest / lowest |
| 35 | مَا يُلَقَّاهَا | *Ma yulaqqaha* | None is granted it |
| 36 | نَزْغٌ | *Nazgh* | Evil suggestion, incitement to evil |
| 38 | لَا يَسْأَمُونَ | *La yas-'amun* | They do not get tired /weary |
| 39 | تَرَى الْأَرْضَ خَاشِعَةً | *Taral-'arda khashi-'a* | You see the earth barren |
| 39 | اهْتَزَّتْ | *'Ih-tazzat* | To be stirred to life |
| 39 | رَبَتْ | *Rabat* | To grow, swell, increase |
| 40 | يُلْحِدُونَ | *Yulhidun* | They pervert the Truth |
| 44 | أَعْجَمِيًّا | *'A'-jamiyya* | Foreign (language) |
| 44 | هُوَ عَلَيْهِمْ عَمًى | *Huwa 'alayhim 'ama* | It (the Holly Qur'an) is blindness for them |
| 47 | أَكْمَامِ | *'Akmam* | Sheaths |
| 47 | آذَنَّا | *'Adhanna* | We assured / inform |

| V. | WORD | TR. | MEANING |
|---|---|---|---|
| 48 | مَحِيص | *Mahis* | Way of escape |
| 49 | دُعَاءِ الْخَيْرِ | *Du-'a-'ilkhayr* | Asking for good (things) |
| 49 | يَئُوسٌ | *Ya-'us* | Hopeless, desperate |
| 49 | قَنُوطٌ | *Qanut* | Despair |
| 50 | هَذَا لِي | *Hadha li* | This is due to my (merit) |
| 51 | نَأى بِجَانِبِهِ | *Na-'a bi-janibih* | (He) got himself remote on his side (instead of coming to Allah) |
| 51 | دُعَاءٍ عَرِيضٍ | *Du-'a-'in 'arid* | Prolonged prayer |
| 53 | آفَاقِ | *'Afaq* | Furthest regions |

# سُورَةُ الشُّورَى

## [42] SURAT ASH-SHURA

## THE CONSULTATION

| V. | WORD | TR. | MEANING |
|---|---|---|---|
| 5 | يَتَفَطَّرْنَ | *Yata-fattarn* | They rent asunder |
| 7 | يَوْمَ الْجَمْعِ | *Yawmal-Jam'* | The Day of assembly |
| 11 | يَذْرَؤُكُمْ | *Yadhra-'ukum* | Multiples you |
| 13 | شَرَعَ | *Shara'* | Established, ordained |
| 13 | أَقِيمُوا الدِّينَ | *'Aqimud-Din* | *Im. pl.* Remain steadfast in religion |
| 13 | كَبُرَ | *Kabur* | Hard, grievous |
| 15 | اسْتَقِمْ | *Astaqim* | *Im.* Stand steadfast |
| 15 | لَا حُجَّةَ | *La hujja* | No contention |
| 16 | حُجَّتُهُمْ دَاحِضَةٌ | *Hujjatuhum dahida* | Their argument is futile |
| 17 | مِيزَانَ | *Mizan* | Balance |
| 18 | مُشْفِقُونَ مِنْهَا | *Mushfiquna minha* | They are fearful of it |
| 18 | يُمَارُونَ فِي السَّاعَةِ | *Yumaruna fis-Sa-'a* | They dispute concerning the Hour |
| 19 | اللهُ لَطِيفٌ بِعِبَادِهِ | *Allahu Latifum-bi-'ibadih* | Allah is very Gracious and Kind to His servants |
| 20 | حَرْثَ الْآخِرَةِ | *Harthal-'Akhira* | The tilth of the Hereafter |
| 21 | كَلِمَةُ الْفَصْلِ | *Kalimatul-Fasl* | Decree (or Word) of Judgement |
| 22 | رَوْضَاتِ الْجَنَّاتِ | *Rawdatil-Jannat* | The Meadows of the Gardens |

| V. | WORD | TR. | MEANING |
|---|---|---|---|
| 23 | يَقْتَرِفْ حَسَنَةً | *Yaqtarif hasanata* | Earns a good righteous deed |
| 32 | جَوَارِ | *Jawar* | Ships |
| 32 | كَالْأَعْلَامِ | *Kal-'a'-lam* | Like mountains |
| 33 | يَظْلَلْنَ رَوَاكِدَ | *Yazlalna rawakid* | They become motionless |
| 34 | يُوبِقْهُنَّ | *Yubiq-hunn* | Causes them to perish, destroys them |
| 38 | أَمْرُهُمْ شُورَى | *'Amruhum Shura* | Their affairs by mutual consultation |
| 39 | بَغْيُ | *Baghy* | Oppressive wrong |
| 45 | يَنْظُرُونَ مِنْ طَرْفٍ خَفِيٍّ | *Yanzuruna min-tarfin khafiyy* | (They are) looking with a stealthy glance |
| 47 | نَكِيرِ | *Nakir* | Denial |
| 52 | إِيمَانُ | *'Iman* | Faith |

| V. | WORD | TR. | MEANING |
|---|---|---|---|

# سُورَةُ الزُّخْرُف

## [43] SURAT AZ-ZUKHRUF
## THE GOLD ADORNMENTS

| | | | |
|---|---|---|---|
| 5 | أَفَنَضْرِبُ عَنكُمُ الذِّكْرَ صَفْحًا | *'Afanadribu 'ankumudh-dhikra safha* | Shall We then (warn you not and) take away the Reminder (the Holy Qûr'an) from you altogether |
| 5 | أَن كُنتُمْ قَوْمًا مُسْرِفِينَ | *'An-kuntum qawmam musrifin* | For that you are a people transgressing beyond bounds |
| 8 | بَطْشًا | *Batsha* | Power |
| 11 | أَنشَرْنَا | *'Ansharna* | We rose to life |
| 13 | لِتَسْتَوُوا عَلَى ظُهُورِهِ | *Litasta-wu 'ala zuhurih* | *pl.* In order that you may sit firm and square on their backs |
| 13 | سَخَّرَ | *Sakhkhar* | Subjected |
| 13 | مُقْرِنِينَ | *Muqrinin* | Those who are able to do a thing |
| 17 | مَثَلًا | *Mathala* | Likeness |
| 18 | يُنَشَّأُ فِي الْحِلْيَةِ | *Yunashsha-'u fil-hilya* | (One who) is brought up among trinkets (i.e.,women) |
| 18 | فِي الْخِصَامِ | *Fil-khisam* | In dispute |
| 20 | يَخْرُصُونَ | *Yakhrusun* | They lie |
| 26 | إِنَّنِي بَرَاءٌ | *'Innani bara'* | I am innocent |
| 28 | كَلِمَةً بَاقِيَةً فِي عَقِبِهِ | *Kalimatam-* | A word lasting |

| V. | WORD | TR. | MEANING |
|---|---|---|---|
| | | *baqiyatan-fi 'aqibih* | among his offspring |
| 31 | الْقَرْيَتَيْنِ | *Al-Qaryatayn* | The two cities (Makka and Ta'if) |
| 33 | مَعَارِجَ | *Ma-'arij* | (Silver) stair-ways |
| 33 | يَظْهَرُونَ | *Yazharun* | They go up |
| 35 | زُخْرُفًا | *Zukhrufa.* | Adornmens of gold |
| 35 | مَتَاعُ | *Mata'* | Enjoyment |
| 36 | مَنْ يَعْشُ | *Many-ya'-sh* | Whosoever withdraws (himself) |
| 36 | قَرِينٌ | *Qarin* | Intimate companion |
| 44 | إِنَّهُ لَذِكْرٌ | *'Innahu la-Dhikr* | This (the Holy Qûr'an) is indeed a Reminder |
| 50 | يَنكُثُونَ | *Yankuthun* | They break their covenant |
| 52 | مَهِينٌ | *Mahin* | Contemptible |
| 53 | مُقْتَرِنِينَ | *Muqtarinin* | Those in procession |
| 54 | اسْتَخَفَّ | *Istakhaff* | Made fool |
| 55 | آسَفُونَا | *'Asafuna* | They provoked Us / angered Us |
| 56 | سَلَفً | *Salaf* | Precedent |
| 57 | يَصِدُّونَ | *Yasiddun* | They raise a clamour / cry aloud |
| 58 | قَوْمٌ خَصِمُونَ | *Qawmun khasimun* | Contentious people |
| 61 | إِنَّهُ لَعِلْمٌ لِلسَّاعَةِ | *'Innahu la-'ilmul-lis-Sa-'a* | He ('Isa عليه السلام) shall be a Sign for (the coming of) the |

| V. | WORD | TR. | MEANING |
|---|---|---|---|
| | | | Hour (of Judgement) |
| 61 | لَا تَمْتَرُنَّ بِهَا | *La tamtarunna biha* | *ni.* Have no doubt about it |
| 67 | أَخِلَّاءُ | *'Akhilla'* | Friends |
| 71 | أَكْوَاب | *'Akwab* | Goblets, cups |
| 75 | لَا يُفَتَّرُ عَنْهُمْ | *La yufattaru 'anhum* | (The punishment) will not be lightened for them |
| 77 | لِيَقْضِ عَلَيْنَا رَبُّكَ | *Liyaqdi 'alayna Rabbuk* | *im.* Let your Lord make an end of us |
| 79 | أَبْرَمُوا أَمْرًا | *'Abramu 'amra* | They settled some plan |
| 83 | يَخُوضُوا | *Yakhudu* | They babble / speak nonsense |
| 88 | وَقِيلِهِ | *Wa qilih* | (Allah has knowledge) of the (Prophet's) ṣaying |
| 89 | فَاصْفَحْ عَنْهُمْ | *Fasfah 'anhum* | *im.* So turn away from them |

| V. | WORD | TR. | MEANING |
|---|---|---|---|

## سُورَةُ الدُّخَان

## [44] SURAT AD-DUKHAN

## THE SMOKE (OR MIST)

| | | | |
|---|---|---|---|
| 3 | لَيْلَةٍ مُبَارَكَةٍ | *Laylatim-mubaraka* | Blessed night (i.e., the Night of Al-Qadr) |
| 4 | يُفْرَق | *Yufraq* | *pv.* Is made distinct |
| 4 | أَمْرٍ حَكِيمٍ | *'Amrin hakim* | Affair of wisdom |
| 10 | دُخَان | *Dukhan* | Smoke |
| 11 | يَغْشَى | *Yaghsha* | Covers, envelops |
| 14 | مُعَلَّمٌ | *Mu-'allam* | *pp.* Taught, instructed, tutored |
| 16 | يَوْمَ نَبْطِشُ | *Yawma nabtish* | On the Day when We shall seize |
| 18 | أَدُّوا إِلَيَّ عِبَادَ اللَّهِ | *'Addu 'ilayya 'iba-dallah* | *im. pl.* Restore to me the servants of Allah |
| 19 | لَا تَعْلُوا | *La ta'-lu* | *ni. pl.* Be not arrogent |
| 20 | تَرْجُمُونِ | *Tarjumun* | *pl.* You stone me |
| 23 | فَأَسْرِ بِعِبَادِي لَيْلًا | *Fa-'asri bi-'ibadi layla* | *im.* Martch forth with My servants by night |
| 23 | إِنَّكُمْ مُتَّبَعُونَ | *'Innakum-muttaba-'un* | *pl.* You will be pursued |
| 24 | رَهْوًا | *Rahwa* | Quiet |
| 27 | فَاكِهِينَ | *Fakihin* | Those who are very joyful / rejoice greatly |
| 31 | عَالِيًا | *'aliya* | Arrogant |

| V. | WORD | TR. | MEANING |
|---|---|---|---|
| 35 | مُنشَرِينَ | *Mun-sharin* | *pp.* Those who shall be resurrected |
| 37 | قَوْمُ تُبَّعٍ | *Qawmu Tubba'* | The people of Tubba' Tubba' is a title or family name of Himyuar kings in Yaman, of the tribe of Hamdan |
| 41 | مَوْلًى | *Mawla* | Friend, protector |
| 45 | مُهْلِ | *Muhl* | Molten brass, boiling oil |
| 46 | حَمِيمِ | *Hamim* | Boiling of scalding water |
| 47 | اعْتِلُوهُ | *A'-tiluh* | *im. pl.* Drag him |
| 47 | سَوَاءِ الْجَحِيمِ | *Sawa-'il-Jahim* | The midst of the Blazing Fire |
| 53 | سُندُسٍ | *Sundus* | Fine silk |
| 53 | إِسْتَبْرَقٍ | *'Istabraq* | Thick silk |
| 54 | حُورٍ عِينٍ | *Hurin 'in* | Maidens with beautiful, big and lustrous eyes |

## سُورَةُ الجَاثِيَة

## [45] SURAT AJ-JATHIYA

### BOWING THE KNEE

| | | | |
|---|---|---|---|
| 5 | تَصْرِيفِ الرِّيَاحِ | *Tasrifir-riyah* | Change of winds |
| 8 | يُصِرُّ | *Yusirr* | Persists obstinately |
| 14 | لَا يَرْجُونَ أَيَّامَ اللَّهِ | *La yarjuna 'Ayyamallah* | They do not hope for the Days of Allah |
| 17 | بَغْيًا بَيْنَهُمْ | *Baghyam-baynahum* | Insolent envy among themselves |
| 20 | بَصَائِرُ لِلنَّاسِ | *Basa-'iru linnas* | Clear evidences to men |
| 21 | اجْتَرَحُوا السَّيِّئَاتِ | *Ijtarahus-sayyi-'at* | They earn evil deeds / do evil deeds |
| 28 | جَاثِيَةً | *Jathiyah* | Bowing the knee |
| 29 | نَسْتَنسِخُ | *Nas-tansikh* | We put on record |
| 32 | مُسْتَيْقِنِينَ | *Mus-tayqinin* | *ap.* Those who are firmly assured |
| 34 | نَنسَاكُمْ | *Nansa-kum* | We (will) forget you |
| 34 | مَأْوَاكُمُ النَّارُ | *Ma-'wakumun-Nar* | *pl.* Your abode is the Fire |

| V. | WORD | TR. | MEANING |
|---|---|---|---|

## سُورَةُ الأَحْقَافِ

## [46] SURAT AL-AHQAF
## THE WINDING SAND-TRACTS

| | | | |
|---|---|---|---|
| 4 | لَهُمْ شِرْكٌ | *Lahum shirk* | They have a share |
| 4 | أَثَارَةٍ مِنْ عِلْمٍ | *'Athara-tim-min 'ilm* | (Any) remnant of knowledge |
| 8 | تُفِيضُونَ | *Tufidun* | *pl.* You talk (so glibily) |
| 9 | بِدْعًا | *Bid-'a* | Innovation, new |
| 12 | مُحْسِنِينَ | *Muhsinin* | *ap.* Those who do well / act righteously |
| 15 | رَبِّ أَوْزِعْنِي | *Rabbi 'awzi'-ni* | *im.* O my Lord! Grant me (the power and ability) |
| 17 | أُفٍّ لَكُمَا | *'Uffil-lakuma* | Fie on you both |
| 18 | حَقَّ عَلَيْهِمُ الْقَوْلُ | *Haqqa 'alayhimul-Qawl* | The word (of torment) proved true against them |
| 21 | أَخَا عَادٍ | *'Akha 'Ad* | The brother of 'Ad (i.e., Hud عليه السلام) |
| 21 | أَحْقَافِ | *'Ahqaf* | Winding sand-tracts |
| 22 | لِتَأْفِكَنَا | *Lita'-fikana* | In order to turn us aside |
| 24 | عَارِضًا | *'Arida* | A Cloud traversing the sky |
| 24 | مُسْتَقْبِلَ | *Mustaqbil* | Proceeding towards |
| 27 | صَرَّفْنَا الْآيَاتِ | *Sar-rafnal-'Ayat* | We have (repeatedly) shown (them) the Signs in various ways |

| V. | WORD | TR. | MEANING |
|---|---|---|---|
| 28 | قُرْبَانًا | *Qurbana* | Means of access (to Allah) |
| 29 | صَرَفْنَا إِلَيْكَ | *Sarafna 'ilayk* | We turned towards you |
| 29 | أَنْصِتُوا | *'Ansitu* | *im. pl.* Listen in silence |
| 33 | لَمْ يَعْيَ بِخَلْقِهِنَّ | *Lam ya'-ya bi-khalqihinn* | He never wearied with their creation |
| 33 | بَلَى | *Bala* | Yea, yes |
| 35 | أُولُوا الْعَزْمِ | *'Ulul-'azm* | Those gifted with firm resolution |

| V. | WORD | TR. | MEANING |
|---|---|---|---|

## سُورَةُ مُحَمَّدٍ

## [47] SURAT MUHAMMAD

MUHAMMAD

| | | | |
|---|---|---|---|
| 1 | أَضَلَّ أَعْمَالَهُمْ | *'Adalla 'a'-malahum* | He has made their deeds to be of none effect |
| 2 | كَفَّرَ عَنْهُمْ | *Kaffara 'anhum* | He has removed from them (their ills) |
| 2 | أَصْلَحَ بَالَهُمْ | *'Aslaha balahum* | He has improved their condition |
| 4 | ضَرْبَ الرِّقَابِ | *Darbar-riqab* | Smite at necks |
| 4 | أَثْخَنْتُمُوهُمْ | *'Athkhan-tumuhum* | *pl.* You thoroughly subdued them |
| 4 | شُدُّوا الْوَثَاقَ | *Shuddul-wathaq* | *im. pl.* Bind a bond firmly (on them) (i.e., take them as captives) |
| 4 | مَنًّا | *Manna* | Generosity |
| 4 | فِدَاءً | *Fida'* | Ransom |
| 4 | حَتَّى تَضَعَ الْحَرْبُ أَوْزَارَهَا | *Hatta tada-'al-harbu 'awzaraha* | Until the war lays down its burdens |
| 4 | فَلَنْ يُضِلَّ أَعْمَالَهُمْ | *Falany-yudilla 'a'-malahum* | He will never let their deeds be lost |
| 5 | بَالَهُمْ | *Balahum* | Their condition |
| 6 | عَرَّفَهَا لَهُمْ | *'Arrafaha lahum* | He has made known to them |
| 8 | تَعْسًا | *Ta'-sa* | Destruction |
| 10 | دَمَّرَ اللَّهُ عَلَيْهِمْ | *Dammarallahu 'alayhim* | Allah brought utter destruction on them |
| 13 | كَأَيِّنْ مِنْ قَرْيَةٍ | *Ka-'ayyim-min-* | How many cities |

| V. | WORD | TR. | MEANING |
|---|---|---|---|
| | | *qarya* | |
| 15 | مَثَلُ الْجَنَّةِ | *Mathalul-Janna* | The description of Paradise |
| 15 | غَيْرِ آسِنٍ | *Ghayri 'asin* | Incorruptible |
| 15 | عَسَلٍ مُصَفًّى | *'Asalim-musaffa* | Clarified honey (clear and pure) |
| 16 | مَاذَا قَالَ آنِفًا | *Ma-dha qala 'anifa* | What has he said just now? |
| 17 | تَقْوَاهُمْ | *Taqwahum* | Their piety |
| 18 | أَشْرَاطُهَا | *'Ashra-tuha* | Its tokens / portents |
| 18 | ذِكْرَاهُمْ | *Dhikrahum* | Their Reminder |
| 19 | يَعْلَمُ مُتَقَلَّبَكُمْ | *Ya'-lamu mutaqallabakum* | (Allah) knows your moving about |
| 20 | مَغْشِيِّ عَلَيْهِ | *Magh-shiyyi 'alayh* | One in swoon |
| 20 | أَوْلَى لَهُمْ | *'Awla lahum* | More fitting for them, woe unto them |
| 21 | طَاعَةٌ | *Ta-'a* | Obedience |
| 21 | عَزَمَ الْأَمْرُ | *'Azamal-'amr* | The matter (preparation for Jihad) is resolved on |
| 22 | هَلْ عَسَيْتُمْ | *Hal 'asay-tum* | Is it to be expected of you? |
| 22 | تَوَلَّيْتُمْ | *Tawal-lay-tum* | *pl.* You are put in authority |
| 24 | أَقْفَال | *'Aqfal* | Locks |
| 25 | سَوَّلَ لَهُمْ | *Sawwala lahum* | Instigated them, beautified for them |
| 25 | أَمْلَى لَهُمْ | *'Amla lahum* | Buoyed them up with false hopes |

| V. | WORD | TR. | MEANING |
|---|---|---|---|
| 26 | يَعْلَمُ إِسْرَارَهُمْ | *Ya'-lamu 'israrahum* | Knows their (inner) secrets |
| 29 | أَضْغَانَهُمْ | *'Adghanahum* | Their rancours |
| 30 | بِسِيمَاهُمْ | *Bisimahum* | By their marks |
| 30 | لَحْنِ الْقَوْلِ | *Lahnil-qawl* | The tone of (their) speech |
| 31 | نَبْلُوَ أَخْبَارَكُمْ | *Nabluwa 'akhbarakum* | We shall test your news |
| 35 | لَا تَهِنُوا | *La tahinu* | *ni. pl.* Do not be weary |
| 35 | وَلَن يَتِرَكُمْ أَعْمَالَكُمْ | *Wa lany-yatirakum 'a'-mala-kum* | And He will never decrease the reawards of your (good) deeds |
| 37 | يُحْفِكُمْ | *Yuhfikum* | Presses you |

| V. | WORD | TR. | MEANING |
|---|---|---|---|

# سُورَةُ الفَتْح

## [48] SURAT AL-FATH

## THE VICTORY

| | | | |
|---|---|---|---|
| 1 | فَتْحًا مُبِينًا | *Fat-ham-Mubina* | Manifest victory |
| 4 | سَكِينَةَ | *Sakina* | Tranquillity |
| 6 | ظَنَّ السَّوْءِ | *Zannas-saw'* | Evil thought |
| 6 | عَلَيْهِمْ دَائِرَةُ السَّوْءِ | *'Alay-him da-'iratus-saw'* | On them is a round of evil [i.e., they will be encircled (or hemmed in) by evil] |
| 9 | تُعَزِّرُوهُ | *Tu-'azziruh* | *pl.* You (may) assist him |
| 9 | تُوَقِّرُوهُ | *Tuwaqqiruh* | *pl.* You honour him |
| 9 | تُسَبِّحُوهُ | *Tusabbihuh* | *pl.* You celebrate His praises |
| 10 | نَكَثَ | *Nakath* | Violated his oath |
| 11 | مُخَلَّفُونَ | *Mukhalla-fun* | Those who lagged behind |
| 12 | يَنْقَلِبَ | *Yanqalib* | Returns |
| 15 | ذَرُونَا نَتَّبِعْكُمْ | *Dharuna nattabi'-kum* | *im.pl.* Permit us to follow you |
| 18 | يُبَايِعُونَكَ | *Yuba-yi-'unak* | They swear fealty to you |
| 18 | فَتْحًا قَرِيبًا | *Fat-han-qariba* | Speedy victory |
| 21 | أَحَاطَ اللَّهُ بِهَا | *'Ahatallahu biha* | Allah has compassed them |
| 24 | بِبَطْنِ مَكَّةَ | *Bi-batni Makka* | In the mids of Makka |
| 24 | أَظْفَرَكُمْ عَلَيْهِمْ | *'Azfarakum 'alay-him* | He gave you the victory over them |

| V. | WORD | TR. | MEANING |
|---|---|---|---|
| 25 | الْهَدْيَ | *Al-hady* | Animals for sacrifice |
| 25 | مَعْكُوفًا | *Ma'-kufa* | Detained |
| 25 | تَطَئُوهُمْ | *Tata-'uhum* | *pl.* You tread them, you trample on them |
| 25 | مَعَرَّةٌ | *Ma'-arra* | Guilt |
| 25 | تَزَيَّلُوا | *Tazayyalu* | They separated / became apart |
| 26 | حَمِيَّةَ | *Hamiyya* | Heat and cant, pride and haughtiness |
| 26 | كَلِمَةَ التَّقْوٰى | *Kali-matat-taqwa* | The word of piety (i.e., none has the right to be worshipped but Allah) |
| 29 | شَطْأَهُ | *Shat-'ah* | Its blade / shoot |
| 29 | آزَرَهُ | *'Azarah* | Made it strong |
| 29 | اسْتَغْلَظَ | *Istaghlaz* | Became thick |
| 29 | اسْتَوٰى عَلٰى سُوقِهِ | *Istawa 'ala suqih* | Stood on its own stem |

| V. | WORD | TR. | MEANING |
|---|---|---|---|

## سُورَةُ الحُجُرات

## [49] SURAT AL-HUJURAT

## THE INNER APARTMENTS

| | | | |
|---|---|---|---|
| 1 | لَا تُقَدِّمُوا | *La tuqaddimu* | *ni. pl.* Do not put yourselves forward, do not obtrude your opinions |
| 2 | أَن تَحْبَطَ أَعْمَالُكُمْ | *'An tahbata 'a'-malukum* | Lest your deeds become vain |
| 3 | يَغُضُّونَ أَصْوَاتَهُمْ | *Yaghudduna 'aswatahum* | They lower their voices |
| 3 | امْتَحَنَ اللَّهُ قُلُوبَهُمْ | *Im-taha-nallahu qulubahum* | Allah has tested their hearts |
| 4 | حُجُرَات | *Hujurat* | inner apartments |
| 6 | تَبَيَّنُوا | *Tabayyanu* | *im.pl.* Ascertain the truth |
| 6 | جَهَالَةٍ | *Jaha-la* | Ignorance |
| 7 | لَعَنِتُّمْ | *La-'anittum* | *pl.* You would certainly be guilty of a crime, you would certainly suffer |
| 9 | تَفِيءَ إِلَى أَمْرِ اللهِ | *Tafi-'a 'ila 'amrillah* | Complies with the command of Allah |
| 9 | أَقْسِطُوا | *'Aqsitu* | *im. pl.* Be fair |
| 9 | مُقْسِطِينَ | *Muqsi-tin* | Those who are fair (and just) |
| 11 | لَا تَلْمِزُوا أَنفُسَكُمْ | *La talmizu 'anfusakum* | *ni. pl.* Do not defame one another |
| 11 | لَا تَنَابَزُوا بِالْأَلْقَابِ | *La tanabazu bil-'alqab* | *ni. pl.* Do not call one another by (offensive) names |

| V. | WORD | TR. | MEANING |
|---|---|---|---|
| 12 | كَثِيرًا مِنَ الظَّنِّ | *Kathiram-minaz-zan* | Much suspicions |
| 12 | لَا تَجَسَّسُوا | *La tajassasu* | *ni. pl.* Do not spy |
| 14 | آمَنَّا | *'Aman-na* | We believe |
| 14 | أَسْلَمْنَا | *'Aslamna* | We have submitted our wills to Allah |
| 14 | لَا يَلِتْ | *La yalit-kum* | Will not belittle /decrease |
| 16 | أَتُعَلِّمُونَ اللَّهَ بِدِينِكُمْ | *'Atu-'allimurallah bi-dinikum* | Will you tell Allah about your religion? |

| V. | WORD | TR. | MEANING |
|---|---|---|---|

# سُورَةُ قٓ

## [50] SURAT QAF

### QAF

| V. | WORD | TR. | MEANING |
|---|---|---|---|
| 3 | رَجْعٌ بَعِيدٌ | *Raj-'um-ba-'id* | Far return |
| 5 | أَمْرٍ مَرِيجٍ | *'Amrim-marij* | Confused state |
| 6 | فُرُوجٍ | *Furuj* | Flaws, rifts |
| 9 | حَبَّ الْحَصِيدِ | *Habbal-hasid* | Grain for harvests |
| 10 | بَاسِقَاتٍ | *Basiqat* | Tall |
| 10 | طَلْعٌ | *Tal'* | Shoots of fruit-stalks |
| 10 | نَضِيدٌ | *Nadid* | Piled one over another |
| 11 | خُرُوجُ | *Khuruj* | Resurrection |
| 12 | أَصْحَابُ الرَّسِّ | *'As-habur-Rass* | The Companions of the Rass ("rass" is an old well or shallow water-pit) |
| 15 | أَفَعَيِينَا بِالْخَلْقِ الْأَوَّلِ | *'Afa-'a-yina bil-khalqil-'awwal* | Were We then weary with the first creation? |
| 15 | فِي لَبْسٍ | *Fi labs* | In confused doubt |
| 16 | حَبْلِ الْوَرِيدِ | *Hablil-warid* | Jugular vein |
| 17 | إِذْ يَتَلَقَّى الْمُتَلَقِّيَانِ | *'Idh yatalaqqal-mutalaq-qiyan* | *lit.* When the two learners learn (i.e., when the two guardian angels note down a man's doings) |
| 17 | قَعِيدٌ | *Qa-'id* | Sitting |
| 18 | رَقِيبٌ | *Raqib* | Watcher |

| V. | WORD | TR. | MEANING |
|---|---|---|---|
| 18 | عَتِيدٌ | *'Atid* | Ready |
| 19 | سَكْرَةُ الْمَوْتِ | *Sakratul-mawt* | Stupor of death |
| 19 | تَحِيدُ | *Tahid* | You escape / avert |
| 22 | حَدِيدٌ | *Hadid* | Sharp |
| 24 | عَنِيدٍ | *'Anid* | Contumacious |
| 27 | مَا أَطْغَيْتُهُ | *Ma 'atghaytuh* | I did not make him transgress |
| 36 | نَقَّبُوا | *Naqqabu* | They wandered through the land |
| 38 | لُغُوبٍ | *Lughub* | Weariness |
| 40 | أَدْبَارَ السُّجُودِ | *'Adbaras-sujud* | After the prostration (i.e., after prayers) |
| 44 | سِرَاعًا | *Sira-'a* | Hastily |

| V. | WORD | TR. | MEANING |
|---|---|---|---|

# سُورَةُ الذَّارِيَات

## [51] SURAT AZ-ZARIYAT
## THE WINDS THAT SCATTER

| | | | |
|---|---|---|---|
| 1 | وَالذَّارِيَاتِ ذَرْوًا | *Wadh-dhariyati dharwa* | By (the winds) that scatter broadcast |
| 2 | فَالْحَامِلَاتِ وِقْرًا | *Fal-hamilati wiqra* | And those (clouds) that lift and bear away heavy weightts |
| 3 | فَالْجَارِيَاتِ يُسْرًا | *Fal-jariyati yusra* | And those (ships) that flow with ease and gentleness |
| 4 | فَالْمُقَسِّمَاتِ أَمْرًا | *Fal-muqassimati 'Amra* | And those (angels) who distribute (provisions, rain, and other blessings) by (Allah's) Command |
| 5 | إِنَّمَا تُوعَدُونَ | *'Innama tu-'adun* | Verily that which you are promised |
| 6 | دِينَ | *Din* | Recompense |
| 7 | حُبُكِ | *Hubuk* | Paths (of stars) |
| 8 | قَوْلٍ مُخْتَلِفٍ | *Qawlim-mukhtalif* | Different saying (i.e., different ideas) |
| 10 | قُتِلَ الْخَرَّاصُونَ | *Qutilal-kharrasun* | Cursed be the conjecturers / liars |
| 11 | غَمْرَةٍ | *Ghamra* | Flood of confusion |
| 11 | سَاهُونَ | *Sahun* | Those who are heedless |
| 12 | أَيَّانَ يَوْمُ الدِّينِ | *'Ayyana Yawmud-Din* | When will be the Day of |

| V. | WORD | TR. | MEANING |
|---|---|---|---|
| | | | Recompense? |
| 17 | يَهْجَعُونَ | *Yahja-'un* | They sleep |
| 19 | مَحْرُومِ | *Mah-rum* | *pp.* Deprived |
| 25 | قَوْمٌ مُنْكَرُونَ | *Qawmum-munkarun* | Unknown people |
| 28 | أَوْجَسَ | *'Awjasa* | Conceived |
| 29 | صَرَّةٍ | *Sarra* | Clamour, loud cry |
| 29 | صَكَّتْ وَجْهَهَا | *Sakkat wajhaha* | She smote her face |
| 39 | تَوَلَّى بِرُكْنِهِ | *Tawalla bi-ruknih* | (Pharaoh) turned back on account of his might |
| 41 | الرِّيحَ الْعَقِيمَ | *Ar-Rihal-'aqim* | The devastating wind |
| 42 | رَمِيمِ | *Ramim* | Rotten ruins |
| 44 | عَتَوْا | *'Ataw'a* | They insolently defied |
| 47 | إِنَّا لَمُوسِعُونَ | *'Inna la-musi-'un* | Verily, We have vast power |
| 48 | فَنِعْمَ الْمَاهِدُونَ | *Fa-ni'-mal-mahidun* | How excellent Spreader are We |
| 50 | فَفِرُّوا إِلَى اللَّهِ | *Fa-firru 'ilallah* | Therefore flee unto Allah |
| 59 | ذَنُوبًا | *Dhanuba* | Portion, lot |

# سُورَةُ الطُّور

## [52] SURAT AT-TUR

### THE MOUNT

| V. | WORD | TR. | MEANING |
|---|---|---|---|
| 1 | وَالطُّورِ | *Wat-Tur* | By the Mount (Sinai) |
| 2 | وَكِتَابٍ مَسْطُورٍ | *Wa Kitabim-mastur* | And by a Book Inscribed |
| 3 | رَقٍّ | *Raqq* | Parchment |
| 3 | مَنْشُورٍ | *Manshur* | *pp.* Unfolded, unrolled |
| 4 | وَالْبَيْتِ الْمَعْمُورِ | *Wal-Baytil-ma'-mur* | And by the much-frequented House |
| 5 | وَالسَّقْفِ الْمَرْفُوعِ | *Was-Saqfil-marfu'* | And by the Conopy Raised High |
| 6 | وَالْبَحْرِ الْمَسْجُورِ | *Wal-Bahril-masjur* | And by the Ocean filled with swell |
| 7 | لَوَاقِعٌ | *La-waqi'* | Will indeed come to pass |
| 8 | دَافِعٍ | *Dafi'* | *ap.* One who averts |
| 9 | تَمُورُ السَّمَاءُ | *Tamurus-sama'* | The heaven will agitate |
| 9 | مَوْرًا | *Mawra* | Dreadful agitation / commotion |
| 10 | وَ تَسِيرُ الْجِبَالُ | *Wa tasirul-jibal* | And the mountains will move away |
| 10 | سَيْرًا | *Sayra* | (Horrible) movement |
| 11 | يَوْمَئِذٍ | *Yawma-'idh* | On that day |
| 12 | خَوْضٍ | *Khawdh* | Shallow trifles |
| 13 | يُدَعُّونَ | *Yuda'-un* | They are pushed down / thrust down |
| 20 | سُرُرٍ | *Surur* | Couches |

| V. | WORD | TR. | MEANING |
|---|---|---|---|
| 20 | مَصْفُوفَةٍ | *Masfufah* | *pp.fg.* Arranged in ranks |
| 21 | مَا أَلَتْنَاهُمْ من عَمَلِهِم | *Ma 'alat-nahum-min 'amalihim* | We shall not decrease the reward of their deeds |
| 21 | رَهِينٌ | *Rahin* | Given in pledge |
| 23 | يَتَنَازَعُونَ | *Yatanaza-'un* | They exchange |
| 23 | كَأْسًا | *Ka'-sa* | Cup |
| 23 | لَا لَغْوٌ فِيهَا وَلَا تَأْثِيمٌ | *La lagh-wun-fiha wa la ta'-thim* | (A cup) free of frivolity, and free of sin |
| 24 | لُؤْلُؤٌ | *Lu'-lu'* | Pearls |
| 24 | مَكْنُونٌ | *Maknun* | Well-guarded |
| 26 | مُشْفِقِينَ | *Mushfiqin* | Those who are afraid |
| 27 | عَذَابَ السَّمُومِ | *'Adhabas-samum* | The Chastisement of the scorching wind |
| 28 | هُوَ الْبَرُّ الرَّحِيمُ | *Huwal-Barrur-Rahim* | He is the Beneficent, the Merciful |
| 30 | رَيْبَ الْمَنُونِ | *Raybal-manun* | Calamity (hatched) by time, adverse fortune |
| 33 | تقول | *Taqaw-wal* | Fabricated, forged |
| 37 | خَزَائِنُ رَبِّكَ | *Khaza-'inu Rabbik* | The treasures of your Lord |
| 37 | مُسَيْطِرُونَ | *Musay-ti-run* | Those who preside over, managers of affairs |
| 38 | سُلَّمٌ | *Sullam* | Ladder |
| 40 | مَغْرَمٍ | *Maghram* | Debt |

| V. | WORD | TR. | MEANING |
|---|---|---|---|
| 40 | مُثْقَلُونَ | *Muthqa-lun* | *pp. pl.* Burdened |
| 42 | مَكِيدُونَ | *Makidun* | Those who are ensnared in a plot |
| 44 | سَحَابٌ مَرْكُومٌ | *Sahabum-markum* | Clouds gathered in heaps |
| 47 | عَذَابًا دُونَ ذَلِكَ | *'Adhaban-duna dhalik* | Another punishment besides this |
| 48 | بِأَعْيُنِنَا | *Bi-'a'-unina* | In Our eyes (i.e., under Allah's loving care and protection) |
| 49 | إِدْبَارَ النُّجُومِ | *'Idbaran-nujum* | The setting of the stars |

# سُورَةُ النَّجم

## [53] SURAT AN-NAJM
## THE STAR

| V. | WORD | TR. | MEANING |
|---|---|---|---|
| 1 | وَالنَّجْمِ إِذَا هَوَى | *Wan-Najmi 'idha hawa* | By the star when it goes down (or sets) |
| 5 | شَدِيدُ الْقُوَى | *Shadidul-Quwa* | One Mighty in Power (i.e., angel Jibril عليه السلام) |
| 6 | ذُو مِرَّةٍ | *Dhu-Mirrah* | One endued with strength (or understanding) |
| 9 | قَابَ قَوْسَيْنِ | *Qaba-qawsayn* | Distance of two bow-lengths |
| 12 | أَفَتُمَارُونَهُ | *'Afatuma-runah* | Will you then dispute with him? |
| 13 | نَزْلَةً أُخْرَى | *Nazlatan 'ukhra* | Second descent (i.e., another time) |
| 14 | سِدْرَةِ الْمُنْتَهَى | *Sidratil-muntaha* | The lote-tree of the utmost boundry (beyond wich none can pass) |
| 15 | جَنَّةُ الْمَأْوَى | *Jannatul-Ma'-wa* | The Paradise of Abode |
| 17 | مَا زَاغَ الْبَصَرُ | *Ma zaghal-basar* | The sight (of the Prophet صلى الله عليه وسلم) never swerved |
| 17 | مَا طَغَى | *Ma tagha* | (His sight) did not transgress beyond (the) limit (ordained for it) |
| 19 | اللَّاتَ وَالْعُزَّى | *Al-Lata wal-'Uzza* | Two idols of the pagan Arabs |
| 20 | مَنَاةَ | *Manat* | Another idol of the pagan Arabs |

| V. | WORD | TR. | MEANING |
|---|---|---|---|
| 22 | ضِيزَى | *Di-za* | Unfair |
| 24 | أَمْ لِلْإِنسَانِ مَا تَمَنَّى | *'Am lil-'insani ma taman-na* | Nay, shall man have (just) anything he hankers after? |
| 32 | لَمَم | *Lamam* | Small faults |
| 34 | أَكْدَى | *'Akda* | Stopped (giving) |
| 37 | وَفَّى | *Waffa* | Fulfilled |
| 46 | تُمْنَى | *Tumna* | *pv.* Is emitted |
| 47 | النَّشْأَةَ الْأُخْرَى | *An-Nash-'atal-'Ukhra* | Second creation (Raising of the Dead) |
| 48 | أَقْنَى | *'Aqna* | Gave satisfaction |
| 49 | شِعْرَى | *Shi'-ra* | Sirius (the mighty star, which was worshipped by the pagan Arabs) |
| 53 | الْمُؤْتَفِكَةَ | *Al-mu'-tafika* | The overthrown cities (of Sodom to which Prophet Lut عليه السلام was sent) |
| 53 | أَهْوَى | *'Ahwa* | Overthrew, destroyed |
| 57 | أَزِفَتْ الْآزِفَةُ | *'Azifatil-'Azifah* | The (Hour) ever approaching draws nigh |
| 61 | سَامِدُون | *Samidun* | *pp.* Those who waste their time in vanities |

# سُورَةُ القَمَر

## [54] SURAT AL-QAMAR
## THE MOON

| V. | WORD | TR. | MEANING |
|---|---|---|---|
| 1 | انْشَقَّ الْقَمَرُ | *Inshaqqal-Qamar* | The moon has been cleft asunder |
| 2 | سِحْرٌ | *Sihr* | Magic |
| 3 | مُسْتَقِرٌّ | *Mustaqirr* | *ap.* Settled, firmly established, lasting |
| 4 | مُزْدَجَرٌ | *Muzdajar* | Deterrent |
| 5 | نُذُر | *Nudhur* | Warners |
| 6 | شَيْءٍ نُكُرٍ | *Shay-'in-nukur* | Terrible thing / affair |
| 8 | مُهْطِعِينَ | *Muh-ti-'in* | Those who hasten with fixed gazes or extended necks |
| 8 | يَوْمٌ عَسِرٌ | *Yawmun 'asir* | Hard day |
| 9 | ازْدُجِرَ | *Izdujir* | *pv.* (He) was driven out (with cries) |
| 10 | مَغْلُوبٌ | *Maghlub* | *pp.* Overcome |
| 11 | أَبْوَابَ السَّمَاءِ | *'Abwabas-sama'* | The gates of heaven |
| 11 | مُنْهَمِرٍ | *Munha-mir* | Pouring forth |
| 13 | دُسُرٍ | *Dusur* | Nails, palm-fibres with which ships are caulked |
| 15 | مُدَّكِرٍ | *Muddakir* | One who receives admonition, one who remembers |
| 19 | مُسْتَمِرٍّ | *Mustamirr* | Continuous, bitter |
| 20 | تَنزِعُ | *Tanzi'* | Plucks out |

| V. | WORD | TR. | MEANING |
|---|---|---|---|
| 20 | أَعْجَازُ نَخْلٍ | *'A '-jazu nakhl* | Roots of palm-trees |
| 20 | مُنْقَعِرٍ | *Munqa- 'ir* | Torn up, uprooted |
| 24 | سُعُرٍ | *Su- 'ur* | Madness |
| 25 | أَشِرٌ | *'Ashir* | Insolent |
| 28 | مُحْتَضَرٌ | *Muhtadar* | Brought forward (by suitable turns) |
| 29 | تَعَاطَى | *Ta- 'ata* | Took (a sword) in the hand |
| 31 | هَشِيمِ | *Hashim* | Dry stubble / sticks |
| 31 | مُحْتَظِرِ | *Muhtazir* | One who builds a fold for cattle |
| 34 | حَاصِبًا | *Hasiba* | A violent tornado bringing a shower of stones |
| 34 | نَجَّيْنَاهُمْ بِسَحَرٍ | *Najjaynahum-bisahar* | We delivered them by early dawn |
| 37 | رَاوَدُوهُ عَنْ ضَيْفِهِ | *Rawaduhu 'an-dayfih* | They sought to snatch away his guests |
| 44 | مُنْتَصِرٌ | *Muntasir* | *ap.* One who is able to defend himself |
| 46 | أَدْهَى | *'Adha* | Most grievous |
| 46 | أَمَرُّ | *'Amarr* | Most bitter |
| 51 | أَشْيَاعَكُمْ | *'Ashya- 'akum* | *pl.* Your likes |
| 53 | مُسْتَطَرٌ | *Mustatar* | *pp.* Written, recorded |
| 54 | نَهَرٍ | *Nahar* | River |
| 55 | مَقْعَدِ صِدْقٍ | *Maq- 'adi Sidq* | Seat of truth |

| V. | WORD | TR. | MEANING |
|---|---|---|---|

## سُورَةُ الرَّحْمان

## [55] SURAT AR-RAHMAN

## THE MOST GRACIOUS

| | | | |
|---|---|---|---|
| 2 | عَلَّمَ الْقُرْآنَ | *'Allamal-Qûr'an* | (Allah) has taught (you mankind) the Qûr'an |
| 4 | بَيَانَ | *Bayan* | Intelligent speech, power of expression |
| 5 | حُسْبَانٍ | *Husban* | Courses (exactly) computed |
| 6 | نَجْمُ | *Najm* | *sr.* and *pl.* Herbs, stars |
| 7 | مِيزَانَ | *Mizan* | Balance (of Justice) |
| 12 | عَصْفِ | *'Asf* | Leaves and stalks for fodder |
| 12 | رَيْحَانُ | *Rayhan* | Sweet-smelling plants |
| 14 | صَلْصَالٍ | *Salsal* | Sounding clay |
| 14 | فَخَّارِ | *Fakh-khar* | Clay of pottery |
| 15 | مَارِجٍ | *Marij* | Smokless flame of fire |
| 19 | يَلْتَقِيَانِ | *Yal-taqiyan* | *dl.* They meet together |
| 20 | لَا يَبْغِيَانِ | *La yabghi-yan* | *dl.* They do not transgress |
| 24 | مُنشَآتُ | *Munsha-'at* | Having lofty sails, *pp.* Raised on high (by the waves) |
| 24 | كَالْأَعْلَامِ | *Kal-'a'-lam* | Like mountains |
| 26 | فَانٍ | *Fan* | Perishable |

| V. | WORD | TR. | MEANING |
|---|---|---|---|
| 27 | ذُو الْجَلَالِ | *Dhul-Jalal* | Full of Majesty |
| 27 | إِكْرَامِ | *'Ikram* | Bounty and Honour |
| 29 | شَأْنٍ | *Sha'-n* | Matter, state |
| 31 | سَنَفْرُغُ لَكُمْ | *Sanafrughu lakum* | We shall settle your affairs |
| 31 | الثَّقَلَانِ | *Ath-thaqalan* | Jinns and men |
| 33 | تَنفُذُوا | *Tanfudhu* | *pl.* You pass beyond |
| 35 | شُوَاظٌ | *Shuwaz* | Flames (of fire) without smoke |
| 35 | نُحَاسٌ | *Nuhas* | (Molten) brass |
| 37 | وَرْدَةً | *Warda* | Rose, rosy |
| 37 | دِهَانِ | *Dihan* | Ointment, grease |
| 41 | نَوَاصِي | *Nawasi* | Forelocks |
| 44 | حَمِيمٍ آنٍ | *Hamimin 'an* | Boiling hot water |
| 48 | ذَوَاتَا أَفْنَانٍ | *Dhawata 'afnan* | (Gardens) with spreading branches |
| 50 | عَيْنَانِ | *'Aynan* | Two springs |
| 52 | زَوْجَانِ | *Zawjan* | Two kinds |
| 54 | إِسْتَبْرَقٍ | *'Istab-raq* | Silk brocade |
| 54 | جَنَى الْجَنَّتَيْنِ | *Janal-jannatayn* | The fruits of the two Gardens |
| 54 | دَانٍ | *Dan* | That which is near at hand |
| 56 | طَمِثْ | *Tmith* | Touched (i.e., deflowered a virgin) |
| 62 | وَمِنْ دُونِهِمَا جَنَّتَانِ | *Wa min-dunihima jan-natan* | And besides these two (Gardens) there are two other |

| V. | WORD | TR. | MEANING |
|---|---|---|---|
| | | | Gardens |
| 64 | مُدْهَامَّتَانِ | *Mud-ham-matan* | (Two Gardens which are) dark-green in colour |
| 66 | عَيْنَانِ نَضَّاخَتَانِ | *'Aynani nadda-khatan* | Two springs pouring forth water in continous abundance |
| 70 | خَيْرَاتٌ حِسَانٌ | *Khay-ratun hisan* | Good and beautiful (Maidens) |
| 72 | مَقْصُورَاتٌ فِي الْخِيَامِ | *Maq-suratun-fil-khiyam* | (Maidens) restrained in (goodly) pavilions |
| 76 | رَفْرَف | *Raf-raf* | Cushions |
| 76 | عَبْقَرِيٍّ | *'Ab-qariy* | Carpets |

# سُورَةُ الوَاقِعَةِ

## [56] SURAT AL-WAQI'A

## THE INEVITABLE EVENT

| V. | WORD | TR. | MEANING |
|---|---|---|---|
| 1 | الْوَاقِعَةُ | *Al-Waqi-'ah* | The inevitable event (i.e., the Day of Resurrection) |
| 3 | خَافِضَةٌ رَافِعَةٌ | *Khafidatur-Rafi-'ah* | It will bring low (some), (and others) it will exalt |
| 4 | إِذَا رُجَّتْ الْأَرْضُ | *'Idha rujjatil-'ard* | When the earth shall be shaken |
| 5 | بُسَّتْ الْجِبَالُ | *Bussatil-jibal* | The mountains shall be crumbled |
| 6 | هَبَاءً | *Haba'* | Dust (floating in the air) |
| 6 | مُنْبَثًّا | *Mum-baththa* | Scattered abroad |
| 8 | أَصْحَابُ الْمَيْمَنَةِ | *'As-habul-May-manah* | The Companions of the Right Hand (i.e., the righteous people) |
| 9 | أَصْحَابُ الْمَشْأَمَةِ | *'As-habul-mash-'amah* | The Companions of the Left Hand (i.e., the damned) |
| 13 | ثُلَّةٌ | *Thulla* | Crowd, number of people |
| 15 | سُرُرٍ | *Surur* | Couches, thrones |
| 15 | مَوْضُونَةٍ | *Maw-dunah* | *pp.* Interwoven (with gold and precious stones) |
| 17 | وِلْدَانٌ | *Wildan* | Boys, youths |
| 17 | مُخَلَّدُونَ | *Mukhalla-dun* | *pl.* Made immortal / eternal |

| V. | WORD | TR. | MEANING |
|---|---|---|---|
| 18 | أَكْوَابٍ | *'Akwab* | Goblets (without spouts or handles) |
| 18 | أَبَارِيقَ | *'Abariq* | Beakers |
| 18 | مَعِينٍ | *Ma-'in* | Flowing wine |
| 19 | لَا يُصَدَّعُونَ | *La yusadda-'un* | They will not suffer from headache |
| 19 | لَا يُنزِفُونَ | *La yunzifun* | They will not suffer intoxication |
| 25 | تَأْثِيمًا | *Ta'-thima* | Accusation of crime |
| 28 | مَخْضُودٍ | *Makhdud* | *pp.* Deprived of throns |
| 29 | طَلْحٍ | *Talh* | Banana tree |
| 29 | مَنْضُودٍ | *Mandud* | *pp.* Spread over one another, piled up in order |
| 30 | ظِلٍّ | *Zill* | Shade |
| 30 | مَمْدُودٍ | *Mamdud* | *pp.* Extended |
| 31 | مَسْكُوبٍ | *Maskub* | *pp.* Poured forth, flowing |
| 37 | عُرُبًا | *'Uruba* | Full of love (for their husbands) |
| 37 | أَتْرَابًا | *'Atraba* | *pl.* Equal in age |
| 43 | يَحْمُومٍ | *Yahmum* | Black smoke |
| 46 | حِنثِ | *Hinth* | Wickedness |
| 55 | هِيمِ | *Him* | Thirsty camels |
| 56 | نُزُلُهُمْ | *Nuzuluhum* | Their entertainment |
| 58 | مَا تُمْنُونَ | *Ma tumnun* | The human seed that you emit |
| 65 | تَفَكَّهُونَ | *Tafakkahun* | *pl.* You would be left in wonderment |

| V. | WORD | TR. | MEANING |
|---|---|---|---|
| 67 | مَحْرُومُونَ | *Mahrumun* | *pp. pl.* Deprived |
| 69 | مُزْن | *Muzn* | Cloud |
| 70 | أُجَاجًا | *'Ujaja* | Saltish (and undrinkable) |
| 71 | النَّارَ الَّتِي تُورُونَ | *An-naral-lati turun* | The fire which you kindle |
| 73 | مَتَاعًا لِلْمُقْوِينَ | *Mata-'al-lil-muq-win* | An article of comfort and convenience for the travellers |
| 75 | أُقْسِمُ | *'Uqsim* | I swear |
| 75 | مَوَاقِعِ النُّجُومِ | *Mawaqi-'in-Nujum* | The settings of the stars |
| 79 | لَا يَمَسُّهُ إِلَّا الْمُطَهَّرُونَ | *La yamassuhu 'illal-mutahharun* | None shall touch it (the Holy Qûr'an) but those who are clean |
| 81 | مُدْهِنُونَ | *Mud-hinun* | Those who hold in low estimation |
| 85 | نَحْنُ أَقْرَبُ إِلَيْهِ | *Nahnu 'aqrabu 'ilayh* | We are nearer to him |
| 86 | غَيْرَ مَدِينِينَ | *Ghayra madinin* | Those who are exempt from (future) account |
| 89 | رَوْحٌ | *Rawh* | Rest |
| 89 | رَيْحَانٌ | *Ray-han* | Provision (*lit.* Sweet-smelling plants) |

| V. | WORD | TR. | MEANING |
|---|---|---|---|

## سُورَةُ الحَدِيدِ

## [57] SURAT AL-HADID

## THE IRON

| V. | WORD | TR. | MEANING |
|---|---|---|---|
| 1 | الْعَزِيزُ | *Al-'Aziz* | The All-Mighty |
| 3 | الْأَوَّلُ | *Al-'Awwal* | The First |
| 3 | الْآخِرُ | *Al-'Akhir* | The Last |
| 3 | الظَّاهِرُ | *Az-Zahir* | The Evident |
| 3 | الْبَاطِنُ | *Al-Batin* | The Hidden |
| 4 | يَلِجُ | *Ya-lij* | Enters |
| 10 | قَبْلِ الْفَتْحِ | *Qablil-Hat-h* | Before the victory (i.e., the conquest of Makka) |
| 10 | حُسْنَى | *Husna* | Goodly (reward) |
| 11 | قَرْضًا حَسَنًا | *Qardan Hasana* | Beautiful loan |
| 13 | انْظُرُونَا | *An-zuruna* | *im.* Wait for us |
| 13 | نَقْتَبِسْ | *Naq-tabis* | (Let us) borrow (a light) |
| 13 | سُور | *Sur* | Wall |
| 14 | فَتَنْتُمْ أَنْفُسَكُمْ | *Fatantum 'an-fusakum* | *pl.* You led yourselves into temptation |
| 14 | تَرَبَّصْتُمْ | *Tarabbastum* | *pl.* You waited (to our ruin) |
| 14 | غَرَّتْكُمُ الْأَمَانِيُّ | *Gharrat-kumul-'amaniyy* | *pl.* (Your false) desires deceived you |
| 16 | أَلَمْ يَأْنِ | *'Alam ya'-n* | Has not the time arrived? |
| 16 | أَمَدُ | *'Amad* | Stretch or span of time, time |

| V. | WORD | TR. | MEANING |
|---|---|---|---|
| 20 | تَكَاثُرٌ | *Taka-thur* | The act of multiplying |
| 20 | كُفَّارَ | *Kuffar* | Tillers, rejecters of truth |
| 20 | يَهِيجُ | *Yahij* | Withers |
| 22 | نَبْرَأَهَا | *Nabra-'aha* | We bring it into existence |
| 23 | لِكَيْلَا تَأْسَوْا | *Li-kayla ta'-saw* | In order that you may not be sad |
| 25 | أَنْزَلْنَا الْحَدِيدَ | *'Anzalnal-Hadid* | We brought forth iron |
| 25 | بَأْسٌ شَدِيدٌ | *Ba'-sun-shadid* | Great might |
| 27 | قَفَّيْنَا | *Qaffay-na* | We caused to follow |
| 27 | الْإِنجِيلَ | *Al-'injil* | The Gospel |
| 27 | رَأْفَةً وَرَحْمَةً | *Ra'-fatanw-wa Rahmah* | Compassion and mercy |
| 27 | رَهْبَانِيَّةً | *Rahbaniyya* | Monasticism |
| 27 | رَعَوْهَا | *Ra-'awha* | They did not observe it |
| 28 | كِفْلَيْنِ | *Kif-layn* | Double portion· |

| V. | WORD | TR. | MEANING |
|---|---|---|---|

# سُورَةُ الْمُجَادِلَة

## [58] SURAT AL-MUJADILA
## THE WOMAN WHO PLEADS

| V. | WORD | TR. | MEANING |
|---|---|---|---|
| 1 | تُجَادِلُكَ | *Tujadiluk* | *fg.* Pleads with you (O Muhammad صلى الله عليه وسلم) |
| 1 | تَحَاوُرَكُمَا | *Taha-wurakuma* | The arguments between both of you |
| 2 | يُظَاهِرُونَ | *Yuzahirun* | They divorce (their wives) by *Zihar* *Az-Zihar* is the saying of a husband to his wife: "You are to me like the back of my mother (i.e., unlawful for me to approach )" |
| 3 | يَتَمَاسَّا | *Yatamas-sa* | *dl.* They touch each other |
| 4 | شَهْرَيْنِ مُتَتَابِعَيْنِ | *Shah-rayni mutatabi-'ayn* | Two successive months |
| 5 | يُحَادُّونَ | *Yuhad-dun* | They oppose |
| 5 | كُبِتُوا | *Kubitu* | (They will) be humbled to dust |
| 6 | أَحْصَاهُ اللَّهُ | *'Ahsa-hullah* | Allah has kept account of it |
| 8 | حَسْبُهُمْ جَهَنَّمُ | *Hasbuhum Jahannam* | Hell is enough for them |
| 10 | لِيَحْزُنَ | *Liyahzun* | In order that he may cause grief |
| 11 | تَفَسَّحُوا فِي الْمَجَالِسِ | *Tafassahu fil-majalis* | *im. pl.* Make room in the assemblies |
| 11 | انشُزُوا | *In-shuzu* | *im. pl.* Rise up |

| V. | WORD | TR. | MEANING |
|---|---|---|---|
| 12 | إِذَا نَاجَيْتُمُ الرَّسُولَ | *'Idha najay-tumr-Rasul* | When you consult the Messenger |
| 13 | أَأَشْفَقْتُمْ | *'A-'ashfaqtum* | Are you afraid? |
| 13 | تَابَ اللَّهُ عَلَيْكُمْ | *Taballahu 'alaykum* | Allah has forgiven you |
| 16 | جُنَّةً | *Junna* | Screen |
| 19 | اسْتَحْوَذَ عَلَيْهِمُ الشَّيْطَانِ | *'Is-tahwadha 'alay-himush-Shay-tan* | Satan has got the better of them |
| 20 | يُحَادُّونَ | *Yuhaddun* | They oppose |
| 20 | أَذَلِّينَ | *'Adhallin* | *pl.* Most humiliatd, lowest |
| 22 | يُوَادُّونَ | *Yuwad-dun* | They love |

| V. | WORD | TR. | MEANING |
|---|---|---|---|

# سُورَةُ الحَشْرِ

## [59] SURAT AL-HASHR
## THE GATHERING

| V. | WORD | TR. | MEANING |
|---|---|---|---|
| 2 | لِأَوَّلِ الْحَشْرِ | *Li-'awwalil-Hashr* | At the first gathering |
| 3 | جَلَاء | *Jala'* | Banishment |
| 4 | شَاقُّوا | *Shaq-qu* | They resisted |
| 5 | لِينَةٍ | *Lina* | Palm-tree |
| 6 | أَوْجَفْتُمْ | *'Awjaftum* | *pl.* You made expedition |
| 6 | رِكَاب | *Rikab* | Camerly |
| 7 | دُولَةً | *Dula* | Circuit |
| 9 | حَاجَةً | *Haja* | Jealousy |
| 9 | خَصَاصَةٌ | *Khasasah* | Poverty |
| 9 | يُوقَ | *Yuq* | *pv.* Is saved |
| 9 | شُحَّ | *Shuh-h* | Covetousness |
| 10 | غِلًّا | *Ghilla* | Rancour |
| 14 | قُلُوبُهُمْ شَتَّى | *Qulubuhum shatta* | Their hearts are divided |
| 15 | وَبَالَ أَمْرِهِمْ | *Wabala 'amrihim* | The evil result of their conduct |
| 19 | أَنْسَاهُمْ أَنْفُسَهُمْ | *'Ansahum 'anfusahum* | (Allah) made them forget themselves |
| 21 | خَاشِعًا | *Khashi-'a* | That which humbles itself |
| 21 | مُتَصَدِّعًا | *Mutasad-di-'a* | That which is cloven or splits itself in two |
| 23 | الْمَلِكُ | *Al-Malik* | The King |

| V. | WORD | TR. | MEANING |
|---|---|---|---|
| 23 | الْقُدُّوسُ | *Al-Quddus* | The Holy One |
| 23 | السَّلَامُ | *As-Salam* | The One Free from all defects |
| 23 | الْمُؤْمِنُ | *Al-Mu'-min* | The Guardian of Faith |
| 23 | الْمُهَيْمِنُ | *Al-Muhay-min* | The Watcher over everything |
| 23 | الْعَزِيزُ | *Al-'Aziz* | The All-Mighty |
| 23 | الْجَبَّارُ | *Al-Jabbar* | The Compeller |
| 23 | الْمُتَكَبِّرُ | *Al-Mutakabbir* | The Supreme |
| 24 | الْبَارِئُ | *Al-Bari'* | The Orginator |
| 24 | الْمُصَوِّرُ | *Al-Musawwir* | The Fashioner |
| 24 | الْأَسْمَاءُ الْحُسْنٰى | *Al-'Asma-'ul-Husna* | The Most Beautiful Names |

| V. | WORD | TR. | MEANING |
|---|---|---|---|

# سُورَةُ الْمُمْتَحَنَة

## [60] SURAT AL-MUMTAHANAH
## THE WOMAN TO BE EXAMINED

| V. | WORD | TR. | MEANING |
|---|---|---|---|
| 2 | يَثْقَفُوكُمْ | *Yath-qafukum* | They overcome you |
| 2 | يَبْسُطُوا إِلَيْكُمْ | *Yab-sutu 'ilay-kum* | They stretch forth |
| 4 | أُسْوَةٌ حَسَنَةٌ | *'Uswatun hasa-na* | Excellent example |
| 4 | إِنَّا بُرَآءُ مِنْكُمْ | *'Inna bura-'a-'u minkum* | We are clear of you |
| 4 | إِلَيْكَ أَنَبْنَا | *'Ilay-ka 'anab-na* | To you (O Allah) we turn in repentance |
| 8 | تَبَرُّوهُمْ | *Tabarruhum* | *pl.* You deal kindly with them |
| 8 | تُقْسِطُوا إِلَيْهِمْ | *Tuqsitu 'ilay-him* | *pl.* You deal justly with them |
| 9 | ظَاهَرُوا | *Zaharu* | They helped / supported |
| 10 | امْتَحِنُوهُنَّ | *Imtahinu-hunn* | *im. pl.* Examine them |
| 10 | أُجُورَهُنَّ | *'Ujurahunn* | Their dower |
| 10 | عِصَمِ الْكَوَافِرِ | *'Isamil-kawa-fir* | The ties (marriage contracts) of unbelieving women |
| 11 | فَاتَ | *Fat* | Passed away, abandoned |
| 12 | يَفْتَرِينَ | *Yaf-tarin* | *fg.* They forge |
| 13 | لَا تَتَوَلَّوْا | *La Tatawallaw* | *ni. pl.* Do not take as friends |

| V. | WORD | TR. | MEANING |
|---|---|---|---|

# سُورَةُ الصَّفِّ

## [61] SURAT AS-SAFF
## THE ROW OR THE RANK

| V. | WORD | TR. | MEANING |
|---|---|---|---|
| 3 | كَبُرَ مَقْتًا | *Kabura maqta* | It is grievously hateful / odious |
| 3 | مَا لَا تَفْعَلُونَ | *Ma la taf-'alun* | That which you do not |
| 4 | سَبِيلِهِ | *Sabilih* | His Cause |
| 4 | صَفًّا | *Saffa* | Row |
| 4 | بُنيَانٌ مَرْصُوصٌ | *Bunyanum-marsus* | Solid structure |
| 5 | زَاغُوا | *Zaghu* | They went wrong |
| 5 | أَزَاغَ اللَّهُ قُلُوبَهُمْ | *'Azagal-lahu qulubahum* | Allah let their hearts go wrong |
| 8 | نُورَ اللَّهِ | *Nurallah* | The Light of Allah |
| 10 | هَلْ أَدُلُّكُمْ | *Hal 'adullukum* | Shall I lead you? |
| 10 | تِجَارَةٍ | *Tijara* | Bargain |
| 10 | تُنجِيكُم | *Tunjikum* | Will save you |
| 14 | حَوَارِيِّينَ | *Hawariyyin* | Disciples |
| 14 | أَيَّدْنَا | *'Ayyadna* | We gave power |

| V. | WORD | TR. | MEANING |
|---|---|---|---|

# سُورَةُ الجُمُعَة

## [62] SURAT AJ-JUMU‘AH

## THE ASSEMBLY (FRIDAY) PRAYER

| | | | |
|---|---|---|---|
| 2 | أُمِّيِّين | *'Um-miyyin* | *pl.* Unlettered |
| 2 | يُزَكِّيهِمْ | *Yuzakkihim* | Purifies them |
| 3 | لَمَّا يَلْحَقُوا بِهِمْ | *Lamma yal-haqu bihim* | They have not yet joined them |
| 5 | حُمِّلُوا التَّوْرَاة | *Hummilut-Tawrat* | They were entrusted with the (obligations of) Taurat |
| 5 | يَحْمِلُ أَسْفَارًا | *Yahmilu 'asfara* | Carries huge tomes |
| 6 | هَادُوا | *Hadu* | They became Jews |
| 8 | عَالِمِ الْغَيْبِ وَالشَّهَادَة | *‘Alimil-ghaybi wash-shahada* | The All-Knower of the unseen and the seen |
| 9 | ذِكْرِ اللَّهِ | *Dhikrillah* | The Remembrance of Allah |
| 9 | ذَرُوا الْبَيْعَ | *Dharul-bay‘* | *im. pl.* Leave off business |
| 10 | فَانتَشِرُوا | *Fanta-shiru* | Then you may disperse |
| 11 | انفَضُّوا | *Infaddu* | They dispersed |

| V. | WORD | TR. | MEANING |
|---|---|---|---|

## سُورَةُ المُنَافِقُونَ

## [63] SURAT AL-MUNAFIQUN

### THE HYPOCRITES

| | | | |
|---|---|---|---|
| 3 | لَا يَفْقَهُونَ | *La-yaf-qahun* | They do not understand |
| 4 | خُشُبٌ | *Khushub* | Timber, wood |
| 4 | مُسَنَّدَةٌ | *Musannadah* | *fg. pp.* Propped up |
| 4 | أَنَّى يُؤْفَكُونَ | *'Anna yu'-fakun* | How are they deluded (away from the Truth) |
| 5 | لَوَّوْا رُءُوسَهُمْ | *Lawwaw ru-'usahum* | They turned away their heads |
| 7 | حَتَّى يَنْفَضُّوا | *Hatta yanfad-du* | Till they disperse |
| 8 | رَجَعْنَا | *Raja'-na* | We returned |
| 8 | أَعَزُّ | *'A-'azz* | The more honourable |
| 8 | أَذَلَّ | *'Adhall* | The meaner |
| 8 | لِلّٰهِ الْعِزَّةُ | *Lil-lahil-'izza* | Honour belongs to Allah |
| 9 | ذِكْرِ اللّٰهِ | *Dhikrillah* | The remembrance of Allah |

| V. | WORD | TR. | MEANING |
|---|---|---|---|

## سُورَةُ التَّغَابُنِ

## [64] SURAT AT-TAGHABUN

## THE MUTUAL LOSS AND GAIN

| V. | WORD | TR. | MEANING |
|---|---|---|---|
| 1 | لَهُ الْمُلْكُ | *Lahul- Mulk* | To Him belongs the Dominion |
| 3 | أَحْسَنَ صُوَرَكُمْ | *'Ahsana suwarakum* | He made your shapes beautiful |
| 5 | وَبَالَ أَمْرِهِمْ | *Wabala 'amrihim* | The evil result of their conduct |
| 8 | نُورِ | *Nuur* | Light (i.e.,the Holy Qûr'an) |
| 9 | يَوْمِ الْجَمْعِ | *Yawmil-Jam'* | The Day of Assembly/Gatherin g |
| 9 | يَوْمُ التَّغَابُنِ | *Yawmut-Taghabun* | Te Day of Mutual Loss and Gain |
| 11 | بِإِذْنِ اللَّهِ | *Bi-'idhnillah* | By the leave of Allah |
| 11 | يَهْدِ قَلْبَهُ | *Yahdi qalbah* | Guides his heart (aright) |
| 16 | وَمَن يُوقَ شُحَّ نَفْسِهِ | *Many-yuqa shuhha nafsih* | And whosoever is saved from his own covetousness |
| 17 | قَرْضًا حَسَنًا | *Qardan Hasana* | Beautiful loan |

# سُورَةُ الطَّلَاق

## [65] SURAT AT-TALAQ

## THE DIVORCE

| | | | |
|---|---|---|---|
| 1 | فَطَلِّقُوهُنَّ لِعِدَّتِهِنَّ | *Fa-talliquhunna li-'iddatihinn* | Divorce them at their prescribed periods |
| 1 | أَحْصُوا | *'Ahsu* | *im. pl.* Count (accurately) |
| 1 | فَاحِشَةٍ مُبَيِّنَةٍ | *Fahishatim-mubayyinah* | Open lewdness |
| 2 | مَخْرَجًا | *Makhraja* | Way out |
| 3 | هُوَ حَسْبُهُ | *Huwa hasbuh* | He (Allah) is sufficient for him |
| 4 | وَاللَّائِي لَمْ يَحِضْنَ | *Walla-'ii lam yahidn* | And those who have no courses (i.e., they are still immature) |
| 4 | يُسْرًا | *Yusra* | Ease, easy |
| 6 | وُجْدِكُمْ | *Wujdikum* | *pl.* Your means |
| 6 | أْتَمِرُوا بَيْنَكُمْ | *Atamiru bayna-kum* | *im. pl.* Take mutual counsel together |
| 6 | تَعَاسَرْتُمْ | *Ta-'asartum* | *pl.* You find yourselves in difficulties |
| 7 | ذُو سَعَةٍ | *Dhu-sa-'a* | Man of means / wealth |
| 8 | عَتَتْ | *'Atat* | *fg.* Opposed, acted arrogantly |
| 8 | عَذَابًا نُكْرًا | *'Adhaban-nukra* | Horrible Chastisement |
| 9 | خُسْرًا | *Khusra* | Perdition |
| 12 | يَتَنَزَّلُ | *Yatanaz-zal* | Descends |

| V. | WORD | TR. | MEANING |
|---|---|---|---|

## سُورَةُ التَّحْرِيم

## [66] SURAT AT-TAHRIM

## HOLDING (SOMETHING) TO BE FORBIDDEN

| | | | |
|---|---|---|---|
| 1 | مَا أَحَلَّ اللَّهُ لَكَ | *Ma 'ahallal-lahu lak* | That which Allah has made lawful to you |
| 1 | مَرْضَاتَ | *Mardat* | The act of pleasing |
| 1 | تَبْتَغِي | *Tabtaghi* | You seek |
| 2 | تَحِلَّةَ أَيْمَانِكُمْ | *Tahillata 'aymanikum* | The dissolution of your oaths |
| 2 | اللَّهُ مَوْلَاكُمْ | *Allahu Mawlakum* | Allah is your Protector |
| 3 | نَبَّأَتْ بِهِ | *Nabba-'at bih* | *fg.* Divulged it |
| 3 | أَظْهَرَهُ اللَّهُ عَلَيْهِ | *'Azharahullahu 'alayh* | Allah made it known to him |
| 4 | صَغَتْ | *Saghat* | *fg.* Inclined |
| 4 | تَظَاهَرَا عَلَيْهِ | *Tazahara 'alayh* | *dl.* You help one another against him |
| 4 | ظَهِيرٌ | *Zahir* | Helper |
| 5 | قَانِتَاتٍ | *Qanitat* | Those (women) who are obedient to Allah |
| 5 | سَائِحَاتٍ | *Sa-'ihat* | Those (women) who fast [*lit.* those (women)who travel] |
| 6 | قُوا أَنفُسَكُمْ | *Qu 'anfusakum* | *im. pl.* Save yourselves |
| 6 | غِلَاظٌ | *Ghilaz* | Stern |
| 6 | شِدَادٌ | *Shidad* | Severe |

| V. | WORD | TR. | MEANING |
|---|---|---|---|
| 7 | لاَ تَعْتَذِرُوا | *La ta-'tadhiru* | *ni.pl.* Make no excuses |
| 8 | تَوْبَةً نَصُوحًا | *Tawbatan-Nasuha* | Sincere repentance |
| 9 | اغْلُظ عَلَيْهِمْ | *Agh-luz 'alayhim* | *im.* Be harsh with them |
| 10 | خَانَتَاهُمَا | *Khanatahuma* | They both betrayed them |
| 10 | دَاخِلِينَ | *Dakhilin* | *ap.* Those who enter in |
| 12 | أَحْصَنَتْ فَرْجَهَا | *'Ahsanat farjaha* | *fg.* Guarded her chastity |

| V. | WORD | TR. | MEANING |
|---|---|---|---|

# سُورَةُ المُلكِ

## [67] SURAT AL-MULK

## THE DOMINION

| | | | |
|---|---|---|---|
| 2 | خَلَقَ الْمَوْتَ | *Khalaqal-Mawt* | Created death |
| 3 | طِبَاقًا | *Tibaqa* | One above another |
| 3 | تَفَاوُت | *Tafa-wut* | Want of proportion |
| 3 | فُطُور | *Futur* | Rifts |
| 4 | كَرَّتَيْن | *Kar-ratayn* | Two other times, twice again |
| 4 | خَاسِئًا | *Khasi-'a* | Dull and discomfited |
| 4 | حَسِيرٌ | *Hasir* | Fatigued |
| 5 | مَصَابِيح | *Masabih* | Lamps |
| 5 | رُجُومًا لِلشَّيَاطِين | *Rujumal-lish-shayatin* | Missiles to drive away Satans |
| 7 | شَهِيقًا | *Shahiqa.* | The (terrible) drawing in of breath |
| 7 | تَفُورُ | *Tafur* | Blazes forth, gushes forth |
| 8 | تَمَيَّزُ | *Tamayyaz* | Bursts |
| 11 | سُحْقًا | *Suh-qa* | Far from (Allah's) mercy |
| 15 | ذَلُولًا | *Dhalula* | Commodious |
| 15 | مَنَاكِب | *Manakib* | Sides, tracts, paths |
| 16 | تَمُورُ | *Tamur* | *fg.* Shakes (as in an earthquake) |
| 19 | صَافَّاتٍ وَيَقْبِضْنَ | *Saffatinw-wa yaq-bidn* | Spreading their wings and folding them in |

| V. | WORD | TR. | MEANING |
|---|---|---|---|
| 20 | جُنْدٌ | *Jund* | Army |
| 20 | غُرُورٍ | *Ghurur* | Delusion |
| 21 | لَجُّوا | *Lajju* | They persisted obstinately |
| 21 | عُتُوٌّ | *'Utuww* | Insolence, pride |
| 21 | نُفُورٍ | *Nufur* | Flight (from the truth) |
| 22 | مُكِبًّا | *Mukib-ba* | Grovelling |
| 22 | يَمْشِي سَوِيًّا | *Yamshi sa-wiyya* | Walks evenly |
| 27 | زُلْفَةً | *Zul-fa* | Near at hand |
| 27 | سِيئَتْ | *Sii-'at* | Grieved |
| 28 | يُجِيرُ | *Yujir* | Delivers |
| 30 | غَوْرًا | *Ghaw-ra* | (Water) running away under ground |
| 30 | مَاءٍ مَعِينٍ | *Ma-'im-ma-'in* | Clear-flowing water |

| V. | WORD | TR. | MEANING |
|---|---|---|---|

## سُورَةُ القَلَم

## [68] SURAT AL-QALAM

## THE PEN

| | | | |
|---|---|---|---|
| 1 | وَالْقَلَمِ | *Wal-qalam* | By the pen |
| 1 | وَمَا يَسْطُرُونَ | *Wa ma yasturun* | And by what they write |
| 6 | بِأَيِّيكُمُ الْمَفْتُونُ | *Bi-'ayyikumul-maftun* | Which of you is afflicted with madness |
| 9 | تُدْهِنُ | *Tud-hin* | You compromise (with them) |
| 9 | يُدْهِنُونَ | *Yud-hinun* | They compromise (with you) |
| 10 | حَلَّافٍ | *Hallaf* | Swearer (i.e., one who swears on all occasions, small or great) |
| 11 | هَمَّازٍ | *Hammaz* | Slanderer |
| 11 | مَشَّاءٍ | *Mash-sha'* | One who goes about |
| 11 | نَمِيمٍ | *Namim* | Calumny, slander |
| 13 | عُتُلٍّ | *'Utull* | Violent, cruel |
| 13 | زَنِيمٍ | *Zanim* | Spurious, illegitimate |
| 16 | سَنَسِمُهُ عَلَى الْخُرْطُومِ | *Sanasimuhu 'alal-khur-tum* | We shall brand him over the nose |
| 17 | يَصْرِمُنَّهَا | *Yas-rimunnaha* | They cut (or gather) its fruits |
| 17 | مُصْبِحِينَ | *Musbihin* | *ap.* Those who enter upon the morning |
| 18 | لَا يَسْتَثْنُونَ | *La yastath-nun* | They do not make |

| V. | WORD | TR. | MEANING |
|---|---|---|---|
| | | | an exception [by saying *Insha Allah* (if Allah wills)] |
| 19 | طَافَ | *Taf* | Went round about, encompassed |
| 19 | طَائِفٌ | *Ta-'if* | *ap.* One who goes round about or encompass (i.e., a common destruction) |
| 20 | صَرِيمِ | *As-sarim* | Dark night, a garden whose fruit has all been gathered |
| 21 | فَتَنَادَوا مُصْبِحِينَ | *Fatanadaw musbihin* | Then they called out one to another as soon as the morning broke |
| 22 | اغْدُوا عَلَى حَرْثِكُمْ | *Igh-du 'ala harthikum* | *im. pl.* Go to your tilth (betimes) in the morning |
| 22 | صَارِمِينَ | *Sarimin* | *ap.* Those who cut or gather fruits |
| 23 | يَتَخَافَتُونَ | *Yatakhafatun* | They converse in secret low tones |
| 25 | غَدَوْا | *Ghadaw* | They went in the morning |
| 25 | حَرْدٍ | *Hard* | Strong intention |
| 25 | قَادِرِينَ | *Qadirin* | *ap.* Those who are able or have power |
| 26 | إِنَّا لَضَالُّونَ | *Inna ladhallun* | We have surely lost our way |
| 28 | أَوْسَطُهُمْ | *'Awsatuhum* | The best among them |
| 30 | يَتَلَاوَمُونَ | *Yatalawamun* | They blame one |

| V. | WORD | TR. | MEANING |
|---|---|---|---|
| | | | another |
| 32 | إِنَّآ إِلَى رَبِّنَا رَاغِبُونَ | *'Inna 'ila Rabbina raghi-bun* | (Truly) we turn to our Lord (wishing for good and forgiveness) |
| 38 | لَمَا تَخَيَّرُونَ | *Lama takhayyarun* | That you choose |
| 39 | لَمَا تَحْكُمُونَ | *Lama tah-kumun* | That you judge |
| 40 | زَعِيمٌ | *Za-'im* | Surety |
| 42 | يَوْمَ يُكْشَفُ عَنْ سَاقٍ | *Yawma yuk-shafu 'an-saq* | The Day that the Shin shall be laid bare (i.e., the Day of Judgement) |
| 43 | خَاشِعَةً أَبْصَارُهُمْ | *Khashi-'atan 'absaruhum* | Their eyes will be cast down |
| 43 | تَرْهَقُهُمْ ذِلَّةٌ | *Tarhaquhum dhillah* | Ignominy will cover them |
| 44 | ذَرْنِي | *Dharni* | *im.* Leave Me alone |
| 45 | أُمْلِي لَهُمْ | *'Umli lahum* | I will grant them a (long) respite |
| 46 | مَغْرَمٍ | *Maghram* | Debt |
| 48 | صَاحِبِ الْحُوتِ | *Sahibil-Hut* | The companion of the fish (i.e., Prophet Yunus عليه السلام) |
| 48 | مَكْظُومٌ | *Mak-zum* | *pp.* Oppressed with silent sorrow |
| 49 | نُبِذَ | *Nubidh* | *pv.* Was cast |
| 49 | عَرَاءِ | *'Ara'* | Bare place, naked shore |
| 50 | اجْتَبَاهُ رَبُّهُ | *Ijtabahu Rabbuh* | His Lord chose him |
| 51 | يُزْلِقُونَكَ | *Yuz-liqunak* | They make you slip |

| V. | WORD | TR. | MEANING |
|---|---|---|---|

## سُورَةُ الحَاقَّة

## [69] SURAT AL-HAQQAH

## THE SURE REALITY

| | | | |
|---|---|---|---|
| 1 | الْحَاقَّةُ | *'Al-Haqqa* | The Sure Reality / Truth |
| 2 | مَا الْحَاقَّةُ | *Mal- Haqqa* | What is the Sure Reality? |
| 4 | الْقَارِعَةِ | *Al-Qari-'ah* | The Day of Noise and Clamour (i.e., the Day of Judgement) |
| 5 | طَاغِيَةِ | *Taghiyah* | Awful cry |
| 7 | سَخَّرَهَا عَلَيْهِمْ | *Sakh-kharaha 'alayhim* | He made it rage against them |
| 7 | حُسُومًا | *Husuma* | Succession (of unlucky nights) |
| 9 | خَاطِئَةِ | *Khati-'ah* | Habitual sinfulness |
| 10 | أَخْذَةً رَابِيَةً | *'Akhdhatar-ra-biyah* | Strong punishment |
| 11 | جَارِيَةِ | *Jariyah* | Floating (ship) |
| 12 | تَذْكِرَةً | *Tadhkira* | Reminder |
| 12 | تَعِيَهَا | *Ta-'iyaha* | Retains its memory |
| 14 | حُمِلَتِ الْأَرْضُ | *Humilatil-'ardh* | The earth is moved |
| 14 | دُكَّتَا | *Dakkata* | They are crushed |
| 15 | وَاقِعَةُ | *Waqi-'ah* | (Great) Event |
| 16 | انشَقَّتِ السَّمَاءُ | *In-shaqqatis-sama'* | The sky will be rent asunder |
| 16 | وَاهِيَةٌ | *Wa-hiyah* | *fg.* Flimsy |
| 17 | أَرْجَائِهَا | *'Arja-'iha* | Its sides |

| V. | WORD | TR. | MEANING |
|---|---|---|---|
| 19 | هَاؤُمْ | *Ha-'um* | Take you (all), come you (all) |
| 19 | كِتَابِيَهْ | *Kitabiyah* | My record / book |
| 21 | رَاضِيَةٍ | *Ra-dhiyah* | *fg.* One who is well pleased |
| 23 | قُطُوفُ | *Qutuf* | Fruits |
| 23 | دَانِيَةٌ | *Daniyah* | *fg. ap.* That which is near at hand or low |
| 27 | قَاضِيَةَ | *Qadhiyah* | That which makes an end (i.e., death) |
| 28 | مَالِي | *Maliy* | My wealth |
| 29 | سُلْطَانِي | *Sul-taniy* | My power |
| 30 | غُلُّوهُ | *Ghulluh* | *im. pl.* Bind him (i.e., bind his hands round his neck) |
| 32 | اسْلُكُوهُ | *Islu-kuh* | *im. pl.* Insert him |
| 34 | لَا يَحُضُّ | *La yahudh* | Does not urge |
| 36 | غِسْلِينٍ | *Ghislin* | The foul pus from the washing of wounds |
| 37 | خَاطِئُونَ | *Khati-'un* | Sinners |
| 44 | تَقَوَّلَ | *Taqawwal* | Invented, fabricated lies |
| 46 | وَتِينَ | *Watin* | Artery of heart |
| 47 | حَاجِزِينَ | *Hajizin* | *pp.* Those who withhold |
| 50 | حَسْرَةٌ | *Hasra* | Cause of sorrow |

| V. | WORD | TR. | MEANING |
|---|---|---|---|

## سُورَةُ الْمَعَارِج

## [70] SURAT AL-MA'ARIJ
## THE WAYS OF ASCENT

| V. | WORD | TR. | MEANING |
|---|---|---|---|
| 1 | سَأَلَ | *Sa-'al* | Asked |
| 1 | سَائِلٌ | *Sa-'il* | Questioner |
| 3 | ذِي الْمَعَارِجِ | *Dhil-Ma-'arij* | The Lord of the ways of ascent |
| 4 | تَعْرُجُ الْمَلَائِكَةُ | *Ta'-rujul-mala-'ika* | The angels ascend |
| 10 | حَمِيمٌ | *Hamim* | Friend |
| 11 | يُبَصَّرُونَهُمْ | *Yubassarunahum* | They shall be made to see |
| 13 | فَصِيلَتِهِ | *Fasilatih* | His kindred |
| 13 | تُؤْوِيهِ | *Tu'-wih* | Shelters him |
| 15 | لَظَى | *Laza* | Blazing fire |
| 16 | نَزَّاعَةً لِلشَّوَى | *Nazza-'atal-lish-shawa* | Taking away (burning completely) the head skin |
| 18 | أَوْعَى | *Fa-'aw-'a* | Hid |
| 20 | جَزُوعًا | *Jazu-'a* | Fretful |
| 21 | مَنُوعًا | *Manu-'a* | One who hold back (his hand), niggardly |
| 37 | عِزِينَ | *'Izin* | Crowds, groups |
| 41 | مَسْبُوقِينَ | *Masbuqin* | Those who are defeated |
| 43 | سِرَاعًا | *Sira-'a* | Suddenly, hastily |
| 43 | يُوفِضُونَ | *Yufidun* | They rush |

| V. | WORD | TR. | MEANING |
|---|---|---|---|

## سُورَةُ نُوح

## [71] SURAT NUH

## NOAH

| V. | WORD | TR. | MEANING |
|---|---|---|---|
| 4 | أَجَلَ اللَّهِ | *'Ajalallah* | The term of Allah |
| 6 | فِرَارًا | *Firara* | Flight |
| 7 | اسْتَغْشَوْا ثِيَابَهُمْ | *Istagh-shaw thiyabahum* | They covered themselves up with their garments |
| 7 | أَصَرُّوا | *'Asarru* | They persisted |
| 13 | لَا تَرْجُونَ لِلَّهِ وَقَارًا | *La tarjuna lillahi waqara* | *pl.* You are not conscious of Allah's Majesty |
| 14 | خَلَقَكُمْ أَطْوَارًا | *Khalaqakum 'atwara* | He has created you in (different) stages |
| 16 | سِرَاجًا | *Siraja* | Lamp |
| 17 | أَنْبَتَكُمْ مِنَ الْأَرْضِ | *'Ambatakum-minal-'ard* | He has produced you from the earth |
| 20 | سُبُلًا فِجَاجًا | *Subulan-fijaja* | Spacious roads |
| 22 | مَكْرًا كُبَّارًا | *Makran-kubbara* | Tremendous plot |
| 23 | وَدًّا | *Wadda* | Names of idols worshipped originally by the antediluvians, and subsequently by the Pagan Arabs |
| 23 | سُوَاعًا | *Suww-'a* | |
| 23 | يَغُوثَ | *Yaghuth* | |
| 23 | يَعُوقَ | *Ya-'uq* | |
| 23 | نَسْرًا | *Nasra* | |
| 26 | دَيَّارًا | *Dayyara* | Any one, single one |
| 28 | تَبَارًا | *Tabara* | Destruction, perdition |

| V. | WORD | TR. | MEANING |
|---|---|---|---|

# سُورَةُ الجِنّ

## [72] SURAT AL-JINN

## THE JINN

| | | | |
|---|---|---|---|
| 1 | عَجَبًا | *'Ajaba* | Wonderful |
| 3 | جَدُّ رَبِّنَا | *Jaddu Rabbina* | The Majesty of our Lord |
| 4 | سَفِيهُنَا | *Safihuna* | The foolish among us (i.e., Iblis) |
| 4 | شَطَطًا | *Shatata* | Extravagant lie |
| 6 | يَعُوذُونَ | *Ya-'udhun* | They take shelter |
| 6 | زَادُوهُمْ رَهَقًا | *Zaduhum rahaqa* | They increased them in sin |
| 8 | حَرَسًا شَدِيدًا | *Ḥarasan-shadida* | Stern guards |
| 8 | شُهُبًا | *Shuhuba* | Flaming fires |
| 9 | رَصَدًا | *Rasada* | Watching in ambush |
| 11 | طَرَائِقَ قِدَدًا | *Tara-'iqa qidada* | Different paths |
| 13 | بَخْسًا | *Bakh-sa* | Short (account) |
| 14 | قَاسِطُونَ | *Qasitun* | Those who swerve from justice, those who act unjustly |
| 14 | تَحَرَّوْا | *Taharraw* | They sought out |
| 15 | حَطَبًا | *Hataba* | Fuel, firewood |
| 16 | طَّرِيقَةِ | *Tariqa* | (Right) way (i.e., Islam) |
| 16 | غَدَقًا | *Ghadaqa* | Abundant, copious |
| 17 | يَسْلُكْهُ | *Yasluk-h* | *pv.* Will cause him to enter |
| 17 | عَذَابًا صَعَدًا | *'Adhaban-sa-'ada* | Ever-growing |

| V. | WORD | TR. | MEANING |
|---|---|---|---|
| | | | chastisement |
| 19 | قَامَ عَبْدُ اللَّهِ يَدْعُوهُ | *Qama 'Abdullahi yad-'uh* | The servant of Allah (the Prophet صلى الله عليه وسلم) stood up to invoke Him |
| 19 | لِبَدًا | *Libada* | Dense crowed |
| 22 | لَنْ يُجِيرَنِي مِنْ اللَّهِ أَحَدٌ | *Lany-yujirani minallahi 'ahad* | None can protect me from (the punishment of) Allah |
| 22 | مُلْتَحَدًا | *Mul-tahada* | Refuge |
| 27 | رَصَدًا | *Rasada* | Band of watching guards (angels) |
| 28 | أَحَاطَ | *'Ahat* | Encompassed, surrounded |
| 28 | أَحْصَى | *'Ahsa* | Took an account of |

## سُورَةُ المُزَّمِّل

## [73] SURAT AL-MUZZAMMIL

## FOLDED IN GARMENTS

| V. | WORD | TR. | MEANING |
|---|---|---|---|
| 1 | الْمُزَّمِّلُ | *Al-Muzzam-mil* | Folded in garments (i.e., the Prophet صلى الله عليه وسلم) |
| 4 | رَتِّلِ الْقُرْآنَ | *Rattilil-Qûr'an* | *im.* Recite the Qûr'an |
| 5 | قَوْلًا ثَقِيلًا | *Qawlan-thaqila* | Weighty word (the Holy Qûr'an) |
| 6 | نَاشِئَةَ اللَّيْلِ | *Nashi-'atal-layl* | Rising by night |
| 6 | أَشَدُّ وَطْئًا | *'Ashaddu wat-'a* | Fitter for earnest devotion |
| 6 | أَقْوَمُ قِيلًا | *'Aqwamu Qila* | More correct in pronunciation |
| 7 | سَبْحًا | *Sabha* | Occupation |
| 8 | تَبَتَّلْ إِلَيْهِ | *Tabattal 'ilayh* | *im.* Devote yourself to him |
| 8 | تَبْتِيلاً | *Tabtila* | A life of complete separation from the world and devotion to Allah |
| 11 | ذَرْنِي وَالْمُكَذِّبِينَ | *Dharni wal-mukadhdhi-bin* | *im.* Leave Me (Alone to deal) with those who deny the truth |
| 11 | أُولِي النَّعْمَةِ | *'Ulin-na'-ma* | Those who are in possession of good things of life |
| 11 | مَهِّلْهُمْ قَلِيلًا | *Mah-hil-hum qalila* | *im.* Give them respite for a little while |
| 12 | أَنكَالًا | *'Ankala* | Fetters |

| V. | WORD | TR. | MEANING |
|---|---|---|---|
| 13 | طَعَامًا ذَا غُصَّةٍ | *Ta-'aman-dha ghussa* | A food that chokes |
| 14 | يَوْمَ تَرْجُفُ الْأَرْضُ | *Yama tarjuful-'ardh* | On the Day when the earth will be in violent shake (i.e., the Day of Judgement) |
| 14 | كَثِيبًا مَهِيلًا | *Kathibam-mahila* | Heap of sand poured out and flowing down |
| 16 | أَخْذًا وَبِيلًا | *'Akhdhanw-wabila* | Heavy punishment |
| 18 | مُنفَطِرٌ | *Munfatir* | Cloven or rent asunder |
| 20 | فَاقْرَءُوا مَا تَيَسَّرَ مِنَ الْقُرْآنِ | *Faq-ra-'u ma ta-yassara minal-Qûr'an* | *im. pl.* So recite as much of the Qur'an as may be easy for you |
| 20 | يَضْرِبُونَ | *Yadribun* | They travel |
| 20 | أَقِيمُوا الصَّلَاةَ | *'Aqimus-Salat* | *im. pl.* Establish regular prayer |

| V. | WORD | TR. | MEANING |
|---|---|---|---|

## سُورَةُ الْمُدَّثِّر

## [74] SURAT AL-MUDDATHTHIR

### ONE WRAPPED UP

| V. | WORD | TR. | MEANING |
|---|---|---|---|
| 1 | الْمُدَّثِّرُ | *Al-Muddaththir* | One who wraps himself in a garment (i.e., the Prophet صلى الله عليه وسلم) |
| 2 | قُمْ فَأَنذِرْ | *Qum fa-'andhir* | *im.* Arise and warn |
| 3 | وَرَبَّكَ فَكَبِّرْ | *Wa Rabbaka fa-kabbir* | *im.* And your Lord do you magnify |
| 4 | وَثِيَابَكَ فَطَهِّرْ | *Wa thiyabaka fatahhir* | *im.* And your garments keep free from stain |
| 5 | وَالرُّجْزَ فَاهْجُرْ | *Warrujza fahjur* | *im.* And all abomination shun |
| 6 | وَلَا تَمْنُن تَسْتَكْثِرُ | *Wa la tamnun-tastakthir* | *im.* And be not liberal in the hope of receiving more |
| 8 | نُقِرَ | *Nuqir* | *pv.* Is sounded |
| 8 | نَاقُورِ | *Naqur* | Trumpet |
| 12 | مَالًا مَمْدُودًا | *Malam-mamduda* | Resources in abundance |
| 13 | وَبَنِينَ شُهُودًا | *Wa banina shuhud* | And sons to be by his side |
| 14 | مَهَّدْتُ لَهُ | *Mahhattu lah* | I made (life) smooth and comfortable for him |
| 16 | عَنِيدًا | *'Anida* | Refractory |
| 17 | سَأُرْهِقُهُ صَعُودًا | *Sa-'urhiquhu sa-'uda* | I will afflict him with (unbearable) |

| V. | WORD | TR. | MEANING |
|---|---|---|---|
| | | | torment |
| 19 | فَقُتِلَ | *Faqutil* | So let him be cursed |
| 22 | عَبَسَ | *'Abas* | Frowned |
| 22 | بَسَرَ | *Basar* | Scowled |
| 24 | يُؤْثَرُ | *Yu'-thar* | *pv.* Derived from old |
| 26 | سَأُصْلِيهِ سَقَرَ | *Sa-'uslihi Saqar* | I will cast him into Hell-Fire |
| 29 | لَوَّاحَةٌ لِّلْبَشَرِ | *Lawwahatul-lil-bashar* | Burning the skins |
| 33 | وَاللَّيْلِ إِذْ أَدْبَرَ | *Wallayli 'idh 'adbar* | And by the night as it retreats |
| 34 | وَالصُّبْحِ إِذَا أَسْفَرَ | *Was-Subhi 'idha 'asfar* | And by the dawn as it shines forth |
| 35 | إِنَّهَا لَإِحْدَى الْكُبَرِ | *'Innaha la-'ihdal-kubar* | This is but one of the mighty (Portents) |
| 37 | يَتَقَدَّمَ | *Yata-qaddam* | Goes forward |
| 38 | كَسَبَتْ | *Kasa-bat* | *fg.* Earned |
| 38 | رَهِينَةٌ | *Rahinah* | Held in pledge |
| 42 | مَا سَلَكَكُمْ | *Ma salakakum* | What has caused you to enter? |
| 45 | نَخُوضُ | *Nakhud* | We talk vanities |
| 50 | حُمُرٌ مُّسْتَنْفِرَةٌ | *Humurum-mustanfirah* | Frightened (wild) donkeys |
| 51 | قَسْوَرَةٍ | *Qaswarah* | Lion |

| V. | WORD | TR. | MEANING |
|---|---|---|---|

## سُورَةُ القِيَامَة

## [75] SURAT AL-QIYAMAH
## THE RESURRECTION

| | | | |
|---|---|---|---|
| 1 | لَا أُقْسِمُ | *La 'uqsim* | I do swear |
| 2 | النَّفْسِ اللَّوَّامَةِ | *An-nafsil-lawwamah* | The self-reproaching soul |
| 4 | بَلَى | *Bala* | Yes |
| 4 | نُسَوِّيَ بَنَانَهُ | *Nusawwiya bananah* | We put together in perfect order the (very) tips of his fingers |
| 5 | يَفْجُرَ | *Yafjur* | Does wrong |
| 5 | أَمَامَهُ | *'Amamah* | (For that which is) before him (i.e., for the future) |
| 7 | فَإِذَا بَرِقَ الْبَصَرُ | *Fa-'idha bariqal-basar* | At length, when the sight is dazed |
| 8 | وَخَسَفَ الْقَمَرُ | *Wa khasafal-Qamar* | And the moon is buried in darkness |
| 9 | وَجُمِعَ الشَّمْسُ وَالْقَمَرُ | *Wa jumi-'ash-shamsu wal-qamar* | And the sun and moon are joined together |
| 10 | أَيْنَ الْمَفَرُّ | *'Aynal-mafarr* | Where (is the refuge) to flee? |
| 11 | لَا وَزَرَ | *La wazar* | There is no place of refuge |
| 14 | بَصِيرَةٌ | *Basirah* | Evidence |
| 15 | وَلَوْ أَلْقَى مَعَاذِيرَهُ | *Wa law 'alqa ma-'adhirah* | Even though he were to put up his excuses |
| 18 | قُرْآنَهُ | *Qur'anah* | Its recital |

| V. | WORD | TR. | MEANING |
|---|---|---|---|
| 22 | نَاضِرَةٌ | *Nadirah* | *fg.* Shining and radiant |
| 24 | بَاسِرَةٌ | *Basirah* | *fg.* Sad and dismal |
| 25 | فَاقِرَةٌ | *Faqirah* | *fg.* Back-breaking calamity |
| 26 | تَرَاقِي | *Taraqi* | Collar-bone |
| 27 | رَاقٍ | *Raq* | *fg.* Enchanter |
| 29 | الْتَفَّتْ | *Il-taffat* | *fg.* Joined with another |
| 30 | مَسَاقُ | *Masaq* | The act of driving |
| 33 | يَتَمَطَّى | *Yatamatta* | Stalks in full conceit |
| 34 | أَوْلَى لَكَ | *'Awla lak* | Woe to you |
| 36 | سُدًى | *Suda* | Neglected |
| 37 | يُمْنَى | *Yumna* | *pv.* Emitted |
| 38 | سَوَّى | *Sawwa* | (Allah) fashioned (him) in due proportion |

| V. | WORD | TR. | MEANING |
|---|---|---|---|

## سُورَةُ الإِنسَان

## [76] SURAT AL-ĪNSAN

## THE MAN

| V. | WORD | TR. | MEANING |
|---|---|---|---|
| 2 | أَمْشَاجٍ | *'Amshaj* | Mingled |
| 4 | سَلَاسِلَا | *Salasila* | Chains |
| 4 | أَغْلَالًا | *'Aghlala* | Yokes |
| 5 | مِزَاجُ | *Mizaj* | Mixture |
| 5 | كَافُورًا | *Kafura* | Comphor |
| 6 | عَيْنًا | *'Ayṇa* | Fountain, spring of water |
| 6 | يُفَجِّرُونَهَا | *Yufajji-runaha* | They cause it to gush forth |
| 7 | مُسْتَطِيرًا | *Musta-tira* | That which spreads itself far and wide |
| 10 | عَبُوسًا | *'Abusa* | Frowning |
| 10 | قَمْطَرِيرًا | *Qam-tarira* | Distress |
| 11 | لَقَّاهُمْ نَضْرَةً | *Laqqahum nadra* | Gave them brightness |
| 13 | زَمْهَرِيرًا | *Zam-harira* | Excessive cold |
| 14 | دَانِيَةً عَلَيْهِمْ ظِلَالُهَا | *Daniyatan 'alay-him zilaluha* | The shades of the (Garden) are close upon them |
| 14 | ذُلِّلَتْ قُطُوفُهَا | *Dhulli-lat-qutu-fuha* | The bunches of fruit (of the Garden) will hang low |
| 15 | أَكْوَابٍ | *'Ak-wab* | Goblets |
| 15 | قَوَارِيرَ | *Qawarir* | Crystals |
| 17 | كَأْسًا | *Ka'-sa* | Cup |

| V. | WORD | TR. | MEANING |
|---|---|---|---|
| 17 | زَنجَبِيلًا | *Zanja-bila* | Ginger |
| 18 | سَلْسَبِيلًا | *Salsabila* | Name of a fountain in Paradise |
| 19 | لُؤْلُؤًا مَنثُورًا | *Lu'-lu-'am-manthur* | Scattered pearls |
| 21 | ثِيَابُ سُندُسٍ | *Thiyabu sundus* | Garments of fine silk |
| 21 | إِسْتَبْرَقٌ | *'Is-tabraq* | Heavy brocade |
| 27 | يَوْمًا ثَقِيلًا | *Yawman-thaqila* | Heavy day |
| 28 | شَدَدْنَا أَسْرَهُمْ | *Shadadna asrahum* | We have made their frame strong |

| V. | WORD | TR. | MEANING |
|---|---|---|---|

## سُورَةُ المُرسلات

## [77] SURAT AL-MURSALAT
THOSE SENT FORTH

| | | | |
|---|---|---|---|
| 1 | وَالْمُرْسَلَاتِ عُرْفًا | *Wal-Mursalati 'urfa* | By the winds sent forth one after another |
| 2 | فَالْعَاصِفَاتِ عَصْفًا | *Fal-'asifati 'asfa* | And by the winds that blow violently in tempestuous gusts |
| 3 | وَالنَّاشِرَاتِ نَشْرًا | *Wan-nashirati nashra* | And by the angels who spread out their wings |
| 4 | فَالْفَارِقَاتِ فَرْقًا | *Fal-fariqati farqa* | And by the angels who separate (truth from falsehood) by a discrimination |
| 5 | فَالْمُلْقِيَاتِ ذِكْرًا | *Fal-mul-qiyati dhikra* | And by the angels who bring the revelations to the Messengers |
| 6 | عُذْرًا | *'Udhra* | Excuse |
| 6 | نُذْرًا | *Nudhra* | Warning |
| 8 | طُمِسَتْ | *Tumisat* | *pv. fg.* Dimmed |
| 9 | فُرِجَتْ | *Furijat* | *pv. fg.* Cleft asunder |
| 10 | نُسِفَتْ | *Nusifat* | *pv. fg.* Blown away, uprooted, scattered abroad |
| 11 | أُقِّتَتْ | *'Uqqitat* | *pv. fg.* Gathered to their time appointed |
| 12 | لِأَيِّ يَوْمٍ أُجِّلَتْ | *Li-'ayyi Yawmin* | For what day are |

| V. | WORD | TR. | MEANING |
|---|---|---|---|
| | | *'ujjilat* | these (portents) deferred? |
| 13 | لِيَوْمِ الْفَصْلِ | *Li-Yawmil-Fasl* | For the Day of sorting out |
| 25 | كِفَاتًا | *Kifata* | A place where things are gathered together |
| 26 | أَحْيَاءً | *'Ah-ya-'* | Living |
| 26 | أَمْوَاتًا | *'Amwata* | Dead |
| 27 | شَامِخَاتٍ | *Shami-khat* | Firm, lofty, tall |
| 27 | مَاءً فُرَاتًا | *Ma-'an furata* | Sweet water |
| 30 | ثَلَاثِ شُعَبٍ | *Thalathi shu-'ab* | Three columns |
| 31 | لَا ظَلِيلٍ | *La zalil* | No shade |
| 31 | لَهَبِ | *Lahab* | Flaming fire, fierce blaze |
| 32 | تَرْمِي | *Tarmi* | *fg.* Throws |
| 32 | شَرَرٍ | *Sharar* | Sparks |
| 32 | قَصْرِ | *Qasr* | Fort, big building, palace |
| 33 | كَأَنَّهُ جِمَالَةٌ صُفْرٌ | *Ka-'annahu jimalatun-sufr* | As if there were (a string of) yellow camels (marching swiftly) |

| V. | WORD | TR. | MEANING |
|---|---|---|---|

## سُورَةُ النَّبَإِ

## [78] SURAT AN-NABA'

## THE (GREAT) NEWS

| | | | |
|---|---|---|---|
| 1 | عَمَّ | *'Amma* | Concerning what? For What? |
| 2 | عَنِ النَّبَإِ الْعَظِيمِ | *'Anin-Naba-'il-'Azim* | Concerning the great news (i.e., the Holy Qûr'an or the Day of Resurrection) |
| 6 | مِهَادًا | *Mihada* | Wide expanse |
| 7 | أَوْتَادًا | *'Awtada* | Pegs |
| 9 | سُبَاتًا | *Subata* | Rest |
| 10 | لِبَاسًا | *Libasa* | Covering |
| 11 | مَعَاشًا | *Ma-'asha* | Means of subsistence |
| 12 | سَبْعًا شِدَادًا | *Sab-'an-shidada* | Seven strong heavens |
| 13 | سِرَاجًا وَهَّاجًا | *Sirajanw-wahhaja* | Blazing lamp (i.e., the sun) |
| 14 | مُعْصِرَاتِ | *Mu'-sirat* | Rainy clouds |
| 14 | مَاءً ثَجَّاجًا | *Ma-'an-thajjaja* | Abundant water |
| 16 | أَلْفَافًا | *'Alfafa* | Trees thickly planted and with interlacing boughs |
| 18 | فَتَأْتُونَ أَفْوَاجًا | *Fa-ta'-tuna 'afwaja* | And you (shall) come forth in crowds (groups) |
| 19 | أَبْوَابًا | *'Abwaba* | Doors, gates |
| 20 | سَرَابًا | *Saraba* | Mirage |

| V. | WORD | TR. | MEANING |
|---|---|---|---|
| 21 | مِرْصَادًا | *Mirsada* | Place of ambush |
| 22 | مَآبًا | *Ma-'aba* | Place of return |
| 23 | أَحْقَابًا | *'Ah-qaba* | Ages |
| 24 | بَرْدًا | *Barda* | Cool |
| 25 | حَمِيمًا | *Ḣamima* | Boiling water |
| 25 | غَسَّاقًا | *Ghassaqa* | Dirty wound discharges (pus) |
| 26 | جَزَاءً وِفَاقًا | *Jaza-'anw-wifaqa* | A fitting recompense (for them) |
| 31 | مَفَازًا | *Mafaza* | Achievement |
| 33 | كَوَاعِبَ | *Kawa-'ib* | Young full-breasted (mature) maidens |
| 33 | أَتْرَابًا | *'Atraba* | Of equal age, of the same age |
| 34 | وَكَأْسًا دِهَاقًا | *Wa ka'-san-dihaqa* | And a full cup (of wine) |
| 35 | لَغْوًا | *Laghwa* | Talk of vanities |
| 35 | كِذَّابًا | *Kidhdhaba* | Untruth, falsehood |
| 37 | خِطَابًا | *Khitaba* | Discourse |
| 40 | تُرَابًا | *Turaba* | Dust |

| V. | WORD | TR. | MEANING |
|---|---|---|---|

## سُورَةُ النَّازِعَات

## [79] SURAT AN-NAZI'AT

## THOSE WHO PULL OUT

| | | | |
|---|---|---|---|
| 1 | وَالنَّازِعَاتِ | *Wan-Nazi-'at* | By those (angels) who pull out (the souls of the disbelievers and the wicked) |
| 1 | غَرْقًا | *Gharqa* | Great violence |
| 2 | وَالنَّاشِطَاتِ نَشْطًا | *Wan-nashitati nashta* | And by those (angels) who gently take out (the souls of the believers) |
| 3 | وَالسَّابِحَاتِ سَبْحًا | *Was-sabihati sabha* | And by those (angels) who glide along (on errands of mercy) |
| 4 | فَالسَّابِقَاتِ سَبْقًا | *Fas-sabiqati sabqa* | And by those (angels) who press forward as in a race |
| 5 | فَالْمُدَبِّرَاتِ أَمْرًا | *Fal-mudabbirati 'amra* | And by those (angels) who arrange to do (the Commands of their Lord) |
| 6 | يَوْمَ تَرْجُفُ الرَّاجِفَةُ | *Yawma tarjufur-rajifah* | The Day everything that can be in commotion will be in violent commotion |
| 7 | تَتْبَعُهَا الرَّادِفَةُ | *Tatba-'u-har-Radifah* | Followed by the oft-repeated (commotions) |
| 8 | وَاجِفَةٌ | *Wajifa* | Palpitating, |

| V. | WORD | TR. | MEANING |
|---|---|---|---|
| | | | throbbing |
| 10 | حَافِرَةِ | *Hafirah* | Former state (of life) |
| 11 | عِظَامًا نَخِرَةً | *'Izaman-nakhirah* | Rotten bones |
| 13 | زَجْرَةٌ وَاحِدَةٌ | *Zaj-ratunw-Wahida* | Single (compelling) cry |
| 14 | سَاهِرَةِ | *Sahirah* | The face of the earth |
| 20 | الْآيَةَ الْكُبْرَى | *Al-'Ayatal-Kubra* | The great sign (i.e., the white shinning hand and the rod that became snake active in motion) |
| 22 | يَسْعَى | *Yas-'a* | Strives |
| 23 | حَشَرَ | *Hashar* | Gathered |
| 25 | نَكَال | *Nakal* | Punishment |
| 28 | رَفَعَ سَمْكَهَا | *Rafa-'a samkaha* | (He) raised its height |
| 29 | أَغْطَشَ | *'Aghtash* | Made dark |
| 29 | ضُحَاهَا | *Duhaha* | Its forenoon |
| 30 | دَحَاهَا | *Dahaha* | Spread it out |
| 31 | مَرْعَاهَا | *Mar-'aha* | Its pasture |
| 32 | وَالْجِبَالَ أَرْسَاهَا | *Wal-jibala 'arsaha* | And the mountains He has fixed firmly |
| 34 | الطَّامَّةُ الْكُبْرَى | *At-tam-matul-Kubra* | The very great calamity (i.e., the Judgement) |
| 36 | بُرِّزَتِ الْجَحِيمُ | *Burrizatil-Jahim* | Hell-Fire shall be placed in full view |
| 42 | أَيَّانَ مُرْسَاهَا | *'Ayyana mursaha* | When will be its appointed time? |

| V. | WORD | TR. | MEANING |
|---|---|---|---|

## سُورَةُ عَبَسَ

## [80] SURAT 'ABASA
## (HE) FROWNED

| | | | |
|---|---|---|---|
| 1 | عَبَسَ | *'Abas* | Frowned |
| 1 | تَوَلَّى | *Tawalla* | Turned away |
| 3 | لَعَلَّهُ يَزَّكَّى | *La-'allahu yazzakka* | He might become pure (from sin) |
| 4 | يَذَّكَّرُ | *Yadhdhakkar* | Receives admonition |
| 6 | فَأَنتَ لَهُ تَصَدَّى | *Fa-'anta lahu tasadda* | To him you attend |
| 10 | فَأَنتَ عَنْهُ تَلَهَّى | *Fa-'anta 'anhu talahha* | Of him you are neglectful |
| 13 | صُحُفٍ | *Suhuf* | Books |
| 14 | مَرْفُوعَةٍ | *Marfu-'a* | *pp.* Exalted (in dignity) |
| 15 | بِأَيْدِي سَفَرَةٍ | *Bi-'aydi safarah* | (Written) by the hands of scribes (angels) |
| 16 | بَرَرَةٍ | *Bararah* | *pl.* Obedient, pious, just |
| 17 | قُتِلَ الْإِنْسَانُ | *Qutilal-'insan* | Be cursed (the disbelieving) man, woe to man |
| 20 | يَسَّرَهُ | *Yassarah* | Made it easy |
| 21 | أَقْبَرَهُ | *'Aqbarah* | Put him in (his) grave |
| 23 | لَمَّا يَقْضِ مَا أَمَرَهُ | *Lamma yaqdi ma 'amarah* | (Man) has not done what He (Allah) has commanded him |
| 26 | شَقَقْنَا الْأَرْضَ | *Shaqaqnal-'ard* | We split the earth |

| V. | WORD | TR. | MEANING |
|---|---|---|---|
| 28 | قَضْبًا | *Qadba* | Fresh vegetation |
| 30 | وَحَدَائِقَ غُلْبًا | *Wa hada-'iqa ghulba* | And enclosed gardens, dense with lofty trees |
| 31 | أَبًّا | *'Abba* | Fodder |
| 33 | صَاخَّةُ | *Sakhkhah* | Deafening noise |
| 38 | مُسْفِرَةٌ | *Musfirah* | Shining |
| 39 | ضَاحِكَةٌ | *Dahika* | Laughing |
| 39 | مُسْتَبْشِرة | *Mustabshira* | Rejoicing |
| 40 | غَبَرَةٌ | *Ghabarah* | Dust |
| 41 | تَرْهَقُهَا قَتَرَةٌ | *Tarhaquha qatarah* | Darkness will cover them |

| V. | WORD | TR. | MEANING |
|---|---|---|---|

# سُورَةُ التَّكْوِير

## [81] SURAT AT-TAKWIR
## THE FOLDING UP

| | | | |
|---|---|---|---|
| 1 | الشَّمْسُ كُوِّرَتْ | *Ash-shamsu kuwwirat* | The sun (with its spacious light) is folded up |
| 2 | النُّجُومُ انكَدَرَتْ | *An-nuju-munkadarat* | The stars fall, losing their lustre |
| 3 | الْجِبَالُ سُيِّرَتْ | *Al-jibalu suyyirat* | The mountains are made to pass away |
| 4 | الْعِشَارُ عُطِّلَتْ | *Al-'isharu 'uttilat* | The pregnant she-camels are left untended |
| 5 | الْوُحُوشُ حُشِرَتْ | *Al-wuhushu hushirat* | The wild beasts are herded together |
| 6 | الْبِحَارُ سُجِّرَتْ | *Al-biharu sujjirat* | The seas become as blazing fire |
| 7 | النُّفُوسُ زُوِّجَتْ | *An-nufusu zuwwijat* | The souls are sorted out, (being joined, like with like) |
| 8 | مَوْءُودَةُ | *Maw-'uda* | Female (infant) buried alive |
| 10 | الصُّحُفُ نُشِرَتْ | *As-suhufu nushirat* | The scrolls (which record the deeds of men) are laid open |
| 11 | السَّمَاءُ كُشِطَتْ | *As-sama-'u kushi-tat* | The sky is unveiled |
| 12 | الْجَحِيمُ سُعِّرَتْ | *Al-Jahimu su'-'irat* | The Blazing Fire is kindled to fierce heat |
| 13 | الْجَنَّةُ أُزْلِفَتْ | *Al-Jannatu 'uzlifat* | The Garden is brought near |
| 14 | عَلِمَتْ نَفْسٌ مَا | *'Alimat nafsum-* | Each soul shall |

| V. | WORD | TR. | MEANING |
|---|---|---|---|
| | أَحْضَرَتْ | *ma-'ahdarat* | know what it has put forward |
| 15 | خُنَّسِ | *Khunnas* | Plants that recede (i.e., disappear during the day and appear during the night) |
| 16 | الْجَوَارِ الْكُنَّسِ | *'Al-jawaril-kunnas* | The plants that move swiftly and hide themselves |
| 17 | وَاللَّيْلِ إِذَا عَسْعَسَ | *Wal-Layli 'idha 'as-'as* | And the night as it dissipates |
| 18 | وَالصُّبْحِ إِذَا تَنَفَّسَ | *Was-subhi 'idha tanaffas* | And the dawn as it breathes away the darkness |
| 20 | مكِين | *Makin* | Held in honour |
| 24 | غَيْب | *Ghayb* | Unseen |
| 24 | ضَنِين | *Danin* | Greedy, grudging |

| V. | WORD | TR. | MEANING |
|---|---|---|---|

## سُورَةُ الإنفِطَار

## [82] SURAT AL-INFITAR

## THE CLEAVING ASUNDER

| V. | WORD | TR. | MEANING |
|---|---|---|---|
| 1 | السَّمَاءُ انفَطَرَتْ | *As-Sama-'unfatarat* | The sky is cleft asunder |
| 2 | الْكَوَاكِبُ انتَثَرَتْ | *Al-kawaki-buntatharat* | The stars are scattered |
| 3 | الْبِحَارُ فُجِّرَتْ | *Al-biharu fujjirat* | The seas are burst forth |
| 4 | الْقُبُورُ بُعْثِرَتْ | *Al-quburu bu'-thirat* | The graves are turned upside down |
| 5 | قَدَّمَتْ | *Qad-damat* | *fg.* Sent forward |
| 5 | أَخَّرَتْ | *'Akh-kharat* | *fg.* Sent back |
| 6 | مَا غَرَّكَ بِرَبِّكَ | *Ma gharraka bi-Rabbik* | What has seduced you from your Lord? |
| 7 | عَدَلَكَ | *'Adalak* | Gave you due proportion |
| 8 | رَكَّبَكَ | *Rakkabak* | Put you together |
| 9 | تُكَذِّبُونَ بِالدِّينِ | *Tukadhdhibuna bid-Din* | *pl.* You deny the Judgement |
| 13 | الْأَبْرَارَ | *Al-'abrar* | *pl.* Pious, righteous |

| V. | WORD | TR. | MEANING |
|---|---|---|---|

## سُورَةُ المُطَفِّفِين

## [83] SURAT AL-MUTAFFIFIN

## THOSE WHO DEAL IN FRAUD

| V. | WORD | TR. | MEANING |
|---|---|---|---|
| 1 | مُطَفِّفِينَ | *Mutaffifin* | Those who give less in measure and weight |
| 2 | اكْتَالُوا | *Iktalu* | They received by measure |
| 2 | يَسْتَوْفُونَ | *Yastawfun* | They take full measure |
| 3 | كَالُوا | *Kalu* | They gave by measure (to others) |
| 3 | وَزَنُوا | *Wazanu* | They weighted (to others) |
| 3 | يُخْسِرُونَ | *Yukhsirun* | They give less than due |
| 7 | كِتَابَ الفُجَّارِ | *Kitabal-fujjar* | The record of the wicked |
| 7 | سِجِّينٍ | *Sijjin* | The register of black deeds |
| 9 | كِتَابٌ مَرْقُومٌ | *Kitabum-marqum* | (There is) a Register (fully) inscribed |
| 14 | رَانَ | *Ran* | Took possession |
| 15 | مَحْجُوبُونَ | *Mah-jubun* | Those who are veiled |
| 18 | كِتَابَ الْأَبْرَارِ | *Kitabal-'Abrar* | The record of the righteous |
| 18 | عِلِّيِّينَ | *'Illiy-yin* | High places |
| 24 | نَضْرَةَ النَّعِيمِ | *Nadratan-Na-'im* | The beaming brightness of bliss |
| 25 | رَحِيقٍ | *Rahiq* | Pure wine |

| V. | WORD | TR. | MEANING |
|---|---|---|---|
| 25 | مَخْتُومٍ | *Makhtum* | *pp.* Sealed |
| 26 | خِتَامُ | *Khitam* | Seal |
| 26 | مِسْكٌ | *Misk* | Musk |
| 26 | فَلْيَتَنَافَسِ | *Fal-yatanafas* | Let those aspire |
| 26 | مُتَنَافِسُونَ | *Mutanafisun* | Those who have aspirations |
| 30 | يَتَغَامَزُونَ | *Yataghamazun* | They wink at each other (in mockery) |
| 31 | فَكِهِينَ | *Fakihim* | Jesting |
| 36 | ثُوِّبَ | *Thuw-wib* | *pv.* Are paid back |

| V. | WORD | TR. | MEANING |
|---|---|---|---|

## سُورَةُ الانشِقَاقِ

## [84] SURAT AL-INSHIQAQ
## THE RENDING ASUNDER

| | | | |
|---|---|---|---|
| 2 | أَذِنَتْ | *'Adhinat* | *fg.* Hearkened |
| 2 | حُقَّتْ | *Huqqat* | *fg.* Needed (to do so) |
| 3 | الْأَرْضُ مُدَّتْ | *Al-'ardu muddat* | The earth is stretched forth |
| 4 | أَلْقَتْ مَا فِيهَا | *'Alqat ma fiha* | (The earth) casts forth what is within it |
| 4 | تَخَلَّتْ | *Takhallat* | *fg.* Becomes empty |
| 6 | إِنَّكَ كَادِحٌ إِلَى رَبِّكَ | *'Innaka kadihun 'ila Rabbik* | You are (ever) toiling on towards your Lord |
| 6 | فَمُلَاقِيهِ | *Fa-mulaqih* | So you will meet Him |
| 11 | يَدْعُو ثُبُورًا | *Yad-'u thubura* | Cries for perdition |
| 14 | يَحُورَ | *Yahur* | Returns |
| 16 | شَفَقِ | *Shafaq* | Readness of the sky after sunset |
| 17 | وَسَقَ | *Wasaq* | Gathered together |
| 18 | اتَّسَقَ | *It-tasaq* | Became full |
| 19 | لَتَرْكَبُنَّ | *La-tarkabunna* | *pl.* You shall surely travel |
| 19 | طَبَقًا | *Tabaqa* | Stage |
| 23 | يُوعُونَ | *Yu-'un* | They secrete (in their breasts) |

| V. | WORD | TR. | MEANING |
|---|---|---|---|

## سُورَةُ البُروج

## [85] SURAT AL-BURUJ

## THE ZODIACAL SIGNS

| V. | WORD | TR. | MEANING |
|---|---|---|---|
| 2 | وَالْيَوْمِ الْمَوْعُودِ | *Wal-Yawmil-Maw-'ud* | And by the promised Day (of Judgement) |
| 2 | شَاهِدٍ | *Shahid* | *ap.* Witness |
| 3 | مَشْهُودٍ | *Mashhud* | *pp.* That which is witnessed |
| 4 | أُخْدُودِ | *'Ukhdud* | Pit |
| 6 | قُعُودٌ | *Qu-'ud* | The act of sitting |
| 8 | نَقَمُوا | *Naqamu* | They disliked / disapproved |
| 12 | بَطْشَ رَبِّكَ | *Batsha Rabbik* | The Grip (Punishment) of your Lord |
| 13 | إِنَّهُ هُوَ يُبْدِئُ | *'Inna-Hu Huwa yubdi'* | It is He Who Creates from the very beginning |
| 13 | يُعِيدُ | *Yu-'id* | Restores (life) |
| 14 | الْوَدُودُ | *Al-Wadud* | Full of love |
| 15 | الْمَجِيدُ | *Al-Majid* | The Glorious |

| V. | WORD | TR. | MEANING |
|---|---|---|---|

سُورَةُ الطَّارِق

## [86] SURAT AT-TARIQ
## THE NIGHT-VISITANT

| V. | WORD | TR. | MEANING |
|---|---|---|---|
| 1 | وَالطَّارِقِ | *Wat-Tariq* | And (by) the night-vistant |
| 3 | النَّجْمُ الثَّاقِبُ | *'An-Najmuth-thaqib* | (It is) the star of piercing brightness |
| 4 | حَافِظٌ | *Hafiz* | Protector |
| 7 | مِنْ بَيْنِ الصُّلْبِ | *Mim-baynis-sulb* | From between the backbone |
| 7 | تَرَائِب | *Tara-'ib* | Breast-bones, ribs |
| 9 | سَرَائِرُ | *Sara-'ir* | Secrets |
| 11 | ذَاتِ الرَّجْعِ | *Dhatir-raj'* | (The Firmament) which gives the returning rain |
| 12 | ذَاتِ الصَّدْعِ | *Thatis-sad'* | (The earth) which splits (with the growth of trees and plants) |
| 13 | إِنَّهُ لَقَوْلٌ فَصْلٌ | *'Innahu la-qawlun-fasl* | Verily! This (the Holy Qûr'an ) is the Word that separates (the truth from falsehood) |
| 16 | وَأَكِيدُ كَيْدًا | *Wa 'akidu kayda* | And I am planning a scheme |
| 17 | فَمَهِّلِ الْكَافِرِينَ | *Fa-mahhilil-kafirin* | So give a respite to the unbelievers |
| 17 | أَمْهِلْهُمْ رُوَيْدًا | *'Amhil-hum ru-waida* | Give respite to them gently (for a while) |

| V. | WORD | TR. | MEANING |
|---|---|---|---|

## سُورَةُ الأَعْلَى

## [87] SURAT AL-‘ALA

## THE MOST HIGH

| | | | |
|---|---|---|---|
| 3 | فَهَدَى | *Fahada* | Then (He) granted guidance |
| 4 | أَخْرَجَ | *'Akhraj* | Brought out |
| 4 | مَرْعَى | *Mar-‘a* | (Green and luscious) pasture |
| 5 | غُثَاءً | *Ghutha'* | Stubble |
| 5 | أَحْوَى | *'Ahwa* | Dark-coloured, swarthy |
| 6 | سَنُقْرِئُكَ | *Sanuqri-'uk* | We shall make you to recite (the Holy Qûr'an) |
| 6 | فَلَا تَنسَى | *Fala tansa* | So you shall not forget |
| 8 | نُيَسِّرُكَ لِلْيُسْرَى | *Nuyassiruka lil-Yusra* | We will make it easy for you (to follow) the simple path |
| 12 | الَّذِي يَصْلَى النَّارَ الْكُبْرَى | *'Alladhi yaslan-Naral-kubra* | (One) who will enter the Great Fire |
| 14 | أَفْلَحَ | *'Aflah* | Prospered |
| 14 | تَزَكَّى | *Tazakka* | Purified himself |

| V. | WORD | TR. | MEANING |
|---|---|---|---|

# سُورَةُ الغَاشِيَة

## [88] SURAT AL-GHASHIYAH
## THE OVERWHELMING EVENT

| | | | |
|---|---|---|---|
| 1 | الْغَاشِيَةِ | *Al-Gha-shiyah* | The Overwhelming Event (i.e., the Day of Judgement) |
| 3 | عَامِلَةٌ | *'Amila* | Labouring (hard) |
| 3 | نَاصِبَةٌ | *Nasibah* | Weary |
| 4 | تَصْلَى نَارًا حَامِيَةً | *Tasla Naran hamiyah* | They will enter the Blazing Fire |
| 5 | آنِيَةٍ | *'Aniyah* | *ap. fg.* Boiling hot (water) |
| 6 | ضَرِيعٍ | *Dhari'* | A bitter thorny plant growing in Hell |
| 7 | لَا يُغْنِي مِنْ جُوعٍ | *La yughni min-ju'* | Will not avail against hunger |
| 8 | نَاعِمَةٌ | *Na-'imah* | *ap. fg.* Joyful |
| 11 | لَاغِيَةً | *Laghiyah* | Harmful speech and falsehood |
| 14 | مَوْضُوعَةٌ | *Mawdu-'ah* | *pp. fg.* Placed |
| 15 | نَمَارِقُ | *Namariq* | Cushions |
| 15 | مَصْفُوفَةٌ | *Masfufah* | *Pp. fg.* Set in rows, arranged in order |
| 16 | زَرَابِيُّ مَبْثُوثَةٌ | *Zarabiyyu mabthuthah* | Rich carpets (all) spread out |
| 22 | مُسَيْطِرٍ | *Musaytir* | One who presides over, manager of affairs |
| 25 | إِيَابَهُمْ | *'Iyabahum* | Their return |

| V. | WORD | TR. | MEANING |
|---|---|---|---|

## سُورَةُ الفَجْر

## [89] SURAT AL-FAJR

### THE DAWN

| | | | |
|---|---|---|---|
| 1 | وَالْفَجْرِ | *Wal-Fajr* | By the dawn |
| 2 | وَلَيَالٍ عَشْرٍ | *Wa la-yalin 'ashr* | By the ten nights (i.e., the first ten days of the .month of Dhul-Hijja) |
| 3 | وَالشَّفْعِ وَالْوَتْرِ | *Wash-Shaf- 'i wal-watr* | By the even and the odd<br>Even is the Day of Slaughtering of the Sacrifices, i.e., 10th of Dhul-Hijja, and odd is the Day of 'Arafat (Hajj), i.e., 9th of Dhul-Hijja |
| 4 | وَاللَّيْلِ إِذَا يَسْرِ | *Wal-layli-'idha yasr* | And by the night when it passes away |
| 5 | قَسَمٌ لِذِي حِجْرٍ | *Qasamul-lidhi hijr* | An adjuration (or evidence) for those who understand |
| 7 | إِرَمَ | *'Iram* | The city of the tribe of 'Ad |
| 7 | عِمَادِ | *'Imad* | Lofty pillars |
| 9 | جَابُوا الصَّخْرَ | *Jabus-sakhr* | They cut (hewed) out (huge) rocks |
| 13 | سَوْطَ عَذَابٍ | *Sawta- 'adhab* | Different kinds of severe torment |
| 14 | إِنَّ رَبَّكَ لَبِالْمِرْصَادِ | *'Inna Rabbaka la-bil-mirsad* | Verily, your Lord is Ever Watchful (over them) |
| 16 | قَدَرَ | *Qadar* | Restricted |

| V. | WORD | TR. | MEANING |
|---|---|---|---|
| 16 | رِزْقَهُ | *Rizqah* | His subsistence |
| 17 | كَلَّا | *Kalla* | Nay |
| 17 | بَل | *Bal* | But |
| 18 | لَا تَحَاضُّونَ | *La tahaddun* | *pl.* You do not urge one another, you do not encourage one another |
| 19 | تَأْكُلُونَ التُّرَاثَ | *Ta'-kulunat-Turath* | *pl.* You devour inheritance |
| 19 | أَكْلًا | *'Akla* | In a greedy devouring manner |
| 19 | لَمًّا | *Lamma* | Altogether, entirely |
| 20 | حُبًّا جَمًّا | *Hubban-jamma* | Much love |
| 21 | دُكَّتْ | *Dukkat* | *pv.* Is pounded |
| 21 | دَكًّا | *Dakka* | Into powder |
| 22 | مَلَكُ | *Malak* | *sr.* and *pl.* Angel, angels |
| 23 | أَنَّى لَهُ الذِّكْرَى | *'Anna lahudh-dhikra* | How will (that) remembrance profit him? |

| V. | WORD | TR. | MEANING |
|---|---|---|---|

## سُورَةُ البَلَد

## [90] SURAT AL-BALAD

## THE CITY

| | | | |
|---|---|---|---|
| 1 | بِهَذَا الْبَلَدِ | *Bi-hadhal-Balad* | By this city (Makka) |
| 2 | حِلٌّ | *Hill* | A man with lawful rights, inhabitant |
| 3 | وَالِدٍ وَمَا وَلَدَ | *Walidinw-wa ma Walad* | The begetter (i.e., Adam (عليه السلام) and that which he begot (i.e., his progeny) |
| 4 | لَقَدْ خَلَقْنَا الْإِنسَانَ | *Laqad khalaqnal-'insan* | Verily, We have created man |
| 4 | كَبَدٍ | *Kabad* | Toil and struggle |
| 6 | أَهْلَكْتُ مَالًا لُبَدًا | *'Ahlaktu malal-lubada* | I havs wasted wealth in abundance |
| 10 | نَجْدَيْنِ | *Najdayn* | *dl.* Two highways (of good and evil) |
| 11 | فَلَا اقْتَحَمَ الْعَقَبَةَ | *Falaqtahamal-'aqabah* | But he has made no effort to pass on the path that is steep |
| 13 | فَكُّ | *Fakk* | Freeing |
| 13 | رَقَبَةٍ | *Raqabah* | Neck, slave |
| 14 | إِطْعَامٌ | *'It-'am* | The act of feeding |
| 14 | مَسْغَبَةٍ | *Masghabah* | Famine, hunger |
| 15 | يَتِيمًا | *Yatima* | Orphan |
| 15 | مَقْرَبَةٍ | *Maqrabah* | Relationship |
| 16 | مِسْكِينًا | *Miskina* | Poor |
| 16 | مَتْرَبَةٍ | *Matrabah* | Poverty [*lit.* (A |

| V. | WORD | TR. | MEANING |
|---|---|---|---|
| | | | person down) in the dust] |
| 17 | تَوَاصَوْا | *Tawasu* | They enjoin to one another |
| 17 | مَرْحَمَةِ | *Mar-hamah* | Mercy, kindness |
| 18 | أَصْحَابُ الْمَيْمَنَةِ | *'As-habul-Maymanah* | The Companions of the Right Hand |
| 19 | أَصْحَابُ الْمَشْأَمَةِ | *'As-habul-mash-'amah* | The Companions of the Left Hand |
| 20 | مُوصَدَةٌ | *Mu'-sadah* | *pp. fg.* Covered over, vaulted over |

# سُورَةُ الشَّمْسِ

# [91] SURAT ASH-SHAMS

## THE SUN

| V. | WORD | TR. | MEANING |
|---|---|---|---|
| 1 | وَالشَّمْسِ | *Wash-Shams* | By the sun |
| 1 | ضُحَاهَا | *Duhaha* | Its brightness |
| 2 | تَلَاهَا | *Talaha* | Followed it |
| 3 | جَلَّاهَا | *Jallaha* | Showed up (the sun's) brightness |
| 4 | يَغْشَاهَا | *Yaghshaha* | Conceals it |
| 5 | وَمَا بَنَاهَا | *Wa ma banaha* | And Him Who Bulit it |
| 6 | وَمَا طَحَاهَا | *Wa ma tahaha* | And Him Who spread it |
| 7 | وَنَفْسٍ | *Wa nafs* | And by the soul |
| 7 | وَمَا سَوَّاهَا | *Wa ma sawwaha* | And Him Who perfected it in proportion |
| 8 | فُجُورَهَا وَتَقْوَاهَا | *Fujuraha wa taqwaha* | Its wrong and its right |
| 9 | أَفْلَحَ | *'Aflah* | Succeeded |
| 9 | زَكَّاهَا | *Zakkaha* | Purified it |
| 10 | خَابَ | *Khab* | Failed |
| 10 | دَسَّاهَا | *Dassaha* | Corrupted it |
| 11 | بِطَغْوَاهَا | *Bi-taghwaha* | Through their transgression |
| 12 | انْبَعَثَ أَشْقَاهَا | *Imba-'atha 'ashqaha* | The most wicked man among them went forth (to kill the she-camel) |
| 13 | نَاقَةَ اللَّهِ وَسُقْيَاهَا | *Naqatallahi wa* | It is the she-camel |

| V. | WORD | TR. | MEANING |
|---|---|---|---|
| | | *suqyaha* | of Allah! (Do not harm it) and bar it not from having its drink |
| 14 | كَذَّبُوهُ | *Kadhdhabuh* | They rejected him |
| 14 | عَقَرُوهَا | *'Aqaruha* | They hamstrung her |
| 14 | دَمْدَمَ | *Dam-dam* | Destroyed, crushed |
| 14 | سَوَّاهَا | *Saw-waha* | Levelled them |
| 15 | عُقْبَاهَا | *'Uqbaha* | Its consequences |

| V. | WORD | TR. | MEANING |
|---|---|---|---|

## سُورَةُ اللَّيْلِ

## [92] SURAT AL-LAIL
## THE NIGHT

| | | | |
|---|---|---|---|
| 1 | وَاللَّيْلِ إِذَا يَغْشَى | *Wal-Layli 'idha yaghsha* | By the night as it conceals (the light) |
| 2 | وَالنَّهَارِ إِذَا تَجَلَّى | *Wan-Nahari 'idha tajalla* | And by the day as it appears in brightness |
| 4 | إِنَّ سَعْيَكُمْ لَشَتَّى | *'Inna sa'-yakum la-shatta* | Certainly, your efforts and deeds are diverse (different in aims and purposes) |
| 6 | الْحُسْنَى | *Al-Husna* | The Best (i.e., Islam) |
| 7 | فَسَنُيَسِّرُهُ | *Fasa-nuyas-siruh* | We will indeed make smooth for him |
| 7 | يُسْرَى | *Yusra* | Path to ease (goodness) |
| 10 | عُسْرَى | *'Usra* | Path to misery |
| 11 | تَرَدَّى | *Taradda* | Fell headlong, went down (in destruction) |
| 12 | إِنَّ عَلَيْنَا لَلْهُدَى | *'Inna 'alayna lal-huda* | Verily We take upon Us to guide |
| 14 | تَلَظَّى | *Talazza* | Blazing fiercely |
| 15 | لَا يَصْلَاهَا | *La yaslaha* | None shall enter it, none shall burn in it |
| 17 | سَيُجَنَّبُهَا | *Sa-yujannabuha* | They shall be removed far from it |

| V. | WORD | TR. | MEANING |
|---|---|---|---|

## سُورَةُ الضُّحَى

## [93] SURAT AD-DUHA

## THE FORENOON (AFTER SUNRISE)

| | | | |
|---|---|---|---|
| 1 | وَالضُّحَى | *Wad-Duha* | By the forenoon (after sunrise) |
| 2 | سَجَى | *Saja* | Became still, grew dark |
| 3 | مَا وَدَّعَكَ رَبُّكَ | *Ma wadda-'aka Rabbuk* | Your Lord has not forsaken you |
| 3 | مَا قَلَى | *Ma qala* | Not displeased |
| 6 | أَلَمْ يَجِدكَ | *'Alam yajidk* | Did He not find you? |
| 6 | آوَى | *'Aawa* | Gave you shelter (and care) |
| 8 | عَائِلًا | *'A-'ila* | Poor, in need |
| 8 | أَغْنَى | *'Aghna* | Made you rich (self-sufficient with self-contentment) |
| 9 | لَا تَقْهَرْ | *La taqhar* | *ni.* Do not treat (him) with harshness / oppression |
| 10 | لَا تَنْهَرْ | *La tanhar* | *ni.* Do not repulse / reproach |

# سُورَةُ الشَّرْح

## [94] SURAT ASH-SHARH

## THE EXPANSION

| | | | |
|---|---|---|---|
| 1 | أَلَمْ نَشْرَحْ | *'Alam nashrah* | Have We not expanded? |
| 1 | صَدْرَكَ | *Sadrak* | Your breast |
| 2 | وَضَعْنَا عَنكَ | *Wada'-na 'ank* | We removed from you |
| 2 | وِزْرَكَ | *Wizrak* | Your burden |
| 3 | الَّذِي أَنقَضَ | *'Alladi 'anqada* | Which weighed down |
| 3 | ظَهْرَكَ | *Zahrak* | Your back |
| 4 | وَرَفَعْنَا | *Wa rafa'-na* | And We raised high |
| 4 | ذِكْرَكَ | *Dhikrak* | Your fame |
| 7 | فَإِذَا فَرَغْتَ | *Fa-'idha faraght* | So when you have finished (from your occupation) |
| 7 | انصَبْ | *Insab* | *im.* Labour hard |
| 8 | ارْغَبْ | *Irghab* | *im.* Turn (all) your attention |

| V. | WORD | TR. | MEANING |
|---|---|---|---|

## سُورَةُ التِّين

## [95] SURAT AT-TIN

## THE FIG

| V. | WORD | TR. | MEANING |
|---|---|---|---|
| 1 | وَالتِّينِ وَالزَّيْتُونِ | *Wat-Tini waz-Zaytuni* | By the fig and the olive |
| 2 | وَطُورِ سِينِينَ | *Wa Turi Sinin* | And the mount of Sinai |
| 3 | وَهَذَا الْبَلَدِ الْأَمِينِ | *Wa hadhal-Baladil-'amin* | And this city of security (Makka) |
| 4 | أَحْسَنِ تَقْوِيمٍ | *'Ahsani taqwim* | The best stature (mould) |
| 5 | رَدَدْنَاهُ | *Radadnah* | We abased him |
| 5 | أَسْفَلَ سَافِلِينَ | *'Asfala safilin* | The lowest of the low |
| 6 | أَجْرٌ غَيْرُ مَمْنُونٍ | *'Ajrun ghayru mamnun* | Uninterrupted reward |
| 7 | دِينِ | *Din* | Recompense (i.e., the Day of Resurrection) |
| 7 | أَحْكَمِ الْحَاكِمِينَ | *Ahkamil-hakimin* | The wisest of Judges |

| V. | WORD | TR. | MEANING |
|---|---|---|---|

## سُورَةُ العَلَق

## [96] SURAT AL-'ALAQ
## THE LEECH-LIKE CLOT

| | | | |
|---|---|---|---|
| 1 | اقْرأْ | *'Iqra'* | *im*. Read |
| 3 | الأكْرَمُ | *Al-'Akram* | The Most Generous |
| 4 | عَلَّمَ | *'Allam* | Taught |
| 5 | مَا لَمْ يَعْلَمْ | *Ma lam ya'-lam* | Which he knew not |
| 6 | يَطْغى | *Yatgha* | Transgress all bounds |
| 8 | رُجْعَى | *Ruj-'a* | Return |
| 9 | أرَأَيْتَ | *'Ara-'ayt* | Have you seen? |
| 9 | يَنْهى | *Yanha* | Forbids |
| 15 | لَئِن لَّمْ يَنتَهِ | *La-'illam yantih* | If he desist not |
| 15 | نَسْفَعَ | *Nasfa'* | We will drag |
| 15 | نَاصِيَةِ | *Nasiyah* | Forelock |
| 16 | كَاذِبَةٍ | *Kadhiba* | Lying |
| 16 | خَاطِئَةٍ | *Khati-'a* | Sinful |
| 17 | فَلْيَدْعُ نَادِيَه | *Fal-yad-'u nadiyah* | Then, let him call (for help) to his council (of comrades) |
| 18 | سَنَدْعُ الزَّبَانِيَةَ | *Sanad-'uz-zabaniyah* | We will call on the angels of punishment (to deal with him) |

## سُورَةُ الْقَدْر

## [97] SURAT AL-QADR

## THE NIGHT OF POWER (OR HONOUR)

| V. | WORD | TR. | MEANING |
|---|---|---|---|
| 1 | أنزَلْنَاهُ | *'Anzalnah* | Verily! We have revealed it (the Holy Qûr'an) |
| 1 | لَيْلَةِ الْقَدْرِ | *Laylatil-Qadr* | The night of power |
| 2 | ومَآ أَدْرَاكَ | *Wa ma 'adrak* | And what will make you know |
| 3 | خَيْرٌ مِّنْ | *Khayrum-min* | Better than |
| 3 | أَلْفِ شَهرٍ | *'Alfi Shahr* | Thousand months |
| 4 | رُوحُ | *Ruh* | Spirit (i.e., Jibril عليه السلام) |
| 4 | بِإِذْنِ ربِّهِم | *Bi-'idhni-Rab-bihim* | By Allah's permission (*lit.* By their Lord's permission) |
| '4 | مِنْ كُلِّ أَمْرٍ | *Min-kulli 'amr* | With all decrees |
| 5 | مَطْلَعِ الْفَجْرِ | *Mat-la-'il-Fajr* | The rise of morn |

# سُورَةُ البَيِّنَةِ

## [98] SURAT AL-BAIYINAH
## THE CLEAR EVIDENCE

| V. | WORD | TR. | MEANING |
|---|---|---|---|
| 1 | مُنفَكِّينَ | *Munfakkin* | Those who depart (from their ways) |
| 2 | صُحُفاً | *Suhuf* | Scriptures |
| 2 | مُطَهَّرَةً | *Mutahharah* | *pp.* Purified, pure and holy |
| 3 | قَيِّمَةٌ | *Qayyimah* | Right and straight |
| 5 | حُنَفَاءَ | *Hunafa'* | *pl.* Inclined to right opinion, orthodox, firm in faith, true |
| 5 | يُقِيمُوا الصَّلاَةَ | *Yu-qimus-Salat* | They establish regular prayer |
| 5 | يُؤْتُوا الزَّكَاةَ | *Yu'-tuz-Za-kat* | They give zakat |
| 5 | دِينُ الْقَيِّمَةِ | *Dinul-Qayyimah* | The right and straight religion |
| 6 | شَرُّ الْبَرِيَّةِ | *Shar-rul-bariyyah* | The worst of creatures |
| 6 | خَيْرُ الْبَرِيَّةِ | *Khayrul-bariyyah* | The best of creatures |

| V. | WORD | TR. | MEANING |
|---|---|---|---|

# سُورَةُ الزَّلزَلَة

# [99] SURAT AZ-ZALZALAH

## THE CONVULSION

| | | | |
|---|---|---|---|
| 1 | زُلْزِلَتْ الْأَرْضُ | *Zulzilatil-'Ard* | The earth is shaken |
| 2 | أَثْقَالَهَا | *'Athqalaha* | Its burdens |
| 3 | مَالَهَا | *Ma la-ha* | What is the matter with her? |
| 4 | تُحَدِّثُ | *Tuhaddith* | Declares |
| 4 | أَخْبَارَهَا | *'Akhbaraha* | Its tidings |
| 5 | أَوْحَى | *'Awha* | Inspired |
| 6 | يَصْدُرُ | *Yasdur* | Proceed |
| 6 | أَشْتَاتًا | *'Ashtata* | Scattered groups |
| 6 | لِيُرَوْاْ أَعْمَالَهُمْ | *Liyuraw 'a'-malahum* | To be shown their deeds |
| 7 | مِثْقَالَ ذَرَّةٍ | *Mithqala dharra* | The weight of an atom |

## سُورَةُ العَادياتِ

## [100] SURAT AL-'ADIYAT

## THOSE THAT RUN

| V. | WORD | TR. | MEANING |
|---|---|---|---|
| 1 | وَالْعَادِيَاتِ | *Wal-'Adi-yat* | By the (steeds) that run |
| 1 | ضَبْحًا | *Dubha* | The act of panting |
| 2 | فَالْمُورِيَاتِ قَدْحًا | *Fal-muri-yati-qad-ha* | And strike sparks of fire (by their hooves) |
| 3 | فَالْمُغِيرَاتِ صُبْحًا | *Fal-mughirati subha* | And push home the charge in the morning |
| 4 | فَأَثَرْنَ بِهِ نَقْعًا | *Fa-'atharna bihi naq-'a* | And raise the dust in clouds the while |
| 5 | فَوَسَطْنَ بِهِ جَمْعًا | *Fa-wasatna bihi jam-'a* | And penetrate forthwith into the midst (of the foe) |
| 6 | كَنُودٌ | *Kanud* | Ungrateful |
| 8 | الْخَيْرِ | *Al-khayr* | Wealth |
| 8 | شَدِيدٌ | *Shadid* | Strong, violent |
| 9 | بُعْثِرَ | *Bu'-thir* | *pv.* Is scattered abroad |
| 10 | حُصِّلَ | *Hussil* | *pv.* Is made manifest |

# سُورَةُ الْقَارِعَة

## [101] SURAT AL-QARI'A
## THE DAY OF CLAMOUR

| V. | WORD | TR. | MEANING |
|---|---|---|---|
| 1 | الْقَارِعَةَ | *'Al-Qari-'ah* | The Day of Clamour (i.e., the Day of Judgement) |
| 4 | فَرَاشِ | *Farash* | Moths |
| 4 | مَبْثُوثِ | *Mabthuth* | Scattered, spread abroad |
| 5 | عِهْنِ | *'Ihn* | Particoloured wool |
| 5 | مَنفُوشِ | *Manfush* | *pp.* Carded |
| 6 | ثَقُلَتْ مَوَازِينُهُ | *Thaqulat mawazinuh* | His balance (of good deeds) will be (found) heavy |
| 7 | عِيشَةٍ | *'Isha* | Life |
| 7 | رَاضِيَةٍ | *Radiyah* | Pleasant, agreeable |
| 8 | خَفَّتْ مَوَازِينُهُ | *Khaffat mawazinuh* | His balance (of good deeds) will be (found) light |
| 9 | فَأُمُّهُ هَاوِيَةٌ | *Fa-'ummuhu Hawiyah* | He will have his home in a (bottomless) pit (in Hell) |
| 10 | مَاهِيَهْ | *Mahiyah* | What it is? |

# سُورَةُ التَّكَاثُر

## [102] SURAT AT-TAKATHUR

## THE PILING UP

| V. | WORD | TR. | MEANING |
|---|---|---|---|
| 1 | أَلْهَاكُمُ | *'Alhakum* | Diverted you |
| 1 | تَكَاثُرُ | *Atakathur* | Mutual rivalry for piling up (the good things of this world) |
| 2 | حَتَّى زُرْتُمُ الْمَقَابِرَ | *Hatta zurtumul-maqabir* | Until you visit the graves (i.e., till you die) |
| 5 | تَعْلَمُونَ | *Ta'-lamun* | *pl.* You know |
| 5 | عِلْمَ الْيَقِينِ | *'Ilmal-yaqin* | Certainty of mind (*lit.* Certainty of knowledge) |
| 6 | لَتَرَوْنَ الْجَحِيمَ | *Latara-wunnal-Jahim* | *pl.* You shall certainly see Hell-Fire |
| 7 | عَيْنَ الْيَقِينِ | *'Aynal-yaqin* | Certainty of sight |
| 8 | لَتُسْئَلُنَّ | *La-tus-'alunna* | *pl.* You shall be asked |
| 8 | نَعِيمِ | *Na-'im* | Delight |

| V. | WORD | TR. | MEANING |
|---|---|---|---|

## سُورَةُ الْعَصْر

## [103] SURAT AL-'ASR

### TIME THROUGH THE AGES

| | | | |
|---|---|---|---|
| 1 | وَالْعَصْرِ | *Wal-'Asr* | By the time |
| 2 | إِنسَان | *'Insan* | Man |
| 2 | لَفِي خُسْرٍ | *Lafi khusr* | In loss |
| 3 | تَوَاصَوْا بِالْحَقِّ | *Tawasaw bil-Haqq* | They join together in the mutual enjoining of truth |
| 3 | تَوَاصَوْا بِالصَّبْرِ | *Tawasaw bis-Sabr* | They join together in the mutual enjoining of patience (and constancy) |

## سُورَةُ الهُمَزَة

## [104] SURAT AL-HUMAZAH

### THE SCANDAL-MONGER

| | | | |
|---|---|---|---|
| 1 | وَيْلٌ | *Wayl* | Woe |
| 1 | هُمَزَةٍ | *Humaza* | Scandal-monger, slanderer |
| 1 | لُمَزَةٍ | *Lumazah* | Backbiter |
| 2 | عَدَّدَهُ | *'Addadah* | Counted it |
| 3 | أَخْلَدَهُ | *'Akhladah* | Made him last forever |
| 4 | لَيُنْبَذَنَّ | *La-yumbadhanna* | Verily, he will be thrown |
| 4 | حُطَمَةِ | *Hutamah* | That which smashes or breaks |

| V. | WORD | TR. | MEANING |
|---|---|---|---|
| | | | to pieces (A name of Hell) |
| 6 | مُوقَدَةٌ | *Muqadah* | *pp*. Kindled |
| 7 | الَّتِي تَطَّلِعُ عَلَى الْأَفْئِدَةِ | *'Allati tattali-'u 'alal-'af-'idah* | Which mounts (right) up to the hearts |
| 8 | مُؤصَدَةٌ | *Mu'-sadah* | Covered over, vaulted over |
| 9 | عَمَدٍ | *'Amad* | Columns |
| 9 | مُمَدَّدَةٍ | *Mumaddadah* | *pp. fg.* Outstretched |

# سُورَةُ الفِيْلِ

## [105] SURAT AL-FIL

## THE ELEPHANT

| | | | |
|---|---|---|---|
| 1 | أَصْحَابِ الْفِيلِ | *'As-habil-Fil* | The companions of the elephant |
| 2 | يَجْعَلْ | *Yaj-'al* | Makes |
| 2 | كَيْدَهُمْ | *Kaydahum* | Their plot |
| 2 | تَضْلِيلٍ | *Tadlil* | To let go astray |
| 3 | طَيْرًا | *Tayr* | Birds |
| 3 | أَبَابِيلَ | *'Ababil* | Folcks (of birds) |
| 4 | سِجِّيلٍ | *Sijjil* | Baked clay |
| 5 | عَصْفٍ مَأْكُولٍ | *'Asfim-ma'-kul* | (An empty field) of stalks and straws, (of which the corn) has been eaten up (by cattle) |

| V. | WORD | TR. | MEANING |
|---|---|---|---|

## سُورَةُ قُرَيْش

## [106] SURAT QURAISH

### THE QURAISH (CUSTODIANS OF THE KA'BA)

| | | | |
|---|---|---|---|
| 1 | لِإِيلَافِ قُرَيْشٍ | *Li-'ilafi Quraysh* | For the Familiarity of the Quraish |
| 2 | رِحْلَةَ | *Rihla* | Journey |
| 2 | شِتَاء | *Shi-ta-'* | Winter |
| 2 | صَيْف | *Sayf* | Summer |
| 3 | رَبَّ هَذَا الْبَيْتِ | *Rabba ha-dhal-Bayt* | The Lord of this House (the Ka'ba in Makka) |

## سُورَةُ الْمَاعُون

## [107] SURAT AL-MA'UN

### NEIGHBOURLY NEEDS

| | | | |
|---|---|---|---|
| 1 | أَرَأَيْتَ | *'Ara-'ayt* | Have you seen? |
| 1 | يُكَذِّبُ بِالدِّينِ | *Yukadhdhibu bid-Din* | Denies the Recompense |
| 2 | يَدُعُّ | *Yadu'* | Repulses |
| 3 | يَحُضُّ | *Yahudd* | Urges, encourages |
| 4 | مُصَلِّين | *Musallin* | *ap*. Those who pray |
| 5 | سَاهُونَ | *Sahun* | *pl.* Neglectful |
| 6 | يُرَاءُونَ | *Yura-'un* | They want to be seen |
| 7 | يَمْنَعُونَ الْمَاعُونَ | *Yamna-'unal-Ma-'un* . | They refuse (to supply even) neighbourly needs |

| V. | WORD | TR. | MEANING |
|---|---|---|---|

## سُورَةُ الكَوْثَر

## [108] SURAT AL-KAUTHAR

### THE ABUNDANCE

| | | | |
|---|---|---|---|
| 1 | أَعْطَيْنَاكَ | *'A '-taynak* | We have granted you |
| 1 | الْكَوْثَرَ | *Al-Kawthar* | *lit.* Good in abundance (name of a river in Paradise) |
| 2 | انْحَرْ | *Inhar* | *im.* Sacrifice |
| 3 | شَانِئَكَ | *Shani-'ak* | The one who makes you angry |
| 3 | أَبْتَرُ | *'Abtar* | One who is cut off (from every good thing in this world and in the Hereafter),childless |

## سُورَةُ الكَافِرُونَ

## [109] SURAT AL-KAFIRUN

### THOSE WHO REJECT FAITH

| | | | |
|---|---|---|---|
| 2 | لَاأَعْبُدُ | *La 'a'-bud* | I do not worship |
| 2 | مَا تَعْبُدُونَ | *Ma ta'-bu-dun* | That which you worship |
| 3 | مَاأَعْبُدُ | *Ma 'a'-bud* | That which I worship |
| 6 | دِينُكُمْ | *Dinukum* | *pl.* Your religion |
| 6 | دِينِ | *Din* | My religion |

| V. | WORD | TR. | MEANING |
|---|---|---|---|

## سُورَةُ النَّصْر

## [110] SURAT AN-NASR

### THE HELP

| | | | |
|---|---|---|---|
| 1 | جَاءَ | *Jaa'* | Came |
| 1 | فَتْحُ | *Fat-h* | Victory (i.e., the taking of Makka) |
| 2 | أَفْوَاجًا | *'Afwaja* | In crowds |
| 3 | فَسَبِّحْ بِحَمْدِ رَبِّكَ | *Fa-sabbih bi-Hamdi Rab-bik* | So celebrate the Praises of your Lord |
| 3 | تَوَّابًا | *Tawwaba* | Oft-Returning (in forgiveness) |

## سُورَةُ المَسَد

## [111] SURAT AL-MASAD

### THE FLAME

| | | | |
|---|---|---|---|
| 1 | تَبَّتْ | *Tabbat* | *fg.* Perished |
| 1 | تَبَّ | *Tabb* | Perished |
| 2 | مَا أَغْنَى | *Ma 'aghna* | Availed not |
| 2 | كَسَبَ | *Kasab* | Gained |
| 3 | سَيَصْلَى | *Sa-yasla* | He will be burnt |
| 3 | نَارًا ذَاتَ لَهَبٍ | *Naran-dhata Lahab* | Fire of blazing flame |
| 5 | جِيدِهَا | *Jidiha* | Her neck |
| 5 | حَبْلٌ مِنْ مَسَدٍ | *Hablum-mim-masad* | A twisted rope of palm-leaf fibre |

| V. | WORD | TR. | MEANING |
|---|---|---|---|

## سُورَةُ الإِخْلَاص

## [112] SURAT AL-IKHLAS
## THE PURITY (OF FAITH)

| | | | |
|---|---|---|---|
| 1 | أَحَدٌ | *'Ahad* | The One |
| 2 | الصَّمَدُ | *As-Samad* | The Eternal, the Absolute<br>The One Who is dependent on no person or things, but all persons or things are dependent on Him |
| 3 | لَمْ يَلِدْ | *Lam yalid* | (He) begetes not |
| 3 | لَمْ يُولَدْ | *Lam yulad* | (He) is not begotten |
| 4 | كُفُوًا | *Kufuwan* | Like, equal |

## سُورَةُ الفَلَق

## [113] SURAT AL-FALAQ
## THE DAWN

| | | | |
|---|---|---|---|
| 1 | أَعُوذُ | *'A-'udh* | I seek |
| 1 | رَبِّ الْفَلَقِ | *Rabbil Falaq* | The Lord of the Dawn / Daybreak |
| 3 | شَرِّ غَاسِقٍ | *Sharri ghasiq* | Evil of darkness |
| 3 | وَقَبَ | *Waqab* | Entered, overspread |
| 4 | النَّفَّاثَاتِ فِي الْعُقَدِ | *An-Naffathati fil-'uqad* | Those (women) who blow on knots |
| 5 | حَاسِدٍ | *hasid* | *ap.* One who envies, envier |

| V. | WORD | TR. | MEANING |
|---|---|---|---|

# سُورَةُ النَّاس

## [114] SURAT AN-NAS
## THE MANKIND

| V. | WORD | TR. | MEANING |
|---|---|---|---|
| 1 | رَبِّ النَّاسِ | *Rabbin-Nas* | The Lord and Cherisher of mankind |
| 2 | مَلِكِ النَّاسِ | *Malikin-Nas* | The King of mankind |
| 3 | إِلَهِ النَّاسِ | *'Ilahin-Nas* | The God of mankind |
| 4 | وَسْوَاسِ | *Waswas* | Whisperer (of evil) |
| 4 | خَنَّاسِ | *Khan-Nas* | The One who withdraws |
| 5 | يُوَسْوِسُ | *Yuwas-wis* | Whispers |
| 6 | جِنَّةِ | *Jinna* | Jinns |